Film and the Shoah in France and Italy

Film and the Shoah in France and Italy

GIACOMO LICHTNER

VALLENTINE MITCHELL
LONDON • PORTLAND, OR

First published in paperback in 2015 by Vallentine Mitchell

Middlesex House,
29-45 High Street,
Edgware, Middlesex HA8 7UU
UK

920 NE 58th Avenue, Suite 300
Portland, Oregon,
97213-3786
USA

www.vmbooks.com

First printed in hardback in 2008

British Library Cataloguing in Publication Data
have been applied for

Library of Congress Cataloging in Publication Data
have been applied for

ISBN 978 0 85303 786 6 (cloth)
ISBN 978 0 85303 949 5 (paper)

Printed by Edwards Brothers Malloy Inc., Ann Arbor, MI

Contents

Illustrations

Foreword

As Giacomo Lichtner reminds us in the pages of his study of French and Italian cinematic 'memory' of these nations' roles in the Holocaust, Robert Rosenstone, Henry Rousso and Peter Novick have been three of the most innovative and important students of the complex process of human remembering and forgetting of these terrible events. Rosenstone has stressed that, in our visual era, films often stand at the centre of our 'revisioning' (his neat and also tricky term) of the past. Rousso has added that they thereby act as 'vectors of memory' of crucial moments of the past. Novick, by contrast, has recounted the way in which, notably in the USA, the Nazi killing of the Jews has cemented itself into being the automatic touchstone of any attempt to assess the meaning of the Second World War as a whole in what is asserted to be the uniquely wicked Judeocide. Simultaneously Novick has wondered bravely if this historiographical victory is altogether a positive one.

Following such leads, Lichtner's book is thus to be read by any who wish to deepen their knowledge of how the French and Italians have confronted or avoided the sad story of their nation's participation in the Holocaust. By now, he demonstrates, officialdom in each country has made at least a formal acknowledgement of sins of omission and of commission readily to be perceived in the 'collaborationism' of the Vichy regime in France and in the actions of the Nazis' 'first ally', the Fascist government in Italy, at its worst amid the oxymorons of its fate from September 1943 to April 1945 as a newly radicalised puppet dictatorship. Nonetheless, as Lichtner frequently underlines, there have been, and remain, plenty of moments when each society has done its best not to see too clearly the horror, the horror, in its wartime past. Forgetting is as predictable a part of filmic (and other) memory, as is the regular intrusion of contemporary events and preoccupations (who could doubt, for example, that Spielberg's *Schindler's List* is as well read by a historian as an implicit and naively boosting commentary on Clinton's USA and the 1990s as it is a convincing probing of the nature of the Nazi Holocaust?) About all these matters, readers will learn much from Lichtner's judicious analysis of the ongoing collision of the processes of remembering and forgetting, accepting and denying.

Like all good books, Lichtner's also alludes to issues that remain at the periphery of his own study and yet plead for further deliberation. Novick has shown how the 'Holocaust' as now understood took more than a decade to establish its meaning. The 'Second World War' is potentially an even more embattled term. Given the marked difference in the war experience of one combatant society and another (and this was the war where more than half the casualties were civilians), should it not be re-branded as the 'Second World Wars'?

Certainly, as Lichtner hints, the comparison between Italy and France offers as many contrasts as it does parallels. For the Third Republic, the auxiliary role of Vichy in the killing of the Jews was set into the general dilemma of the country's 'strange defeat'. When made subject to devastating but potentially meretricious Nazi Blitzkrieg in the summer of 1940, in its military, psychological and cultural collapse, did the French nation expose a profound hollowness that it may still be better to forget than focus on too starkly?

For Italy, that country which had fallen under Fascist rule as early as 1922, it may be that the national 'Second World War' began then, or, at least in January 1925, when Mussolini assumed full-scale, 'totalitarian' dictatorship (the adjective it is always worth underlining spread from Italian into universal discourse). Any Italian reckoning with its crimes and follies thus possesses an ample possible range and it is easy to see how partially Italians have confronted many pasts that they cheerfully prefer to pass away. Has the acceptance, remarked on by Lichtner, in recent times, even by Gianfranco Fini, heir of his nation's post-1945 neo-fascist traditions, that the killing of the Jews was 'total evil', hidden either a continuing refusal to peruse or an active attempt to conceal and forget Fascist Italy's more numerous body count of Slavs, blacks and Arabs, whether in its colonial wars before 1940 or in Italy's version of the wartime imposition of the Nazi-fascist New Order on the Balkans?

Another problem may lurk here. As Novick has warned generally, too heavy an emphasis on the 'uniqueness' of the

Holocaust leads readily to the total 'otherising' of its perpetrators. Even so austere a biographer as Sir Ian Kershaw concludes Hitler was in some sense 'mad' and therefore, to a marked degree, incomprehensible. Thus separated from 'us' in our normality, the killers are reduced to offering the lesson that the world is full of 'bad guys' and good guys (as George W. Bush's ineffable rhetoric has so frequently put it with such disastrous effect). But quite a bit of Fascist murder, despite carrying traits from the times, equally bore the common traditions of European imperialism and connects Fascist Italian history as much with that of nineteenth-century Britain, Belgium or Imperial Germany (and with 1950s and early 1960s France in Algeria) as it does with the Nazis. When fully reviewed, there is no escape clause from Fascist murder in the excuse that Mussolini and his aides were 'mad' nor in any claim that their massacres were 'unique'.

Questions, questions. Readers of the foreword to a history of cinematic representations of the Holocaust should not be too surprised to learn that Lichtner's book will not resolve all the dilemmas that swirl around our memory of so cataclysmic an event as the Second World War. It will, however, nourish that eternal vigilance that was first expressed by historians who themselves lived through some version of the war, a vigilance posited on a commitment to reading the past with eternal criticism.

R.J.B. Bosworth
University of Western Australia/Reading University

Acknowledgements

The history of twentieth-century Europe is also a history of displacement and trauma. At the beginning of this book I wish to acknowledge Anna Gross and her seven children, Zoltan, Marcel, Derek, Lajos, Béla, Dezsö and Gyula; Stella Passigli and her two sons, Enzo and Rodolfo. This work is for them.

In researching and writing this book, I have become indebted to a number of people. The guidance of Nick Atkin and David Laven was instrumental in taking this project through the doctoral dissertation stage. Nick and David are not only rigorous and thoughtful scholars, but also supportive, generous and patient friends. I am thankful to Simon Kitson and Frank Tallett, whose comments actively encouraged the creation of this book and offered it direction. I would also like to thank Roy Wolfe, who has been a consistent source of fundamental material. The project was supported financially by generous grants from the University of Reading and Victoria University of Wellington. The History Programme at Victoria has been encouraging throughout the past two years, and I am particularly grateful to Giselle Byrnes, Susan Foley, Andrew Francis, Stephen Levine and Don MacRaild for their support.

I am deeply thankful to Richard Bosworth for enriching this work with a grave and thought-provoking foreword, and to all those colleagues and friends who helped in the final preparation of the manuscript. In particular, I wish to acknowledge the helpful feedback of Vallentine Mitchell's anonymous reviewers, and mention Charlotte MacDonald, Russell Campbell and Daphne Hassett, from whose experience and wisdom I have been fortunate to benefit. I would also like to express my gratitude to Heather Marchant and the editorial and production teams at Vallentine Mitchell for their work in publishing this book, and to the producers of all the films whose images illustrate this book. Every effort has been made to obtain permission for the images, but we will rectify any omissions if we receive new information on the copyright holder.

Finally, I would like to pay tribute to my father Rudi and my mother Cristina, who are quite extraordinary parents, resilient, honest and unpretentious. By the strength of their remembrance the family history has continued. For my part, that sense of continuity is best embodied by my beautiful daughter, Rebecca Lulu, *l'amore di papà*, who carries with grace her grandmother's name and her mother's smile; Nikki, who has seen this book take form and its author grow up along the way. *Sei una meraviglia.*

Introduction: Screened Memories

There is a man at a drawing desk. A mouse-shaped mask covers his face. Flies are hovering around him while he tells us: 'In September 1986, after eight years of work, the first part of MAUS was published. It was a critical and commercial success'. A larger plan shows that his chair and his desk, his work, are balanced upon a heap of mouse-faced corpses, their mouths open, gasping for air. Art Spiegelman's cartoon describes perfectly the difficulties encountered by those trying to represent the Shoah.[1] Whatever our language, artistic or otherwise, during that pursuit we perform a balancing act surrounded by death. This does not prevent us from expressing ourselves freely and adequately, but it carries the considerable danger that, should we at any point lose our footing, we will inevitably trample over the dead.

Our own balancing act begins from a momentous day in 2005 when Italy's Foreign Minister, Gianfranco Fini, landed in Tel Aviv. The result of a long and difficult mediation, his trip meant far more than a routine diplomatic encounter between friendly states. Fini has been, since 1992, the leader of Alleanza Nazionale (National Alliance, AN), the modern evolution of the old Movimento Sociale Italiano (Italian Social Movement, MSI), itself the post-war incarnation of Mussolini's Fascist Party. Israeli Premier Ariel Sharon welcomed Fini on a tour which included a visit to Yad Vashem, Jerusalem's Holocaust Memorial museum. There, Fini stigmatised fascism as 'absolute evil'. By publicly renouncing the legacy of Mussolini, Fini's decade-long effort to establish democratic credentials for his party had seemingly come to an end. But Fini's march towards the middle ground came at a price for AN, which suffered the defection of Alessandra Mussolini's right-wing faction without achieving any evident electoral reward.

The spectre of fascism continues to haunt the Italian political spectrum and popular culture. Even a brief visit to one of AN's political rallies reveals unsavoury echoes of the past which question the party leadership's reformist zeal. In the 2006 elections, Berlusconi's coalition sought and obtained the alliance of Alessandra Mussolini's new formation, Alternativa Sociale (Social Alternative, AS), and other openly neo-fascist groups; racist and fascist slogans during sporting occasions are a common occurrence and, on several occasions in 2005 and 2006, SS Lazio footballer Paolo di Canio greeted his fans with the fascist salute. As expected, his gesture sparked outrage among many and earned him fines and a short suspension. Di Canio's passion, however, also drew calls to respect all political opinions and their physical expression – as though di Canio was Jesse Owens at the Berlin Olympics. These pleas, sponsored by Cabinet ministers and senior members of AN, were not isolated but part of a concerted, decade-long revisionist effort aimed at establishing equal legitimacy between fascism and anti-fascism, and between their respective political and cultural legacies. This effort began in the early 1990s, when Berlusconi's brand-new Forza Italia movement, the Lega Nord (Northern League) and AN filled the power vacuum left by the traditional parties in the wake of corruption scandals. Also aided by the left's post-Cold War identity crisis, these forces set about wresting popular culture and memory from what they saw as communist controls, with initiatives such as the attempted censorship of allegedly 'Marxist' textbooks,[2] and the establishment of a National Day of Remembrance for the victims of Tito's post-war ethnic cleansing of Italians.[3]

Italy is not alone in this ambivalent attitude towards the legacy of the extremist right-wing ideologies of the twentieth century. Extreme right-wing political groups, with revisionist, nationalist and xenophobic agendas, have been gaining ground in Austria, Belgium, Germany and Holland, among other places. In France, there has been a long history of scandals since the 1978 remarks of Holocaust deniers Darquier de Pellepoix and Robert Faurisson. The words of the latter,[4] a respected Lyon professor, were perhaps more shocking than those of the former,[5] once the head of Vichy's Commissariat Général aux Questions Juives (Commissariat for Jewish Affairs, CGJQ). In 1980, anti-Semitic terrorist attacks in the Marais once more raised the fear of persecution and, in 1987, Jean-Marie Le Pen, a former Poujadist and leader of the Front

National (National Front, FN) relegated the gas chambers to 'a point of detail in the Second World War'.[6]

At the same time, France has been more active than Italy in pursuing justice. In 1987, the German head of the Gestapo in Lyon, Klaus Barbie, was tried for crimes against humanity. He was accused of orchestrating the deportation of Lyon's Jews and personally murdering de Gaulle's right-hand man, Jean Moulin.[7] Significantly, the trial of Klaus Barbie created a link between the Final Solution and the repression of the Resistance in France, establishing the latter as a crime against humanity.[8] The trials of French collaborators such as René Bousquet, Paul Touvier and Maurice Papon were less straightforward.[9] The first was never tried: arrested in 1991, he was murdered at his Parisian flat in 1993; the second, pardoned in 1971 and charged again in 1989 with the murder of seven Jews, was convicted only in 1994, after the defence's argument that Touvier's offences did not constitute crimes against humanity was met by widespread protests; the third, arrested in 1983, did not face a court until 1997, when, like Touvier, he was sentenced to life imprisonment for his 'administrative' involvement in the deportation of 15,000 Jews.

The trials of French collaborators and German Nazis, which characterised Mitterrand's presidential terms, have confirmed further the contradictions of France's obsession with its past. Yet even they have not closed the Vichy chapter. Perhaps the most remarkable example of all was the exploit of Jean-Marie Le Pen in the French presidential elections of 2002. Le Pen, who as a veteran of the Algerian War embodies in his person the related ghosts of Vichy and decolonisation, constantly reminds France that the memory of the Second World War and the Shoah are dynamic and by no means closed chapters of European history. Ever-increasing calls to recognise the reasons and dignity of the defeated as well as those of the victors have not brought about reconciliation and closure. They have instead muddied the waters of history in the vain conviction that the truth is somewhere in the middle. The Second World War and the Shoah remain ever popular subjects of investigation not only with scholars, but also with the general public.

It is interesting that hindsight and alleged emotional detachment should not have eased but increased the controversies over how the Shoah and the Second World War should be remembered. These issues continue to haunt Italy and France, because of their similarly traumatic wartime experiences and also because of the ways in which these have been approached historically. The history of the Second World War and its remembrance in these two European countries, which have always shared close cultural and historical links, present remarkable similarities and intriguing differences, which demand a comparative approach. On the one hand, after 1943, both France and Italy had similar experiences of occupation, collaboration and resistance. After 1945, both had difficulties in dealing with the legacy of the German occupation and both nations had to confront the treatment of their Jewish populations. Moreover, France and Italy have experienced parallel if by no means identical political and social developments in the post-war period. On the other hand, when the populations of France and Italy finally have faced this particular part of their past, their approach has been different, sometimes markedly so.

In both countries an initial period of uneasiness surrounded the Shoah, during which the domestic role in the persecution of the local Jewry was completely overlooked in favour of a wholesale apportioning of blame to the foreign invaders. In France, the traumatic experience of decolonisation also contributed to the revisiting of *les années noires* (the years of German occupation). So too did the return to power and eventual fall of General de Gaulle, which facilitated further links between the two conflicts.[10] Italy did not undergo the same experience. Unlike France, it had no place at the victors' table: a fact which, in a way, allowed Italy to forego the effort of reconciling its wartime self with its post-war self. Though all residues of the past were by no means purged, the armistice of 8 September 1943, the Resistance and the 1946 expulsion of the Savoy dynasty allowed at least the illusion of a clean slate. Decolonisation was not an issue. Nor did Italy possess a figure of de Gaulle's personality and personal history. Furthermore, the comparatively low percentage of Italian Jewry murdered during the war enabled Italy to archive the genocide more convincingly than its neighbour as an event alien to a country of warm-hearted and generous Christians. With France stunned into revisionism and Italy somewhat safe in a cosy self-reassurance, it is hardly surprising that the former initiated a far-reaching work on memory which the latter is only beginning to embrace.

Since the late 1980s, the study of historical memory has

increasingly established itself as an area of research, and it was in France that the analysis of memory first emerged with the publication of Pierre Nora's oft-cited *Les Lieux de Mémoire*.[11] In the gargantuan three tomes and seven volumes he edited and inspired, Nora elaborated the concept of 'mnemonic sites' or 'realms of memory'.[12] With this expression, he defined the physical, psychological and temporal sites around which popular memory clusters, allowing the nation to form common images of its past and shared understandings of its identity. The major flaw of Nora's work was that it favoured the *lieux de mémoire* over the equally interesting *lieux d'amnésie* or *non-lieux de mémoire*: it ignored the more recent and controversial 'realms of memory', dedicating a mere twenty pages to Vichy.[13] There was no mention of Algeria.

One of the darker sides of French popular memory was instead analysed by Henri Rousso, whose work initiated much interest in the study of the memory of the Second World War in France.[14] In *Le Syndrome de Vichy* (*The Vichy Syndrome*), Rousso diagnosed the ways in which France has failed to come to terms with its wartime past.[15] This 'illness', he argued, manifested itself in two ways: first, through the unwillingness to face up to the Vichy regime and the phenomenon of collaboration; second, through the inability to contextualise the war experience and move forwards from it. The 1990s have seen the field of memory turned into a veritable market. In Italy, there has not been a work as groundbreaking as Rousso's, and research on memory does not come close to rivalling that in France in terms both of quantity and quality. Perhaps this is because scholars are concentrating on the necessary reassessment of the history of fascism, the Second World War and the Shoah in Italy.

The recent increase in works on the Italian Jewish experience during fascism suggests that this reappraisal is needed before scholars can turn to the subject of how these historical events have been perceived and remembered in the post-war period. Recent works – mostly authored by Jewish scholars such as Liliana Picciotto Fargion, Giorgio Israel and Michele Sarfatti – suggest that Italy is undergoing a process similar to the one experienced by France since the 1970s. Nonetheless, memory has commanded some interest in Italy, too. Mario Isnenghi's edited collection, *I Luoghi della Memoria*, though a less ambitious Italian equivalent of Nora's work by which it was inspired, was a direct answer to the political revisionism of Berlusconi's modern right, and launched a re-evaluation of key people and moments in Italian history since the unification.[16] Isnenghi's work is part of a broader interest in memory, which, since the late 1990s, has accompanied the political attempt to reinterpret the past, and in particular the years of the Second World War. Following Claudio Pavone's essay on *Alle Origini della Repubblica*,[17] works in Italian and English have followed more recently, by scholars such as Luisa Passerini,[18] Richard Bosworth and Patrizia Dogliani,[19] Davide Rodogno and others,[20] particularly in an effort finally to re-evaluate the memory of Italian fascism and the ever-seductive myth of *Italiani brava gente*.[21]

In this book, memory is not understood in the ways suggested by Nora. The French historian considered memory a primitive or sacred form, antithetic to the rational and secular discourse of history. This opposition is central to Nora's thesis. With the contrast between history and memory he justifies the modern concern with the latter: 'We speak so much of memory because there is so little of it left.'[22] Both these premises are suspect. Nora laments the disappearance of a rural world built on memory, but this reveals a partial and Franco-centric interpretation. Rural communities and communities which make memory a central part of their culture and identity still exist, though perhaps not in the French countryside. New groups and new memories appear constantly: remembrance and the reinterpretation of the past, in part institutionally sanctioned, have by no means ceased to exist with the end of traditional French rural communities. Much current work on memory follows the same rationale, pitting memory against history, though, according to Kerwin Lee Klein, 'few authors openly claim to be engaged in building a world in which memory can serve as an alternative to history'.[23]

Instead, this study attempts to break the praxis of understanding the study of memory either as a supplement or as an antonym of historical discourse, and considers popular memory as an integral part of historical discourse. There is no contrast between the study of history and the analysis of how history is perceived by a specific group or in a specific country: the latter is simply a branch of the former. Moreover, memory is history because it affects history; in line with Halbwachs's understanding of collective memory as a political phenomenon, the way we perceive history affects our interpretation of the present and, therefore, our actions. Past and present are inextricably related, not only because one is the product of the other, but because current perceptions of the past perpetuate it and give it a new form, which exists independently of its original essence and in turn can affect present events. At times, perceptions of the past shaped by popular or institutional efforts are so powerful that they replace the original events to the extent that memory can seem to replace fact.

In a similarly circular fashion, cinema and society cohabit in a dual relationship: on the one hand, cinema reflects society's desires of self-representation, its taboos and myths; on the other hand, it shapes these very ideas with its uniquely far-reaching arm. This book is concerned with this specific aspect of popular memory-formation: namely, film's ability to reflect or affect popular attitudes towards history. In particular, this study has three complementary purposes: firstly, to offer a detailed analysis of key cinematic works on the Shoah; secondly, to link the popular and institutional reception of these works to society's attitudes towards the Shoah; thirdly, to show how these attitudes have changed over time, so as to evince the role film has played in the transmission of history and memory. To achieve this last aim in particular, this study does not examine all Holocaust films made in France and Italy between 1956 and 1998, but those which best reflect the change in popular perception of the Shoah in these two countries.

Alongside this crucial selection principle, all the selected films answer three broad criteria. The first criterion was that these films should be directed by French and Italian film-makers, released in at least one of these countries and at least partially funded by national producers. This is not to say that foreign Holocaust films, such as Steven Spielberg's *Schindler's List* (1993), have not influenced popular perceptions of history in these countries. Yet only by studying domestic films could one truly gauge the relationship between cinema as a cultural product and the society that has produced it; the analysis of the reception of foreign films will always present only half of that dual relationship.

The second criterion was chronological: the study opens with Alain Resnais's *Nuit et Brouillard* (*Night and Fog*, 1956) and ends forty years later with *Train de Vie* (*Train of Life*) and Roberto Benigni's *La Vita è Bella* (*Life is Beautiful*, 1997). These serve as bookends which demonstrate the extent to which the representation of the Shoah has changed and yet its unchanging ability to generate controversy.

The third criterion was that all selected films should be concerned, to some extent, with the Shoah. This involved a wholly subjective interpretation for which the author does, of course, take full responsibility. Hence, works such as Luchino Visconti's *Vaghe Stelle dell'Orsa* (*Sandra*, 1965) and *La Caduta degli Dei* (*The Damned*, 1969), Vittorio De Sica's *I Condannati d'Altona* (*The Condemned of Altona*, 1962), François Truffaut's *Le Dernier Metro* (*The Last Metro*, 1980), and others commonly referred to as Holocaust films, do not feature prominently here. Although they might all touch, to different extents, on the fate of the Jews, their primary concerns are elsewhere.

Three of the works discussed in these pages are documentaries that have not only deeply affected the representation of the Shoah, but also forever changed documentary film-making. Alain Resnais's *Night and Fog* (1956), Marcel Ophuls's *Le Chagrin et la Pitié* (*The Sorrow and the Pity*, 1971) and Claude Lanzmann's *Shoah* (1985) form the backbone of this study. These warranted three dedicated chapters, which are interlinked by comparative case studies on a number of fiction films. Documentary and fiction are clearly distinct forms of film-making: while both are creative forms of art, the former has by definition a relationship with reality which the latter can disregard; documentary and fiction respond to different rules and attract different audiences. This study does not, therefore, seek to equate them or subject them to an unqualified comparison. Nevertheless, for the purpose of this book, both are legitimate, and indeed necessary, sources. Firstly, in presenting a specific interpretation of the past, both use artifice and manipulative artistic techniques. Secondly, all the documentary films discussed in the following chapters are unusual inasmuch as they secured a theatrical release and were widely discussed in the press. Thus, while the audience they attracted may have been quantitatively and qualitatively different to that of fiction films, these documentaries fulfil the crucial criterion of having entered the public discourse through theatrical distribution.

There is no doubt that cinema is only one of the 'vectors of memory' that shape popular beliefs: trials, political pressures, commemorative ceremonies, public places of remembrance, family narratives and literature also affect a country's memories of an historical event. Yet film is a unique tool for the cultural historian. Historians today seldom question the fact that the mass media play a part in the creation of popular perceptions of history, and scholars such as Robert Rosenstone have gone some way to explaining the growing influence of the visual media on popular understanding of history.[24] While the use of film for the purposes of propaganda has been widely studied by historians, the much subtler role of film in shaping national identities and popular memories through the representation, partial representation, or actual misrepresentation of a nation's past has largely been ignored. Fiction film, in particular, has been employed by historians mostly as a visual aid in teaching, and in general regarded as second-class evidence. A notable exception, which informs this book's approach, is the work of Pierre Sorlin, who has successfully studied cinema as a cultural product inextricably linked to the social, political and economic context that produces it.[25]

Historians are understandably suspicious of the subjective nature of the medium, fearful of its ability to distort history and, perhaps less justifiably, protective of the audiences it may mislead. Abundant factual inaccuracies and cinema's lack of accountability fully explain the historians' concerns. Nonetheless, this author believes that the premise behind these concerns is fundamentally wrong: so far scholars have thought of the inaccuracies of historical films as a risk; one must instead begin to consider them a certainty and an opportunity. If one assumes that inaccuracies are inevitable characteristics of the historical film, then it becomes obvious that, while continuing to point them out, one must also exploit those very inaccuracies as a valuable source for the study of a nation's cultural history. Hence, this book does not ask, 'Is this film an accurate representation of history?' but 'What do this film's specific inaccuracies say about the understanding of history at the time of its production?'

In this study, films are never employed by themselves as the assumed reflection of popular attitudes towards the Shoah. Rather, the textual analysis of each film places it firmly within the context of its production. When was the film made? Who made it and who financed it? What were the concerns, the fashion or the taboos of society at the time? What were the cinematic styles in vogue? What was the country's attitude to the historical events tackled in the film at the time of production? For instance, in Italy in 1974, the impending referendum on the legality of abortion undoubtedly affected the reception of Liliana Cavani's *Il Portiere di Notte* (*The Night Porter*), which was released only weeks before it. The aim of this method of analysis is not to grade each work according to 'historical accuracy', but rather to understand what shapes the interpretation of history conveyed by the film. How were the film-makers' choices influenced by the opinions of their contemporary society? How do they shed light on these? And finally, how, if at all, did the representation of the past affect popular attitudes towards history?

The textual analysis of films provides the answer to only one side of the argument: how popular and institutional attitudes towards the Shoah influence representation. To understand fully what these attitudes were, and then if and how they were changed by a motion picture, it was paramount to consider the films' reception. In recent times, the subject of film reception has attracted much interest from media and film scholars. Alongside the traditional question about the language of cinema and film production, researchers are increasingly studying 'the experiences of viewing for cinema audiences'.[26] Within the field of film studies, Janet Staiger has argued strongly for the adoption of a 'historical materialist approach to modes of reception', aimed at shifting the practice of film interpretation from a text-based one to an audience-based one.[27] Staiger, and others such as Elizabeth Ellsworth,[28] have reflected on the fact that differentiations of age, class, nationality, cultural background, gender and race, are more marked among audiences than among critics.[29]

The increase in reception-studies scholarship is significant. It signals a shift from the understanding of film as 'a container holding immanent meaning' to an approach that seeks to analyse all the different interpretations given to that meaning.[30] The purpose of reception studies is not to establish which of these varying interpretations is right, but to consider the range of political, social and cultural contexts that inform them. This book shares that aim. However, unless it is understood as an inherently contemporary methodology,[31] reception-studies theory does not solve the problem of how to reconcile the potential interpretative differences between film critics and the cinema audiences. Because it relies on the analysis of audiences, it is impossible for researchers to apply this method to past films in its conventional form: that is, through the selection and observation of groups of spectators.[32]

Whether a specific film was the expression of the dominant view or of counter-culture, a parallel quantitative–qualitative analysis of the text and its reception is arguably the most appropriate way to test the dynamics of the interaction between cinema and society: on the one hand, this method allows for and reveals the ambivalent role of cinema as both mirror and initiator of social trends; on the other hand, it interprets popular and institutional attitudes towards the historical events in question. Crucially, this process also reveals the critics' reaction to the ways in which the Shoah was represented. The extent to which historical inaccuracies were identified exposed the general degree of knowledge and understanding amongst reviewers. By considering the range of opinions expressed by a regionally diverse and politically polarised press, this analysis highlights the sensitive nature of the interpretation of history. In this way, the chapters that follow uncover not just attitudes towards each film but also, more generally, how the understanding of the Shoah in France and Italy has changed over time, why these changes have occurred, and with what consequences for politics, history and the memory of those who did not come back.

NOTES

1. Art Spiegelman, *The Complete Maus: A Survivor's Tale* (London: Penguin, 2003).
2. Simona Casalini, 'Lazio, AN censura i libri di testo "troppo filo-marxisti"', *La Repubblica*, 10 November 2000. Storace's censorious efforts won him the nickname 'Epurator', from the Italian verb for purge; Curzio Maltese, 'L'Epurator della Storia', *La Repubblica*, 10 November 2000.
3. Gianni Oliva, *La Resa dei Conti: Aprile–Maggio 1945: Foibe, Piazzale Loreto e Giustizia Partigiana* (Milano: Mondadori, 1999), is one of the works more closely associated with this revisionist political effort. On the *foibe* see Glenda Sluga, who has approached the topic from the wider issue of ethnicity and identity, rather than to avenge the long silence that has surrounded the massacres: Glenda Sluga, *The Problem of Trieste and the Italo-Yugoslav Border: Difference, Identity, and Sovereignty in Twentieth-Century Europe* (Albany, NY: State University of New York Press, 2001); Sluga, 'Trieste: Ethnicity and the Cold War, 1945–1954', *Journal of Contemporary History*, 29 (1994), pp.285–304; and Sluga, 'Fascism, Anti-Fascism, and Italianità: Contesting Memories and Identities', in Richard Bosworth and Patrizia Dogliani (eds), *Italian Fascism: History, Memory and Representation* (London: Macmillan, 1999).
4. Faurisson's views were published in 'La question des chambre à gaz', *Le Monde*, 29 December 1978. For a comprehensive rebuttal of Faurisson's views see Pierre Vidal-Naquet, *Les Assassins de la Mémoire* (Paris: La Découverte, 1982), especially the essays, 'Un Eichmann de Papier' and 'De Faurisson et de Chomski'.

5. Darquier de Pellepoix claimed that 'at Auschwitz only lice were gassed'. *L'Express*, 28 October 1978.
6. Robert Gildea, *France since 1945* (Oxford: Oxford University Press, 1996), p.67.
7. On Moulin see Daniel Cordier, *Jean Moulin: L'Inconnu du Panthéon*, 3 vols (Paris: Lattés, 1989–93) and Alan Clinton, *Jean Moulin, 1899–1943: The French Resistance and the Republic* (Basingstoke: Palgrave, 2002).
8. Richard J. Golsan, *Vichy's Afterlife: History and Counter-History in Postwar France* (Lincoln, NE: University of Nebraska Press, 2000).
9. On Bousquet and Touvier see Richard Golsan, *Memory, the Holocaust and French Justice: The Bousquet and Touvier Affairs* (Hanover, NH: University of New England, 1996). On Papon see Jean Bruno and Frédéric de Monicault, *L'Affaire Papon: Bordeaux, 1942–1944* (Paris: Tilandier, 1997) and Golsan (ed.), *Memory and Justice on Trial: The Papon Affair* (New York: Routledge, 2000).
10. An extensive literature exists on General de Gaulle. Among the numerous biographies of the general, the most comprehensive are Julian Jackson, *De Gaulle* (London: Cardinal, 1989); Jean Lacouture, *De Gaulle*, 2 vols (London: Harper Collins, 1990); and Andrew Shennan, *De Gaulle* (London: Longman, 1994). De Gaulle also wrote extensive memoirs, which form essential primary sources on his person and ideology: Charles de Gaulle, *Mémoires de Guerre*, 3 vols (Paris: Plon, 1989). Also published in English as *War Memoirs*, 6 vols (London: Collins, 1955).
11. Pierre Nora (ed.), *Les Lieux de Mémoire* (Paris: Gallimard), Tome I, *La République* (1984); Tome II, *La Nation*, vols 1–3 (1986), Tome III, *Les France*, vols 1–3 (1992). In English it has been published as Pierre Nora and Lawrence Kritzman (eds), *Realms of Memory: Rethinking the French Past*, vols 1–3 (New York: Columbia University Press, 1996–98).
12. Both expressions are owed to translations by Arthur Goldhammer: 'mnemonic sites' in Henry Rousso, *The Vichy Syndrome: History and Memory in France since 1944* (Cambridge, MA: Harvard University Press, 1991); 'realms of memory' in the English title of Nora's book.
13. What I have termed here *lieux d'amnésie*, or 'realms of amnesia', have elsewhere been called *non-lieux de mémoire*. See, for example, *Revue d'Histoire de la Shoah: Le Monde Juif*, 181 (July–December 2004).
14. Henri Rousso, *Le Syndrome de Vichy: De 1944 à Nos Jours* (Paris: Editions du Seuil, 1987).
15. Ibid.
16. Mario Isnenghi (ed.), *I Luoghi della Memoria: Personaggi e Date dell'Italia Unita*, 3 vols (Bari: Laterza, 1997).
17. Claudio Pavone, *Alle Origini della Repubblica* (Torino: Bollati Borlinghieri, 1995).
18. Luisa Passerini, *Fascism in Popular Memory: The Cultural Experience of the Turin Working Class* (Cambridge: Cambridge University Press, 1987).
19. Bosworth and Dogliani (eds), *Italian Fascism*.
20. Davide Rodogno, *Il Nuovo Ordine Mediterraneo: Le Politiche di Occupazione dell' Italia Fascista in Europa (1940–1943)* (Torino: Bollati Boringhieri, 2003) and Rodogno, 'Italiani Brava Gente?', *European History Quarterly*, 35, 2 (April 2005), pp.213–40. See also Filippo Focardi, *La Guerra della Memoria: La Resistenza Nel Dibattito Politico Italiano Dal 1945 a Oggi* (Bari: Laterza, 2005).
21. Angelo del Boca, *Italiani, Brava Gente?* (Vicenza: Neri Pozza Editore, 2005).
22. Pierre Nora, 'Between Memory and History', pp.7–24.
23. Kerwin Lee Klein, 'On the Emergence of "Memory" in Historical Discourse'. *Representations*, 69 (Winter 2000), pp.127–50, p.128.
24. Robert Rosenstone (ed.), *Revisioning History: Film and the Construction of a New Past* (Princeton, NJ: Princeton University Press, 1995); and Rosenstone, *Visions of the Past: The Challenge of Film to our Idea of History* (Cambridge, MA: Harvard University Press, 2001).
25. Among Sorlin's numerous works, see especially Pierre Sorlin, *European Cinemas, European Societies 1939–1990* (London: Routledge, 1991).
26. Janet Staiger, *Perverse Spectators: The Practices of Film Reception* (New York: New York University Press, 2000), p.11.
27. Ibid., p.23.
28. Elizabeth Ellsworth, 'Illicit Pleasures: Feminist Spectators and *Personal Best*', *Wide Angle*, 8, 2 (1986).

29. Janet Staiger, *Interpreting Films: Studies in the Historical Reception of American Cinema* (Princeton: Princeton University Press, 1992). On her work see also Barbara Page, 'Theory and Historicity in Film Studies', *College English*, 54, 8 (December 1992), pp.948–50, and Michael Isenberg, 'Review of *Interpreting Films: Studies in the Historical Reception of American Cinema*', *The American Historical Review*, 98, 2 (April 1993), pp.596–7.
30. Ibid.
31. Klaus Bruhn Jensen, 'The Past in the Future: Problems and Potentials of Historical Reception Studies', *Journal of Communications*, 43, 4 (Autumn 1993), pp.20–8; and Thomas Lindlof, 'The Qualitative Study of Media Audiences', *Journal of Broadcasting and Electronic Media*, 35, 1 (Winter 1991), pp.23–42.
32. Lindlof, 'The Qualitative Study of Media Audiences'.

1

A Resistant Make-up: The Making and Reception of *Nuit et Brouillard*

> There was a Prime Minister whose name was Mendès, and he also had another name, but he was too small for such a big name. It was he who lost France enormous territories.[1]

Pronounced in 1955 amidst the panicked atmosphere of a disbanding empire, this anti-Semitic slur aimed at Pierre Mendès-France by a Poujadist MP was the latest episode in a decade in which France had struggled to come to terms with the darker legacies of the Second World War. As Henry Rousso has argued, in the years between 1944 and 1954, France had employed the positive, unifying memories of the Resistance and the Liberation to eclipse the more uncomfortable and divisive issues of the defeat of 1940, the Vichy regime, German occupation and French collaboration with it. This process took place at a popular and institutional level for reasons ranging from the psychological desire to escape traumatic memories, to a political design strongly to reaffirm France as a victor, while marginalising the Communist Party and allowing the recycling of a largely compromised elite.[2]

Even before the end of the war, de Gaulle had set in motion this process – which Rousso has called 'unfinished mourning'. He had done so by means of several strategic decisions: first, by setting out the continuity between the Third and Fourth Republics through the mediation of the Free French; second, by all but ignoring Vichy; third, by merging the two world conflicts into a 'thirty-years war', in the context of which the defeat of 1940 was but a lost battle within a triumphal war. With a stroke of genius, de Gaulle had established an orthodoxy according to which virtually all French people had in some way taken part in the Resistance. Moreover, this uplifting portrait did not displease the communists, who had quickly established their leadership of the Resistance by claiming the inflated figure of 75,000 martyrs, but still had the problem of dealing with their own late entry in the Resistance.[3] Thus, during this first phase, the inability and unwillingness to deal thoroughly with Vichy caused the nation's mourning to be incomplete.

The disappearance of the physical reminders of the war and the emergence of other, more pressing concerns caused a change in emphasis in French understanding of its wartime past. Between 1954 and 1971, Rousso argued, a period of repression of memory ensued. Algeria is crucial to this second phase for a number of reasons. Firstly, the Algerian conflict stirred the memory of the occupation because for many French men and women, Algeria was part of France.[4] Algeria had been a French colony since 1830 but, unlike other French territories in North Africa, had been divided into three *départements* and was considered an integral part of the nation. It was not so much a case of retaining a French Algeria, but rather of protecting an Algerian France. By defending what in their eyes was the indivisibility of the motherland, these people felt they were replicating the struggle against Nazi occupation. Hence, many left-wing sympathisers and former *résistants*, such as François Mitterrand and Guy Mollet, joined former supporters of Vichy in the call to repress the Algerian nationalists.[5] Christian Democrat Georges Bidault, who in 1943 had been the head of the Conseil National de la Résistance (National Resistance Council, CNR), in 1962 called for the formation of a new CNR.[6] Secondly, the Algerian revolt questioned the long-standing French belief in the country's civilising mission, challenging the idea that imperialism could be compatible with the spirit of 1789 – or indeed that of 1943–45. Thirdly, the atrocities of French regular and paramilitary troops in Algeria struck a chord with many who remembered the Nazi use of torture: how could one be justified and the other barbaric? Furthermore, the Algerian conflict brought back echoes of Vichy's racial persecutions: Frenchmen of Algerian descent were arbitrarily arrested and, as the quote at the beginning of this chapter testifies, Prime Minister Mendès-France was openly attacked for being Jewish. Fourthly, the stark and often violent internal divisions between supporters and opponents of decolonisation recalled the internecine struggle between Vichy and the Resistance. Fifthly, the Algerian War directly facilitated the return to power, in 1958, of de Gaulle. Because the general was the living symbol of the Second World War and the embodiment of the resistancialist myth, his political resurrection was crucial to the re-emergence of popular and institutional discourses around Vichy.[7]

In 1954, the publication of de Gaulle's memoirs had further set out this myth: here he simultaneously played down Vichy's significance and emphasised his radio appeal on 18 June as the beginning of the Resistance, which in turn he glorified as an abstract concept of national defiance independent of the *résistants* themselves.[8] In the same year, the Jewish historian Robert Aron, who had been a 'non-conformist' in the 1930s and close to Vichy during the 1940s, had published his own interpretation of Pétain's regime in his *Histoire de Vichy*.[9] Using sources including the trials of key Vichy notables, he articulated the idea of Vichy as a shield which had prevented total German occupation and exploitation of France and its resources, sparing it the harsher fate which befell other defeated nations. Practically, he argued, Vichy had served a purpose complementary to that of de Gaulle's Free France, defending national interest in the face of the occupier as the general carried on the war effort on France's behalf from London and Algiers. Although the visions of de Gaulle and Aron differed significantly, they were not too far apart. For instance, both created a distinction between a vast majority of French men and women who had kept their integrity and their patriotism, and a small portion who had sought actively to collaborate with Germany. Also, both facilitated, albeit for different reasons, the recycling of the moderate right into national politics.

When Rousso uses the word 'repression' to describe this period, he does not intend it in strict psychoanalytic terms. Vichy had not been removed from popular memory; on the contrary, the experience of the Second World War remained central to French memory. From as early as 1951, the Comité d'Histoire de la Deuxième Guerre Mondiale (Committee for the History of the Second World War, CHDGM) was set by the government, under the direction of Henri Michel, whose *Histoire de la Résistance, 1940–1944* had defined the orthodox view of the Resistance.[10] Even before then, the processes of commemoration had a clearly institutional flavour. As Wieviorka reminds us, the unveilings of several monuments to the martyrs of the concentration camps in Paris's Père Lachaise cemetery, between 1946 and 1949, were highly symbolic events: these were used not only to commemorate victims and create bonds between survivors, but also – particularly by the Parti Communiste Français (French Communist Party, PCF) – to stake a claim on the legacy of the Resistance. As ashes from Auschwitz were scattered around the site dedicated to the memorial, on 30 June 1946, '180,000 French men women and children' were commemorated to the sound of the Marseillaise.[11]

The figure of 180,000 was obtained by adding 120,000 Jewish victims to 60,000 French victims. Wieviorka points out that, while the former figure was thought to be correct until the 1960s – and then revised to around 75,000 – the latter was deliberately exaggerated to deny that Auschwitz had been primarily a camp for the extermination of Jews. 'The memory of Auschwitz thus became a component of communist memory. To achieve that, it was necessary to silence the fact that the only French children who died there, and whose memory is honoured on that monument, were Jewish.'[12] It is also worth pointing out, however, that the writing on the memorial said French, not communist, and that the Marseillaise, not the socialist Internationale, was played at the unveiling. Thus the hijacking of Jewish identity was twofold: political and national. The identity of Jewish victims, and especially of foreign and denaturalised Jews deported from France, was strangled between communist and nationalist memories of martyrdom.[13]

Since the Père Lachaise ceremonies, it would take six years of complex negotiations for the Mémorial du Martyr Juif Inconnu (Memorial to the Unknown Jewish Martyr) to be inaugurated. Even within the French Jewish community, afraid of upsetting the new national harmony, there was opposition to the project. Eventually, however, the Mémorial became the repository of the archives of the Centre de Documentation Juive Contemporaine (Contemporary Jewish Documentation Centre, CDJC), which had started collecting material on the Shoah while Paris was still under German occupation. Thus, while the war and the Shoah were both remembered in this period, the memory of the Shoah was still an essentially Jewish one.[14] Hence, Rousso's 'repression' should not be understood as uniform silence, but as the emergence and embracing of a sanitised version of the past which – Gaullist or communist – became the only acceptable one: a 'civic religion' of the Resistance.[15]

In the midst of this complex and sensitive scenario came Alain Resnais's 1956 documentary, *Nuit et Brouillard* (*Night and Fog*). There is little doubt that the film is a milestone both in the memory of the occupation and the Shoah in France,[16] and in French cinema and, as such, it has attracted much interest, especially from film scholars, and much is known about its making, style and tormented reception.[17] Further than that, Resnais's film has long been acknowledged as one of the essential filmic texts on the Holocaust, as well as a key example of documentary film-making.[18] More recently, the film has been examined as a new, post-traumatic cinema that contributed to a post-traumatic historical consciousness by breaking down the boundaries between past and present.[19]

In the context of this book, however, *Night and Fog* is examined as the mediator between three sensitive aspects of France's relationship with its past in this difficult, initial post-war period of hardship and adjustment: firstly, the memory of the occupation and the Resistance; secondly, the understanding of the full extent and nature of the persecution of the Jews during the Second World War; and thirdly, the contemporary concerns with the events unfolding in Algeria. Because of this unique role, Resnais's film bears witness to the contradictory processes of remembrance and repression of the past in 1950s France. These French paradoxes are revealed in and by Resnais's documentary. The representational choices made by the film-makers are evidence of the simultaneous French interest in the death camps and misunderstanding of their primary purpose as an arena for the slaughter of European Jewry. At the same time, the institutional commissioning of the film testifies to a clear interest in the war, while the subsequent censorship suggests a simultaneous unwillingness to acknowledge any French involvement in the crimes *Night and Fog* describes. Finally, the permanence until the present day of Resnais's work both in popular imagination and in French governmental pedagogic strategies in prevention of racism, is not only testament to its extraordinary qualities, but also to its ability to lend itself to ever-shifting interpretations.

THE MAKING OF *NIGHT AND FOG*

In January 1955, on the tenth anniversary of the liberation of Auschwitz, the CHDGM approached Anatôle Dauman and his production company, Argos Films. Its commission was a documentary film on the Nazi concentration camps, which would build on an anthology of testimonies of ex-deportees, edited by Henri Michel and Olga Wormser for the CHDGM in 1954.[20] In November 1954, this had inspired an exhibition at the Institut Pédagogique National (National Pedagogical Institute) in Paris, aimed at 25,000 pupils of Parisian schools.[21] Right from its conception, then, the film was steeped in the historiography of the period and in the educational mission with which the CHDGM had been entrusted. This is confirmed by the fact that historians Wormser and Michel, who directed the committee, took on the role of historical consultants for the film.

Dauman immediately proposed the project to Alain Resnais, who was at the time a young film-maker admired for a couple of short films, one on Picasso (*Guernica*, 1950) and the other on pre-colonial African art (*Les Statues Meurent Aussi, Statues Also Die*, 1953) both of which had been censored because of their political implications.[22] Resnais, who was close in his thinking to the film theorist André Bazin and the circle of intellectuals around the film journal *Les Cahiers du Cinéma*,[23] would in the 1960s become associated with the French New Wave. A committed left-wing intellectual, in 1960 Resnais signed the *Manifeste des 121*, an appeal endorsed by 121 French intellectuals reaffirming the right of oppressed people to self-determination. Within this controversial document, they endorsed Algeria's right to armed revolt, and encouraged French conscripts to North Africa to desert. Resnais would continue his political activism well into the 1970s: in a telegram to President Nixon, he referred to American actions in Vietnam as '*méthodes hitlériennes*'.[24]

Resnais's political commitment would inevitably affect the making of *Night and Fog*. Initially, Alan Resnais refused the project on the principle that such a film could not be shot by someone without first-hand experience of the camps.[25] Eventually Dauman and Resnais agreed that the left-wing poet Jean Cayrol, a survivor of Mauthausen, would write the commentary while Resnais would collect and arrange the images. Alongside him, the renowned French short-film director Chris Marker, who had also co-authored *Statues Also Die*, became Resnais's assistant. Marker edited the first version of Cayrol's commentary to fit the images, and suggested that the East German composer Hans Eisler write the musical score.[26]

The title was inspired by the Nacht und Nebel Erlass (Night and Fog Decree) issued on 7 December 1941 by Field Marshal Keitel, reportedly on Hitler's behalf.[27] The decree concerned the treatment of civilians in the occupied territories suspected of crimes against the Reich. These individuals were 'to vanish without a trace',[28] and their families were not to be informed of their whereabouts, or even of their arrest. In some cases these prisoners were deported to concentration camps including Auschwitz, where their clothes were marked 'NN'. It was also the title of Jean Cayrol's collection of poems, *Poèmes de la Nuit et du Brouillard*, published in 1946.[29] Through Cayrol's poems, the expression 'Night and Fog' ceased to refer only to victims of the specific operation and became symbolic of the deportations as a whole. Arguably, then, this title reflected perfectly the approach Resnais and the CHDGM intended to take: an approach that would refer directly to political persecution while maintaining a universal resonance at a symbolic level.

Given the patronage of the CHDGM and the involvement of three production companies, the film did not experience significant financial difficulties. More problematic was the collection of the wartime footage needed by Resnais, with the film eventually comprising shots collected from a variety of archives in France, Belgium, Holland and Poland.[30] The film-makers were able to obtain much of the relevant Soviet material from Polish archives, but their access to British material was limited to that held in the Dutch Institute of War Documentation. Resnais used post-liberation images out of context, to represent life within the active camps. The script of *Night and Fog* was published in *L'Avant-Scène du Cinema* in 1961,[31] and Raskin has later matched the original Argos Films shooting script with the commentary.[32] This confirms that shots of prisoners sharing their soup or helping each other stand, which Resnais used to express the inmates' ability to maintain peer solidarity in the face of persecution, were in fact post-liberation takes.

It is worth raising the issue of accuracy about a document often used for educational purposes. This criticism, however, should not be interpreted as tantamount to accusing the film-makers of

Figure 1.1. *Night and Fog*: 'Resnais's camera-eye panned over 1955 Auschwitz's infamous ramp, overrun by vegetation, trying to grasp what time and peace had conspired to hide.' (*Nuit et Brouillard*, by Alan Resnais © 1956, Argos Films.)

dishonesty. Rather, this incident points to the potential that archival footage has to mislead when employed in historical representation. Another often overlooked example of this is Resnais's inclusion, as archival footage, of a fictional scene. The black-and-white shot of the arrival of a convoy at Auschwitz, far from being original, originates from Wanda Jakubowska's *Ostatni Etap* (*The Last Stage*, Poland, 1948), widely acknowledged as the first Holocaust film. The shot, credited in the shooting script but not in the film's credits,[33] blends so well with the archival material that it is almost impossible to notice its lack of authenticity.[34] In an age where any inaccuracy may be exploited as 'evidence' that the Shoah never happened, it is essential to avoid, or at least acknowledge, any discrepancies. In 1955, however, there were different problems. *Night and Fog* should be analysed both in the context of the mid-1950s and from a present-day vantage point.

It seems quite clear that in making *Night and Fog*, Resnais was not attempting a realistic representation of the Shoah. Instead, he sought to make a commemorative and a political point applicable to all instances of totalitarian repression, regardless of their specific nature. A number of choices he made in the structure of the film support this interpretation. To begin with, the director's insistence on having a survivor write the commentary suggests his awareness of the problems of imagining and representing the camps. It was not merely a first-hand experience or an individual story of survival that Resnais sought, but the psychological and linguistic ability to understand and express the Nazi persecution. Resnais was thus exploring the very modern contrast between the perception of survivors who had witnessed the Nazi extermination factories in their macabre industrial efficiency, and that of the person attempting to understand the Shoah from black-and-white archival footage, memoirs and often scant material remains.

In *Night and Fog*, Resnais's camera-eye panned over 1955 Auschwitz's infamous ramp, broken barracks and blown-up gas chambers, overrun by vegetation, trying to grasp what time and peace had conspired to hide (Figure 1.1).[35] It is important to remember that, in 1955, Auschwitz was not the international centre of commemoration that it is today. It was an eerie and abandoned place, which the opposing tides of defeat and victory had failed either to erase completely or to convert into some new incarnation. Avoiding the cliché of portraying it in tones of grey and blue, the colours of the desolate Polish sunshine in which Resnais shoots the Auschwitz scenes succeed in conveying an uncomfortably peaceful atmosphere. Resnais himself explained:

> By making all the film in black-and-white I was afraid of obtaining, from those old stones, barbed wire and laden skies, a filmic romanticism that would not have been at all genuine. The colours and the silent parts are there to show the difference.[36]

Shooting present-day Auschwitz in colour allowed Resnais to create a contrast with the archival footage, which mirrors the one mentioned earlier between Resnais the investigator and Cayrol the survivor. The passage of time and the clash between the quest for memory and the difficulty of relating to the past, are central to *Night and Fog*.

The relationship between colour and black and white is only one of several contrasts in the dual approach pursued by Alain Resnais. Another significant one is that between motion and stillness. In the modern-day filming, Resnais made widespread use of tracking and panoramic shots, achieving a constant sense of motion; on the contrary, almost without exception the archival images are still images edited together. Inspired by André Bazin, Italian neo-realism and the French poetic-realism of the 1930s, Resnais embraced the principle that emotional visual material should be met by an inversely proportional dispassionate treatment.[37] Thus, as Albrecht Dumling has argued, the soundtrack of East German composer Hans Eisler is purposely at odds with the images: the peaceful notes reminiscent of Arcadian pastures accompany harrowing pictures of severed heads and heaps of human hair. By being dissonant with the images, the music creates a separate level of perception, not allowing the audience to be desensitized by the flow of horrific images.[38] Nonetheless, while watching *Night and Fog* it is easy for the viewer to wonder if Eisler's tranquil score really underplays the images or if, by creating such a strident contrast, it reinforces them.

NIGHT AND FOG AND THE JEWS: MISSION OR OMISSION?

Night and Fog is a commemoration in the shape of a search, and the start of this investigation is the scene of the crime, where the evidence has aged. 'Even a quiet country scene, even a field with crops harvested and crows flying can lead to a concentration camp.'[39] The beginning of *Night and Fog* is a long, colour travelling shot of contemporary Auschwitz, taken in summer. It passes by fields of wheat, then the old electrified fence, once a source of dread and delivery for prisoners. Then it enters the camp. Despite the eeriness of the place, the untrained eye will have difficulties understanding the extent and nature of what has taken place. The glare of the sun conceals the bitter cold of winter; the gentle breeze fails to reveal the lashing wind; the long dry grass hides the enveloping mud of autumn and spring. At first glance, there is no way of knowing that well over 1,000,000 human beings were murdered here, or realising the abysmal conditions in which prisoners were forced to exist. While he leads us into 1955 Auschwitz, Resnais is setting the crux of the film: the complexity of comprehending the concentration camp experience through second-hand knowledge. 'The camera is the only visitor now [...]; a strange grass grows where once the inmates trod the earth, no current passes through the wires, no step is heard but ours.'[40]

The second step is calling the witnesses: a jumpcut, in sharp contrast with the long, smoothly edited modern-day sequences, transforms the scenario into black-and-white archival footage of a pre-war Nazi rally. This is Cayrol's territory; the film-maker–survivor dualism begins here. The historical reconstruction is divided into eleven black-and-white parts, but these can be arranged in three larger chapters: the building of the camps and the deportations; the physical and social structure of the camp; the extermination procedure. Each part is punctuated by a colour sequence shot in the present, exploring from a modern perspective the events described by the commentary and evoked by the historic images: for instance, the archival footage referring to the extermination process is met by Resnais's camera moving around the remains of a gas chamber. By this process, Resnais constantly reminds us of the starting point of the investigation.

'1933, la machine se met en marche.'[41] The first chapter takes its cue from the Nazi rise to power and explores the building of the camp system, interpreted in both a material and a conceptual way. If the film is a little hasty in its analysis of the years leading to the genocide or its motives, its explanation of Nazi Germany as a machine is incisive and ahead of its time. Resnais's interpretation here is evidently Marxist: he understands the establishment of the concentration camp system as that of an industry, whereby contractors compete for the building commissions, architects and engineers are called in, housing for the workforce is provided. Even the cultural heritage of the location is taken into consideration, as demonstrated by the conservation of Goethe's oak tree at Mauthausen. The feeling with which the film leaves the viewer is that these death factories were the natural development of the National Socialist ideology, matched by the willingness of industrialists to collaborate, and the acquiescence of the population as a whole.

The film then deals with the deportations. Resnais tries to explain who the deportees were and whence they came. Here, one of the major controversies around *Night and Fog* becomes evident: who, in fact, were the prisoners detained, exploited and killed in these camps? 'Burger, a German worker; Stern, a Jewish student from Amsterdam; Schmulski, a shopkeeper from Krakow; Annette, a schoolgirl from Bordeaux'.[42] The reference to the paradigmatic Dutch student is the only occasion in which the voice-over in *Night and Fog* mentions Jews. Resnais's film gives no sense of any Jewish dimension to the crime it discusses. Faced with this astonishing absence one can respond either by ignoring it, or by accusing the film of deliberate deceit. In the first reaction, one assumes that the film-makers took as read the specific anti-Jewish nature of the persecution; in the second there is the expectation of a perennially lurking anti-Semitism. There are arguments in favour of both these explanations, yet both are inadequate.

There are indeed signs that the film-makers were aware of the particular Nazi measures against the Jews, and that they attempted to convey this subtly, choosing not to discriminate between victims. In saying that they were 'rounded up in Warsaw, deported from Lodz, Prague, Brussels, Athens, Zagreb, Odessa or Rome',[43] the commentary names well-known sites of mass Jewish deportations, although it would be wrong to assume that in 1956 the general audience would automatically have made such a connection. The line that follows, on the other hand, 'rounded up at the Vél d'Hiv',[44] also names a place which certainly would have been recognisable to most French audiences as the location where Parisian Jews were held. The commentary continues, '*résistants* captured at Compiègne',[45] in this instance specifically identifying a different persecuted group. Jewish stars are evident on many of the prisoners seen in the archival material. While he displays footage of Hitler, Goebbels, and German soldiers marching, Resnais at no point mentions Nazism. Yet no commentator has ever questioned the nationality of the persecutors.

These facts may be employed to argue that the lack of direct references to anti-Semitism in *Night and Fog* stems neither from ignorance nor from willing historical revisionism, but simply from taste and style. Having taken into consideration the period in which the film was made, and the corpus of Resnais's work as well as that of his collaborators, it is arguable that Resnais consciously opted for a universal approach which would relate the Shoah to the general issue of totalitarianism and fit perfectly his stance against colonialism. There is contrasting evidence, however, which makes the issue less simple to resolve. To begin with, there is the sentence, 'those caught in the act, or by error, or by ill luck, head for the camps',[46] which follows the statements reported in the last paragraph and concludes the first part of *Night and Fog*. To suggest that people sent to the death camps of

Poland were randomly chosen is to deny a long-term racial strategy. *Night and Fog*'s failure to acknowledge this clearly goes well beyond problems of nomenclature or semantics and is a serious oversight. Moreover, this is particularly unfortunate as it risks preserving an image of the Nazis as mindless monsters, popular in immediate post-war representation, contradicting the film's own remarkable point on the unique kind of Nazi hyper-rationality which made the aberration of the concentration camp possible.

Another statement in Cayrol's commentary further complicates matters. In describing the social structure of the camps, the commentary states:

> [The prisoners are] classified in ways as yet incomprehensible, dressed in the blue striped uniform sometimes marked Nacht und Nebel, Night and Fog. The deportee wearing the red triangle of the 'political prisoners' answers first to the green triangle of the common criminals. Above them the kapo, almost always a common criminal.[47]

On the one hand, the film discusses the camps with simultaneous attention to detail and to the historical phenomenon as a whole; on the other, it omits any reference to Jewish prisoners, or any group of prisoners other than political deportees and criminals. This is a baffling omission which reinforces the feeling that the film-makers, in line with their own political allegiance and the dominant opinion of the time, deliberately emphasised the persecution of political prisoners and neglected the persecution of Jews. It is easy to hypothesise that Cayrol's own experience as a political deportee may have something to do with this, as he may well have privileged, in his commentary, certain aspects of the persecution. Yet this is only a partial explanation. Clearly the film was never intended as a rendition of Cayrol's unwritten memoirs, as the insistence on Auschwitz, not Mauthausen where Cayrol had been a prisoner, makes quite clear.

The failure of Resnais's film to address the Jews as the main victims of Auschwitz can probably be best explained by looking at the fashion in which the Shoah was more generally approached at the time *Night and Fog* was made. The way Resnais tackled the topic revealed a wider interest in totalitarianism and oppression. His interpretation of the camp system referred to the idea of a *univers concentrationnaire*, an alternative society characterised by its own rules, even its own class system. Furthermore, the fact that this universe, conceptually and practically, was the product of ordinary human beings did not escape Resnais. Yet, at the same time, the main purpose of the concentration camp system, and in particular of its extermination facilities, eluded him and his collaborators, including survivor Jean Cayrol.

Thus, the customary description of Resnais's approach as 'universal' is inaccurate. This explanation applies a modern concept, the idea of commemorating not just Jews but all victims of Nazi persecution, to a film that is steeped in the culture of France in the 1950s. From the title onwards, *Night and Fog* was conceived as a general commemorative and educational work on the deportations, with a particular attention to the persecution of French *résistants*. The film reflects contemporary French society's interest in the subject, but also its inability and unwillingness to understand or discuss the attempted genocide of the Jews as anything other than a side issue in the wider struggle between fascism and anti-fascism. It is in no way an indictment of the film to suggest that political deportees take centre stage in it. Rather, it is a credit to Resnais that his work managed to focus primarily on the death camps, their inception, construction and functioning, revealing an interest in humanity's ability to imagine and create such aberrations.

This same approach is revealed by the film's finale. A lengthy tracking shot of the infamous Auschwitz ramp picks up the story where Cayrol's commentary had left it: 'Today there is sunlight on those lines. We follow them slowly, seeking what? Traces of the bodies that fell out when the cars were opened? Of survivors driven by rifle butts through the door?'[48] Once again, and as on many occasions in the narration, the film-makers insist on the elusive nature of memory and its difficult relation with history. The effect is to remind the audience constantly that the film is uncovering a horrible past through the help of testimonies and historical research, but that, no matter how painstaking the reconstruction, it cannot transmit the horror in full. *Night and Fog* deliberately does not encourage its audience to identify with the victims. Instead, commemoration and memory here go hand in hand; reconstruction and remembrance become two aspects of the same work aimed at exposing forgotten truths.

By means of this dual approach *Night and Fog* successfully, if briefly, examines the prisoners' arrival and first sight of the camp; it analyses the social structure of the camp; looks at the camp's work pattern; it examines the infirmary, the medical experiments and the camp jail; and it discusses the underground resistance organisations. The camp's organisation as a micro-society, with its own regulations and social dynamics, seems particularly to interest Resnais. He marvels at the camp ethics, dwelling on the chilling irony of mottos such as 'arbeit macht frei' and 'a flea means death'. His camera points out the infirmary, the role of which is reversed from the one of hope and care that it possesses in the outside world; it lingers on a still of the Buchenwald camp zoo; and, with sarcasm, it pans around the utter absurdity of a camp prison.

As one follows Resnais's camera further into 1955 Auschwitz, the archival footage becomes harsher. The pace of the editing increases as the film draws closer to its peak, to revealing the extermination process, and the disposal and recycling of the corpses. It is at this point that Cayrol's words fail, and the commentary stops. Throughout, the harrowing images are contrasted with Eisler's soothing score, which prevents them from becoming unsupportable. Even so, this part of the film remains disturbing and difficult to watch. The viewer is relieved when, for the last time, black-and-white relinquishes its place to colour, and the emaciated corpses become once again only memories in the Auschwitz scenery. One understands, then, that the whole film has been intended to lead to this; Resnais's mystified gaze and Cayrol's reconstruction finally merge and abandon the past to turn their glance to the present:

> As I talk to you, cold marsh waters fill the ditches, as cold and sluggish as our memories. War has dozed off, one eye still open. Grass grows again around the blocks, an abandoned village still full of menace. [...] From this strange observatory, who watches to warn of new executioners? Do they really look so different from us? Somewhere among us remain undetected kapos, officers, informers. There are all those who did not believe, or only sometimes; and those of us who see the monster as being buried under these ruins, finding hope in being finally rid of this totalitarian disease, pretending to believe it happened but once and in one country, not seeing what goes on around us, not heeding the unending cry.[49]

With the exception of the two unfinished documentaries attempted by the British and American Army Film Units in 1946, *Night and Fog* is the first Western European Holocaust film. Yet its originality transcends this fact. Resnais's film is groundbreaking because it links the Nazi genocide to other atrocities. In doing so, it urges the viewers not only to learn from what the film has shown but to act on what they have learnt to prevent future sufferings. *Night and Fog*'s ending makes it relevant for three generations of viewers: those who watched in the 1950s were reminded of the Second World War; in the 1970s it conjured up thoughts of Vietnam; now it triggers memories of genocides in Rwanda, Bosnia or East Timor.

In the 1980s, Resnais repeatedly stated that he filmed *Night and Fog* with Algeria in mind. In particular, he referred to his concern with detention camps for French Algerians which were already taking shape in 1955.[50] However, Philip Dine has cast considerable doubt over Resnais's 1980s statements. Despite producing no evidence to disprove them, he has convincingly suggested that 1955 was too early on in the Algerian conflict for it to have inspired the film.[51] Indeed, Dine seems to imply that the director may have overstated the link between the film and Algeria in order to improve his already considerable credentials as an enlightened intellectual. In fact, two separate points must be made with regards to the film and its ending: on the one hand, we have the film's main body, which undoubtedly is not about Algeria; on the other hand, we have the ending of the film, which, by directly addressing the audience in the first person plural and the present tense, clearly contains contemporary implications. These may or may not have been about Algeria, but I see no good reason to disbelieve Resnais. On the contrary, if we interpret the director's statements as recognition that the film contained a general concern about contemporary human rights, these statements become easier to reconcile with the film's timing.

This notwithstanding, there is no evidence to suggest that his contemporaries interpreted the film as an allegory of the events unfolding in Algeria. Moreover, few people saw the film in 1956. There were a number of reasons for this. Most significantly, the film was not released for general distribution because of its unpopular format and disturbing theme. Resnais's subtle final reference may have played a part in the film's unpopularity, but evidence suggests that if an allusion to Algeria was indeed made, it was too subtle to bother the censors. As we shall see, other references to less contemporary matters did not escape their vigilance. But, while it is well known that censorship banned the film from the Cannes Film Festival, there is no evidence to suggest that censorship prevented the film from being released more widely. The last part of this chapter will examine the problematic reception of *Night and Fog*, and finally consider how and why its status changed over time, from being an unwelcome reminder of the dark years to becoming a highly regarded work of art and institutional tool against a resurgent right-wing militancy.

UNACCEPTABLE, BUT TO WHOM? THE RECEPTION OF *NIGHT AND FOG*[52]

> M. Maurice Lémaire, Secretary of State for Industry and Commerce, in agreement with the Foreign Affairs Ministry, confirms the French selection to the Cannes Film Festival. The only alteration is in the 'short films' category, where *Nuits Royales* replaces *Night and Fog*, which has been withdrawn from the competition following a request from the German embassy.[53]

Night and Fog was due to be presented at the 1956 Cannes Film Festival, a celebration of French culture and expression of France's renewed grandeur. Only a few weeks before the festival, however, on 6 April, the French Ministry of Industry and Commerce requested that the film be banned. The organising committee duly obliged, replacing *Night and Fog* with another French short film, *Nuits Royales*, which had received no votes in the initial selection process.[54] *Night and Fog* was not the only film to be withdrawn. On 28 March, Jack Lee's *A Town like Alice*, a British film about a group of women captured by the Japanese in Malaysia, was removed from the festival after a complaint by the Japanese ambassador.[55] Meanwhile, Luis Buñuel's *Cela s'Appelle l'Aurore* (*That is the Dawn*, 1956), which critiqued bourgeois politics, religion and hypocritical family values, was also rejected. Its place was taken by Jean Delannoy's *Marie Antoinette*, a tribute to the French queen's martyrdom in which, according to *France-Observateur*, every individual with remotely revolutionary sympathies was portrayed as a bloodthirsty brute. It is evident that the organisers were steering well clear of controversy by rejecting difficult topics as well as difficult personalities.

The headline of Doniol-Valcroze's article leaves no doubt on its polemical approach to government interference: 'The deportation never took place.'[56] His conclusion echoed his anger at the 'official historical truth' of the French authorities: 'why would it be shameful simply to tell the truth in front of the assembly of nations present in Cannes?' By the festival's own regulations, a film could be removed if it was deemed that its content could cause offence to one of the participating nations. The same rule had been applied in 1955 to exclude the Norwegian film *Blodveien* (Kåre Bergstrøm and Rados Novakovic, 1955), again following a German protest.[57] Nor is the other suggested explanation – that the festive spirit of the *kermesse* would have been incompatible with *Night and Fog*'s harrowing theme – very convincing.[58] Though the Cannes Film Festival is a glamorous and often frivolous occasion, there is no evidence to suggest it ever refused films because of serious or tragic subject matter.

The extreme sensitivity of Adenauer's Germany to the subject of Nazism and Nazi atrocities is perhaps more easily explainable than France's apparent willingness to bow to West German grievances.[59] The French position is especially surprising coming from a government that included former resisters and deportees such as the Foreign Secretary, Christian Pineau.[60] France's effort in establishing strategic Western European alliances such as the European Coal and Steel Community (ECSC) is well known, yet the answer lies only partially with the need to cultivate good neighbourly relations. Instead, the affair points to the French government's own discomfort with some of the issues discussed in Resnais's film. Indeed, the French authorities welcomed the opportunity to attribute the withdrawal of *Night and Fog* to German sensibilities rather than to their own wishes. In doing so, they managed to renew the opposition between Nazism and Resistance while also maintaining positive relations with the West German government in the build-up to the Treaty of Rome. Three pieces of evidence point specifically to this conclusion: first, the French censorship board's refusal to pass *Night and Fog* before certain 'adjustments'; second, the much-reported official warnings of possible German interference; third, the fact that in

1956 *Night and Fog* was invited to the Oberhausen Film Festival in West Germany, without a ban being imposed by Bonn.

All the contemporary reviews reporting the exclusion of *Night and Fog* seemed certain of German responsibility, while blaming the French government for its acquiescence. A sense of self-righteous anger at what was perceived as German arrogance lurks in these newspaper articles, suggesting an all-too-fresh memory of times when Germany was indeed able to decide what French cinemas should or should not screen. In the French communist periodical *Libération*,[61] Simone Dubreuilh expanded on this by inventing a conversation between a supporter of Resnais and a conservative man wondering what all the fuss is about.[62] In their imaginary exchange, Dubreuilh's character 'A' suggests that the film must be genuinely offensive or false, for the German government to intervene so decidedly, while character 'B' rebukes him. The rhetorical construction continues along these lines, with bigoted objection followed by enlightened riposte. However, while Dubreuilh's two interlocutors disagree over why the German government requested the film's exclusion, and whether it had a right to do so, there is no suggestion in this dialogue that the responsibility might lie, even in part, elsewhere.

The aforementioned Jacques Doniol-Valcroze even suggested that West Germany must still identify itself with Nazism, if a representation of its atrocities offended it. More interestingly still, it reported indirectly an earlier statement made by Foreign Secretary Pineau warning that 'today's Germans cannot meddle in this affair without giving the impression of sanctioning Nazism'.[63] Surprisingly, however, in another article published exactly a week later in the same paper, Doniol-Valcroze retracted his own sweeping accusations. According to this second, rather subdued instalment: 'with less confused festival regulations, there never would have been a *Night and Fog* affaire',[64] and 'Secretary of State Lémaire was in no way influenced' by a German intervention, which had indeed taken place.[65] Doniol-Valcroze, who was also a member of the selection committee, stated that he had had a meeting with Mr Lémaire on 16 April and could vouch for the latter's good faith.

The 'affaire-*Night and Fog*' had been resolved in the space of a week and a few lines. The unravelled mystery conveniently revealed confusion as the culprit and at the same time restored French dignity. A compromise was agreed: *Night and Fog* was

Figure 1.2. *Night and Fog*: by obscuring the *képi* the censors sought to erase an historical fact. (*Nuit et Brouillard*, by Alan Resnais © 1956, Argos Films.)

screened in Cannes during the festival, though not within its official programme. It is difficult to establish to what extent the whole affair had been stirred up by an over-zealous press. What is certain, however, is that the scandal raised by the exclusion of Resnais's film from the Cannes Film Festival and the alleged West German meddling, diverted attention from the French censorship board's own intervention against the film.

The story is well known: *Night and Fog* was granted a censorship visa only at the price of a minor adjustment. One particular shot, about five minutes into the documentary, showed a still taken in the French concentration camp of Pithiviers. On the left of the shot was the head of a French gendarme, easily distinguishable by his *képi* (Figure 1.2).[66] At the request of the censors, Resnais agreed to obscure the gendarme's hat without removing the shot from the film. It became a dark shadow in the top left-hand corner of the shot: it is a stain, which censorship has rendered indelible. The official reason for the cut was that the image brought the gendarmerie into disrepute, but it is not difficult to imagine the discomfort the French government would have felt at the implication that French police took part in the guarding and running of concentration camps. Although the newspapers reported the vanished gendarme in the days immediately following *Night and Fog*'s exclusion from Cannes, they put much greater emphasis on the German protest. In a France willingly in the grip of the Gaullist resistancialist myth, it is hardly surprising that the government was not alone in wishing to reject the *képi*'s implications.

Why Resnais agreed to introduce such a serious alteration to *Night and Fog* is difficult to understand. Certainly, it earned him some criticism. René Vautier, who was at the time the secretary of the Comité d'Action Contre la Censure (Committee of Action Against Censorship), reported his own reaction:

> I said to Resnais: 'All right then, show your film in Germany like that! I hope they will ask you to avoid all allusions to Germans, and that we should see the Jews walk willingly in the crematoria, and lock the door behind them.[67]

Yet, Germany is indeed the key to Resnais's compliance. His priority seems to have been that his film be shown on the other side of the Rhine, in particular at the Oberhausen Film Festival to which he had been invited. On 11 June 1956, Jean Cayrol, responding to the controversy stirred up by the film, wrote: 'France hurriedly sweeps under the carpet those pages of history which it does not like anymore [...] it does not accept the greatest murder of all time other than in the form of a clandestine memory' [*dans la clandestinité de la mémoire*].[68] Indeed, in 1956, the potential role of a film like *Night and Fog* was to reintroduce into the public memory, even though crippled, those images that had shocked people in the immediate aftermath of the camps' liberation.

The other result of the controversy was that the event of *Night and Fog* overshadowed the film *Night and Fog*. So much of the media's reception of Resnais's film was concerned with German plots to eclipse it and with perceived right-wing French censorship that no one seemed to analyse either the film's content or its style. Although reviewers obviously discussed the content of the film, they did not examine it in any depth. Only one article about the film appeared on the day after its eventual screening, on 1 May 1956. The unsigned piece in *Le Monde* was genuinely emotional and described *Night and Fog* as 'the most harrowing testimony ever realised',[69] which the government had deemed likely to put at risk 'our intellectual comfort and the joyous atmosphere of international entente which reigns here'.[70]

It was not until 1959 that a detailed analysis of Resnais's work appeared, published by the Institut des Hautes Etudes Cinématographiques based in Paris, and authored by Vincent Pinel. In its suggestion for further reading, the author points out how little had been written on the film to that date. Perhaps this absence is explained in Truffaut's words:

> It is almost impossible to speak about this film in the vocabulary of cinematic criticism. It is not a documentary, or an indictment, or a poem, but a meditation on the most important phenomenon of the twentieth century. [...] The power of this film [...] is rooted in its tone, the terrible gentleness [sic]. [...] When we have looked at these strange, seventy-pound slave labourers, we understand that we are not going to 'feel better' after seeing *Night and Fog*; quite the opposite.[71]

Alternatively, the relative uninterest in *Night and Fog* can be explained by its format and subject matter. It is hardly surprising that a harrowing thirty-minute documentary on the concentration camps did not command a vast audience. Undoubtedly there is some truth in this. Yet to attribute *Night and Fog*'s failure to attract viewers in 1956 simply to commercial unsuitability would be reductive. It would also mean ignoring the wide distribution the film obtained in later years, and the box office success of other, much lengthier, documentary films such as *Le Chagrin et la Pitié* (*The Sorrow and the Pity*) and *Shoah*.

Thus, while it would be preposterous to suggest that *Night and Fog* had changed popular perception of the Shoah through far-reaching distribution to mass audiences, in the way that *Schindler's List* has perhaps done, it is not unreasonable to say that the film has had a significant, long-lasting, inter-generational influence on memory and representation in France. While Resnais's documentary did not enjoy widespread popularity at the time of its release, over the years its influence grew to make it the reference point for films on the Shoah, particularly in France.

Night and Fog was first shown on French television in 1957, on the morning of Easter Sunday. In his book, *Le Crime et la Mémoire*, the historian Alfred Grosser remembers regarding it as a revelation.[72] But the full institutional acceptance of *Night and Fog* started to take place during the 1960s when renewed interest in the Holocaust gave the film a new lease of life. In the 1970s and 1980s it began to be used in schools, where its short running time and its approach – fairly uncontroversial given the deletion of the *képi* – facilitated easy use.

A further transformation of Resnais's film is even more striking: during the decades after its first release, the interpretation of the *Night and Fog* has changed dramatically. Though Resnais's work was not physically altered until the 2003 DVD release, which reintroduced the censored *képi*, shifting public perceptions turned a film which had consciously avoided almost all references to Jewish victims into one entirely about the attempted genocide of the Jews. In 1956, *France-Observateur* had said 'victims',[73] *Libération* 'innocent individuals',[74] *Le Monde* 'human beings',[75] but no reviewer had mentioned Jews; instead, on 19 December 1979, a short piece in the satirical paper *Le Canard Enchaîné* described the film as 'a cry of horror in the face of the massacre of the Jews'.[76] In the same article, the shot of the camp of Pithiviers is transformed into one of Drancy. This was a telling blunder, which confirmed further the effects of popular perception of history on the reading of films and other documents on a specific period. Drancy was not simply a much more famous French transit camp, but one that by 1979 would immediately be linked in popular imagination with the Jews, because of its role in the mass deportation of the Jewish population of Paris. *Night and Fog* had now become a film about the massacre of Europe's Jewry.

In April 1987, during the trial of Klaus Barbie, the then Prime Minister Jacques Chirac asked teachers to show *Night and Fog*,[77] and three years later, on 15 May, the film was broadcast simultaneously on all five French television channels, as part of government initiatives following the desecration of the Jewish cemetery of Carpentras.[78] Finally, in 1993, during the Paul Touvier trial, the Minister of National Education, Jack Lang, distributed a tape of the film to all public and private secondary schools,[79] so that it could be shown to first- and final-year students. These events represent the definitive institutional recognition for *Night and Fog*. They also reveal a further shift in the use of the film: from a commemorative tool to a preventive one, employed no longer to address the past but to respond to modern events and to combat anti-Semitism, racism and denial of the Shoah. Or, in the less kind words of Vincent Löwy, '*Night and Fog* has thus become the most representative film in the teaching of official history, with its onerous silences and its touched-up photos, a vision at once reconciliatory and idealist'. [80] This argument will be tested in the near future by whether or not the film continues to be shown in schools now that it is available in its integral uncensored version.

It is not easy to quantify the impact *Night and Fog* has had on the popular memory of the Shoah in France. However, its simultaneous broadcast in 1990, and the ministerial encouragement of its educational use give a sense of how powerful its impact has been. At the same time, there is no better description of how changing times can alter the way we look at a film, almost to the point of altering the film itself. And yet the film's images, text and musical score are still the same – or virtually the same – as when it was first made. It conserves its gross generalisations, its omissions, its half-truths and the main historiographical problem of nonchalantly skipping in space and time, talking now about Auschwitz while showing images of Mauthausen, now about 1933 while displaying images of 1939. On top of this, there is the sensation that Cayrol's status as a survivor qualified him to talk about things he had neither experienced nor survived, such as Auschwitz. This approach entailed and entails obvious dangers so that, paradoxically, if there is a danger in *Night and Fog*, it is exactly in the sort of institutional and educational use to which it has been put.

Nevertheless, if we consider *Night and Fog* in the context of its age, it remains a historically valuable piece of art, not as rigorous as some later works but with an outstanding understanding of dehumanisation as perhaps the ultimate Nazi crime. In terms of representation as well, *Night and Fog* may well have been surpassed by now, but it remains unique and in 1956 was absolutely innovative. In 1956, it helped reintroduce into social discourse, if only briefly, the issues and images of the Shoah. In the following decades it consistently performed a service to history teaching and memory. Today, it still conveys a real passion for memory and a respectful curiosity for the mechanisms of the human mind, even when criminal.

NOTES

1. In Jacques Capedevielle and Renè Mouriaux, *L'Entre-Deux de la Modernité: Histoire de Trente Ans* (Paris: FNSP, 1988), p.57; quoted in Robert Gildea, *France since 1945* (Oxford: Oxford University Press, 1996), p.20.
2. On the Fourth Republic see, among others, 'La Coagulation: The Fourth Republic, 1944–1958', in Nicholas Atkin, *The Fifth French Republic* (Basingstoke: Palgrave-Macmillan, 2005), pp.8–36; and Jean-Pierre Rioux, *The Fourth Republic, 1944–1958* (Cambridge: Cambridge University Press, 1987).
3. Atkin, *Fifth French Republic*, p.12. On the communist Resistance see Serge Courtois, *Le PCF dans la Guerre* (Paris: Ramsay, 1980) and Jean-Pierre Azéma *et al.*, *Le Parti Communiste Français des Années Sombres, 1938–1941* (Paris: Seuil, 1986).
4. See Phillip Naylor, *France and Algeria: A History of Decolonization and Transformation* (Gainesville, FL: University Press of Florida, 2000) and Benjamin Stora, *Algeria 1830–2000* (Ithaca, NY: Cornell University Press, 2001).
5. Gildea, *France*, pp.20–9; Atkin, *Fifth French Republic*, pp.42–54.
6. Atkin, *Fifth French Republic*, pp.42–54.
7. The work of Benjamin Stora on the French and Algerian experiences of the Algerian conflict is the starting point for any analysis of the subject. See Stora, *Algeria 1830–2000*; Stora, *La Gangréne et l'Oubli: La Mémoire de la Guerre d'Algérie* (Paris: La Découverte, 1992) and Stora, *Imaginaires de Guerre: Algérie-Viètnam, en France et aux Etats-Unis* (Paris: La Découverte, 1997). Alongside these, see Jean-Pierre Rioux (ed.), *La Guerre d'Algérie et les Français* (Paris: Fayard, 1990). On the representation of the war in French literature and cinema, the seminal work remains Philip Dine, *Images of the Algerian War* (Oxford: Clarendon Press, 1994).
8. Charles de Gaulle, *War Memoirs*, 6 vols (London: Collins, 1955).
9. Robert Aron and Georgette Elgey, *Histoire de Vichy: 1940–1944*, 2 vols (Paris: Fayard, 1954).
10. Henri Michel, *Histoire de la Résistance, 1940–1944* (Paris: CHDGM, 1950 and 1958).
11. The actual monument to the Auschwitz dead was unveiled three years later, on 26 June 1949. It stands alongside several other memorials to Nazi camps and one to the deportees of forced labour (*travail forcé*). Annette Wieviorka, *Déportation et Génocide: Entre la Mémoire et l'Oubli* (Paris: Hachette Littératures, 1992); pp.136–42.
12. Wieviorka, *Déportation et Génocide*, p.40.
13. Ibid.

14. See 'Deuxième Partie: Les Premiers Témoignages', in Wieviorka, *Déportation et Génocide*, pp.161–313, and Serge Klarsfeld, *Vichy-Auschwitz: La 'Solution Finale' de la Question Juive en France*, 2 vols (Paris: Fayard, 1983), pp.378–9, for a useful guide to early Jewish memoirs of the camps.
15. Gildea, *France*, p.64.
16. Christian Delage, '*Nuit et Brouillard:* A Turning Point in History and Memory of the Holocaust', in Toby Haggith and Joanna Newman (eds), *Holocaust and the Moving Image* (London: Wallflower Press, 2005).
17. On the reception of *Night and Fog* in France, and also Germany, Great Britain and Israel, see Ewout van der Knaap (ed.), *Uncovering the Holocaust: The International Reception of Night and Fog* (London: Wallflower Press, 2006).
18. André Pierre Colombat, *The Holocaust in French Film* (Metuchen: The Scarecrow Press, 1993); Sandy Flitterman-Lewis, 'Documenting the Ineffable: Terror and Memory in Alain Resnais's *Night and Fog*', in Barry Keith Grant and Jeanette Sloniowski (eds), *Documenting the Documentary: Close Readings of Documentary Film and Video* (Detroit, MI: Wayne State University Press, 1998). See also Annette Insdorf, *Indelible Shadows: Film and the Holocaust*, third edition (Cambridge: Cambridge University Press, 2003), pp.39–41 and 212–13, and Ilan Avisar, *Screening the Holocaust: Cinema's Images of the Unimaginable* (Bloomington, IN: Indiana University Press, 1988), pp.12–18.
19. Joshua Hirsch, *Afterimage: Film, Trauma and the Holocaust* (Philadelphia, PA: Temple University Press, 2004).
20. Henri Michel and Olga Wormser (eds), *Tragédie de la Deportation 1940–1945: Témoignages de Survivants des Camps de Concentration Allemands* (Paris: Hachette, 1954).
21. *Le Monde*, 10 November 1954.
22. Richard Raskin, *Nuit et Brouillard* (Aarhus: Aarhus University Press, 1987), pp.25–32.
23. James Monaco, *Alain Resnais* (New York: Oxford University Press, 1979), p.9.
24. Vincent Löwy, *L'Histoire Infilmable: Les Camps d'Extermination Nazis à l'Écran* (Paris: L'Harmattan, 2001), p.59.
25. Ibid.
26. Thierry Jousse, 'Jean Cayrol Récrit le Commentaire de *Nuit et Brouillard*', *Les Cahiers du Cinéma*, Special Issue (January 1995), p.77.
27. Document 090-L at the Nuremberg War Crimes Tribunal. See Raskin, *Nuit et Brouillard*, p.15.
28. Raskin, *Nuit et Brouillard*, p.16.
29. Jean Cayrol, *Poèmes de la Nuit et du Brouillard* (Paris: Seghers, 1946).
30. Raskin, *Nuit et Brouillard*, p.70.
31. *L'Avant-Scène du Cinema*, 15 February 1961.
32. Ibid., pp.101–2.
33. Ibid., p.83.
34. The shot appears 7:04 minutes into the film.
35. Resnais's decision to film modern-day camps would be echoed thirty years later, in 1985, by Claude Lanzmann in *Shoah*, to which Chapter Six of this book is dedicated.
36. Alain Resnais in Roy Armes, *The Cinema of Alain Resnais* (London: Zwemmer, 1968).
37. This principle is associated most strongly with the works of Jean Renoir, and formed the basis of Bazin's theory, and hence of French New Wave cinema. On Renoir see Giorgio De Vincenti, *Jean Renoir: La Vita, i Film* (Venice: Marsilio, 1996). Bazin published his theories in André Bazin, *Qu'est-ce que le Cinéma?* (Paris: Éditions Cerf, 1958).
38. Albrecht Dumling, 'Eisler's Music for Resnais's *Night and Fog*: A Musical Counterpoint to the Cinematic Portrayal of Terror', in *Historical Journal of Film, Radio and Television* (October 1998).
39. Raskin, *Nuit et Brouillard*, p.73.
40. Ibid., p.74.
41. Ibid.
42. Ibid., pp.76–7.
42. Ibid., p.78.
44. Ibid., p.79
45. Ibid.

46. Ibid., p.80. The exact words here are 'des-pris-sur-le fait, des pris-par-erreur, des pris-au-hasard, se met en marche vers le camps'.
47. Ibid., pp.85–6.
48. Ibid., p.84.
49. Ibid., p.130.
50. Ibid., p.51.
51. Dine, *Images of the Algerian War*, p.223.
52. On the reception of *Night and Fog* in France, and also Germany, Great Britain and Israel, see van der Knaap (ed.), *Uncovering the Holocaust.*
53. *Le Figaro*, 7 April 1956.
54. In fact, the makers of *Nuit Royales* refused to take the place of Resnais's film. Jacques Doniol-Valcroze, 'L'affaire *Nuit et Brouillard*', *France-Observateur*, 19 April 1956.
55. Jacques Doniol-Valcroze, 'Il n'y a jamais eu des deportations', *France-Observateur*, 12 April 1956. Here, Lee's film is reported only with the French title, *Ma Vie Commence en Malaysie.* Doniol-Valcroze makes no reference to the director.
56. Ibid.
57. Ibid. Again, Doniol-Valcroze does not report the name of the film-makers and refers to the film only by the French title, *La Route Sanglante.*
58. See Antoine de Baecque and Serge Toubiana (eds), 'Histoires de Cannes', *Les Cahiers du Cinéma*, Special Issue (April 1997).
59. Norbert Frei, *Adenauer's Germany and the Nazi Past: The Politics of Amnesty and Integration* (New York: Columbia University Press, 2002).
60. Richard Vinen, *France, 1934–1970* (Basingstoke: Macmillan, 1996); p.78; Nicholas Atkin, *The French at War, 1934–44* (London: Pearson Education, 2001), pp.80–2.
61. The journal *Libération* was founded in 1945 by Emmanuel d'Astier de la Vigérie, and eventually closed in 1954. Except for its political outlook, it is unrelated to the popular left-wing daily founded in 1973.
62. Simone Dubreuilh, *Libération*, 12 April 1956.
63. Doniol-Valcroze, 'Il n'y a jamais eu des deportations'.
64. Jacques Doniol-Valcroze, *France-Observateur*, 19 April 1956.
65. Ibid.
66. The original photo is held at the Centre de Recherches et d'Etudes Historiques de la Seconde Guerre Mondiale. The 2001 DVD edition of the film has reinstated the image in its original place.
67. René Vautier, 'Traces de poudres', in *Les Inrockuptibles*, 24 December 1997, p.44.
68. Jean Cayrol, *Le Monde*, 11 June 1956.
69. Jean de Baroncelli, *Le Monde*, 1 May 1956.
70. Ibid.
71. François Truffaut, *The Films of my Life* (New York: Simon & Schuster, 1978).
72. Alfred Grosser, *Le Crime et la Mémoire* (Paris: Flammarion, 1989), p.121.
73. Doniol-Valcroze, 'Il n'y a jamais eu des deportations'.
74. Dubreuilh, *Libération.*
75. De Baroncelli, *Le Monde.*
76. *Le Canard Enchaîné*, 19 December 1979.
77. Löwy, *Histoire Infilmable*, p.63.
78. Ibid., pp.63–4.
79. Ibid., p.64.
80. Ibid.

2

The Shoah in Black and White: 1959–61

The 1960s saw the turn of the tide in public awareness of the Shoah. For Jews and non-Jews alike, in Europe as in Israel and the United States, this decade was a period of transition from the widespread amnesia of the late 1940s and 1950s, towards the culture of analysis and remembrance which has been gaining momentum ever since. In particular, the audacious capture and public trial of Adolf Eichmann by the Israeli state in 1961 marked a watershed between refusal to remember and the resolve not to forget. It would be wrong, however, to imagine that the Eichmann trial alone brought about a sudden change in popular, or even institutional, attitudes to the Shoah.

In Italy, the overdue if timely publication in 1958, by Turinese publisher Einaudi, of Primo Levi's *If This Is A Man*, seems to suggest that change was already under way before the Eichmann trial. Earlier, in 1947, Einaudi and many others had refused to publish Levi's manuscript. Natalia Ginzburg, herself Jewish, anti-fascist and one of Italy's best twentieth-century writers, was working as a reader for Einaudi when the Turinese author first submitted it. Ginzburg rejected its publication on the grounds that 'the time was not right'.[1] But if we can assume that Ginzburg was no anti-Semite, then her rejection suggests a much deeper, generalised unease with the subject. Another explanation is that Levi did not fulfil contemporary Italian expectations about men of letters. As a professional chemist, he was considered something of an amateur, whose style of writing was too concise and direct to warrant publication.[2]

Ten years later, the time and the audience were at last deemed ready for *If This Is A Man*. Moreover, in 1962, Einaudi published

Levi's second work, *La Tregua* (*The Truce*),[3] as well as Bassani's *Il Giardino dei Finzi-Contini* (*The Garden of the Finzi-Contini*),[4] a dramatised autobiographical account of life in the Ferrara Jewish community during the later stages of fascism and the occupation. The publication of Bassani, an author of established reputation, is less remarkable than that of Levi. If the Eichmann trial played a part in Italy's attitude to the Shoah, this may have been as a catalyst of a change already afoot. Yet the impression remains that in Italy, at this time, the Shoah was regarded as a foreign matter that did not concern it significantly. Certainly, there appears to be no direct link between Eichmann's trial and the production of Holocaust-related cinematic work in Italy.

Three Italian Holocaust films were produced between 1959 and 1961: Roberto Rossellini's *Il Generale della Rovere* (*General della Rovere*, 1959), Gillo Pontecorvo's *Kapò* (*Kapo*, 1960) and Carlo Lizzani's *L'Oro di Roma* (*The Gold of Rome*, 1961). All three films were conceived before the Eichmann trial, even though *The Gold of Rome*'s release in Italy coincided with his sentencing by the Jerusalem High Court. Two chapters will argue that these films are not the result of a new interest in the Shoah, but of the neo-realist revival that took place between 1959 and 1963. First, this chapter will analyse *General della Rovere* and *The Gold of Rome* as the direct products of this revival. Then, the next chapter will seek to compare Italian developments with parallel ones taking place in France, by comparing *Kapo* with a French film, Armand Gatti's *L'Enclos* (*The Enclosure*), which was released in France in 1961 alongside Pontecorvo's film.

Lizzani's was the first Italian film to deal with the deportation of Italian Jews and is still one of only a handful of films to have done so. *General della Rovere*, instead, is only loosely connected to the Shoah, though the persecution of the Jews encroaches upon the narrative towards the end of the film. Nonetheless, it was important to include *General della Rovere* for a number of reasons: first, because the film contains a scene of Jews praying, which is rare in Italian filmography, and was a first in 1959; second, because in its finale the film implies an awareness that Jews were persecuted for specific reasons, and not only when they were involved in anti-fascist activities; third, because the triumph of Rossellini's film at the 1959 Venice Film Festival sparked a new lease of life for neo-realism, which saw over forty films made between 1959 and 1963, with themes concerning either the Resistance or fascism. Hence, *General della Rovere* is at least partly responsible for the neo-realist renaissance, of which *Kapo* and *The Gold of Rome* are products.

THE LEGACY OF NEO-REALISM

It is important briefly to consider neo-realism as the dominant film school of post-war Italy. This heterogeneous film school had flourished between 1945 and the 1950s, bringing considerable theoretical, technical and thematic innovation to Italian cinematography. Although neo-realism was not the international cinematic revolution it has sometimes been hailed as, it certainly helped restore Italian dignity abroad while expressing both anxieties about Italian society and a rekindled political passion after the fall of fascism.[5] Treating themes such as Italy's war experience and its post-war socio-economic and political situation, neo-realism spread through Italian film production and throughout film genres. Stretching from the rigour of Visconti's Gramscian *La Terra Trema* (*The Earth Trembles*, 1947) to the slapstick comedy of Zampa's *Vivere in Pace* (*To Live in Peace*, 1947), neo-realism proved to be a malleable but resilient style.

Early neo-realist films – such as Rossellini's *Roma, Città Aperta* (*Rome, Open City*, 1945) and *Paisà* (1946), and De Sica's *Sciuscià* (*Shoeshine*, 1946) and *Ladri di Biciclette* (*Bicycle Thieves*, 1947) – were able to maintain the momentum of the Resistance and the hopes surrounding the liberation through to the social critique of post-fascist Italian society. Occasionally openly communist – but more often only perceived as communist – the best neo-realist examples linked Resistance and revolution in a way that politics had been unable to achieve. These few films perhaps justify Lino Micciché's somewhat idealistic definition of neo-realism as 'an aesthetic full of the past and an ethic full of a utopian future'.[6] In fact, neo-realism dealt with the future more comfortably than with the past. In its less ideologically charged examples, neo-realism conveyed the message that wartime Italians had essentially been victims, or at best unwilling and incompetent sidekicks of the Germans. This suited the emerging Christian Democratic rhetoric of the time while helping Italy in its effort to move swiftly on from the fascist parenthesis.

'Neo-realism's problems started with the desire to label it', said Rossellini to an audience of young French film-makers during the

1959 Venice Film Festival.[7] Rossellini was referring to the central theoretical debate of the 1950s, concerning what should be regarded as neo-realism and what should not. This was a pointless controversy, which started just as neo-realism's momentum was fading. Whether or not one agrees with Micciché's theory that neo-realism ended in 1952, it is certain that, by the mid-1950s, it had lost the significance and inspiration of the first post-war lustrum. Rather than just ending, neo-realism had evolved. Economic reconstruction and the fading memories of the war deprived neo-realism's themes of social justice of their former urgency; its styles had become over-exploited; its political and social relevance surpassed long before. Thus the vast majority of what was hailed as neo-realist in the 1950s was either a more or less professional exercise lacking punch, or a caricature of earlier works.

What is particularly interesting about Rossellini's 1959 Venice statement is that he made it at the presentation of *General della Rovere*, which was a stylistic and thematic return to his neo-realist days, after the experimentation of *Viaggio in Italia* (*Voyage in Italy*, 1954), and most of his 1950s work.[8] *General della Rovere* signalled Italy's neo-realist revival by winning the Venice Film Festival of 1959, ex aequo with Mario Monicelli's bitter First World War comedy, *La Grande Guerra* (*The Great War*). This double Italian victory was hailed not only as a successful return to the themes and moods of neo-realism, but also as a triumph of Italian cinema over US production, which throughout the 1950s generated, on average, three quarters of the annual ticket income.[9]

This neo-realist renaissance was enthusiastically received for three particular reasons: first, there was the intellectual gratification of those, mostly on the left, who were nostalgic for neo-realism; second, the eruption of Italian national pride over the successes of Rossellini and Monicelli; third, there were the financial concerns of Italian producers. One of these, Dino de Laurentiis, financed *The Great War* and was one of the minds behind the reprise of the whole genre. Micciché suggested that another possible factor in the resurgence of neo-realism was the 'ideological desert of the era'.[10] Yet the connection seems to be indirect rather than direct. In other words, a stagnant ideological environment may well explain the lack of a sort of 'Italian New Wave', similar to those developed in France, England,

Poland, Czechoslovakia and Brazil, by a new generation of film-makers who challenged hegemonic culture.[11] Italy's cultural stagnation in the 1960s, however, does not adequately account for this intense, if short-lived, return to neo-realism.

There were 'serious' and 'comic' trends to this new batch of films on the Italian wartime experience. The latter contained little or no historical critique, its only aims being escapism and entertainment. At times, however, what these comedies suggested was not that Italians wanted to reinterpret fascism, or even have a laugh at its expense, but that the Italian middle classes, swollen in size and wealth by the Economic Miracle, wanted to exorcise their own ideological ambivalence by caricaturing both fascism and anti-fascism. Films such as Luciano Salce's *Il Federale* (1962), Luigi Comencini's *Tutti a Casa* (*Everybody Go Home*, 1960), Dino Risi's *La Marcia su Roma* (*March on Rome*, 1962) and Giuseppe de Santis's notorious *Italiani Brava Gente* (*Attack and Retreat*, 1963) mocked key events in Italy's fascist period. They shared not only laughs, but an uplifting moral about Italian national character. These films implied that Italians, whatever their political side, were disorganised but loving; not fond of war but brave in need; individualistic but fundamentally generous. With few exceptions, the 'serious' branch was also ideologically ambiguous. Often, the two styles merged into a sort of 'war-melodrama', with the insertion of sporadic gags or comical characters destined to soften the tone and relieve the tension.[12]

These films, comical or otherwise, imposed a much wider view of anti-fascism, which reflected the desires and concerns of Italian society in the 1960s. By 1960 the Resistance theme, stripped of its political arguments and moral values, had been reduced to a consolatory memory. In this reminiscence, the spectators, still mindful of past hardships, could gratify themselves either with their new comfortable life or with their former heroism, whatever their role had been. Thus these historical films were primarily, though often inadvertently, contemporary: they reflected the increasingly well-off Italy of the Economic Miracle, just as immediate post-war neo-realism had captured the widespread hardships of war and reconstruction. These films justified and absolved contemporary political torpor by glorifying past bravery. The new neo-realism hurt no one: it was financially viable to producers; uplifting to audiences of all social classes; unthreatening to the political status quo.

In fact, the Resistance films of the early 1960s revived and enhanced many of the worst characteristics of the earlier brand of neo-realism while lacking the urgency it obtained from the extreme proximity to the events. Thus, these films blamed the Germans for all atrocities; they depicted fascists as cowardly, greedy and idiotic but generally harmless and not devoid of compassion; they focused almost exclusively on fascism's demise, not on its rise to power or the twenty years of its not unpopular rule; they deliberately exaggerated the extent of popular participation in the Resistance. All in all, these later films lacked the social consciousness of the immediate post-war neo-realist works, simply because society had changed dramatically. The newspapers of the time paint an interesting picture of a changing country in which sexual liberation cohabited with ecclesiastical bigotry. The cinemas were invaded by titillating films set in exotic countries, such as *Nuda tra le Tigri* (*Naked amongst Tigers*) and *Tunisi Top Secret*,[13] to name two of seemingly countless titles out in 1959, at the same time as *General della Rovere*. Even products of different genres often sported scantily-dressed leading ladies in their newspaper adverts. These films, rigorously rated unsuitable for minors, hardly concerned the regulating authorities. Their advertisements appeared in all papers, political position and cultural aspirations notwithstanding. This clearly demonstrates the political ability of the Democrazia Cristiana (Christian Democrats, DC), who retained their clerical image and Vatican support while allowing the mass media to back popular demand for a degree of sexual liberation. Indeed, despite a global and irreversible decline, cinema, which in 1955 had attracted 819,424,000 people, in 1959 still mustered an audience of just under 750,000,000.[14]

The attitude of the Church deserves highlighting. The Vatican newspaper *L'Osservatore Romano* did not have an entertainment page or any columns of film critique – scarcely surprising, given the Catholic Church's aversion for this sort of leisurely pursuit. Mindful, however, that it could not altogether stop the faithful from watching, the ecclesiastical broadsheet did have a daily list of films and their censorship rating as determined by the Conferenza Episcopale Italiana (Italian Episcopal Conference, CEI). Here, at least, the Church could shun all compromises with the changing moral values of its acolytes, while retaining its monopoly over censorship. Instead of regulating viewing through determined limitations, the Vatican discerned between different levels of indecency. Thus, four of the five rating categories identified different levels of unsuitability: films rated 'E' (excluded) were described as 'morally unacceptable'; 'S' (advised against) as 'of negative content'; 'A' as 'containing adult material'; and 'Ar' as of adult themes, with the added threat of undisclosed 'dangerous elements'.[15] Meanwhile, the DC continued to play both sides: on the one hand, the party's daily paper, *Il Popolo*, gave details of the CEI's recommendations alongside its own critical advice; on the other hand, it advertised all films indiscriminately, and jovially reported the gossip of suntanned stars and starlets of the silver screen, popular music and the increasingly fashionable television.

In this context, Rossellini's film was met enthusiastically, particularly by the left, which mistakenly saw it as a chance to use the Resistance as a political tool. The Communist Party had built its popularity and its credibility on the anti-fascist struggle. Aware of the subversive power of some early neo-realist films, the PCI no doubt hoped *General della Rovere* would inject new vitality in the Resistance-film genre, introduce a new generation to the glory and cost of the partisan war, and thus help shift the political balance back towards the left. It could not see, however, that the film's ideological message was not about the cathartic power of the communist cause, but about the unconscious martyrdom of a *qualunquista*, an apathetic and selfish Guicciardinian man. Most left-wing commentators failed to see that if the past may have belonged to marmoreal champions of the working class, the present and future were firmly in the hands of apolitical, bourgeois Italian anti-heroes.

UNCONSCIOUS BRAVERY: *GENERAL DELLA ROVERE*

In line with the modern reinterpretation of the anti-fascist struggle outlined above, the protagonist of neo-realist renaissance films were almost always male, middle-aged and petty-bourgeois. They were quite content with life; they did not belong to persecuted political or ethnic minorities; they were affected by fascism only through the shortages and general gloom of wartime. This is exactly the sort of leading man Vittorio De Sica plays in Rossellini's *General della Rovere*. The director identifies Bardone straightaway by showing him unwrapping a sugar cube, eating it and nonchalantly throwing away the wrapper in unsatisfied fashion. This subtle gesture, in the opening sequence, tells the viewer that Bardone is relatively well off, as well as quite selfish. Rossellini immediately clarifies Bardone's ideological stance by showing him helping out some stranded German soldiers with an 'acquiescence that borders obsequiousness'.[16] The story soon reveals that Bardone makes his money by impersonating a respectable retired colonel, and by persuading wealthy families of arrested Italian men that he can earn their release through his contacts at the German headquarters.

Bardone is not a collaborator; he has no fondness for the occupying forces, but his cynicism is that of all those who put survival above justice or commitment. Caught by the Germans in his double-dealings, Bardone is offered an escape from execution in the form of yet another new identity. He is asked to impersonate an Italian army general and Resistance leader, whom the Nazis have accidentally killed while on his way to a secret meeting. Having infiltrated Milan's San Vittore prison as the general, Bardone is asked to make contact with the Resistance chief nicknamed Fabrizio, and subsequently identify him for the Germans.

In a further twist, Bardone's new gamble results not, as anticipated, in physical survival but in the rediscovery of bravery, morality, and the ultimate deliverance of his soul. In a cathartic ending, Bardone, who has successfully recognized Fabrizio, decides to die at the hands of a firing squad rather than reveal Fabrizio's identity to the German authorities. Although by no means free from melodramatic overtones, the sequence immediately preceding the execution holds the key to both the film's modernity, and its connection with Rossellini's neo-realist beginnings. Men find themselves locked overnight in a cell, aware that ten of them will be chosen to be executed in response to partisan action. Detained alongside Bardone are people picked up in routine checks and a number of Jews. In 'a night like this', during which 'people talk', Colonel Mueller hopes the fake general will be approached by Fabrizio.

In this sequence, a middle-class man complains that he is innocent because he has 'done nothing'. This incensed bourgeois wears not a black shirt but a suit; though we are told that he has benefited economically from the regime's corruption, he is not a fascist fanatic. He is the average Italian man: a less charismatic and altogether greyer version of Bardone, sitting on the fence. When one of the Jews retorts that they too 'have done nothing', the unidentified man answers: 'but you are Jews'. Other than the general bitterness about his persona, there is no anger and no pity in his voice. It is reasonable to believe that this man is not anti-Semitic, yet the persecution of the Jews does not seem to be repugnant to him. He may think it natural because of atavistic cultural prejudice, religious indoctrination or more recent, yet intense, fascist propaganda; he may even think it unfortunate, but he is altogether untouched by it because it does not physically touch him.

Here, a film that is not about Jews or about the Shoah gives the viewer a rare exchange between two Italians, one Jew and one gentile, and a synthetic yet incisive picture of middle-class Italian attitudes towards Jewish persecution. Moreover, as the hour of the execution approaches, Rossellini focuses on the group of Jewish men as they recite a prayer in Hebrew. He subtitles only one sentence: 'Our souls are in your hands now, and the sword is above our heads; God of Vengeance, do not forget us.' The selective translation is extremely meaningful but was disregarded altogether by reviewers at the time. This long shot acts as a pause in this scene, the overall mood of which helps support the idea of a dedication by Rossellini to those who died.

During this poignant group sequence, the Resistance chief does indeed make contact with Bardone. Fabrizio is a stylized hero rather than a complex human being: aware and humble, brave and wise, unpretentiously selfless as well as young and handsome. He is an intellectual, but unlike Rossellini's other intellectual Resistance fighters, such as Manfredi in *Rome, Open City*, he contains no element of social criticism or political aspiration. He merely expresses a general hope for a better future. He is an almost angelic messenger who delivers serenity by statements. First, he rebukes the whingeing man: 'Why did you do nothing? Maybe if we all had done something we would not be in this situation now.' Then, in a conversation with the fake General della Rovere, he concludes: 'what gave me the strength to bear such responsibility was that I believed to be fighting for a better world. Will we see it? Will the others see it? I think so.'

In *Rome, Open City*, one of Rossellini's characters, the communist typographer Francesco, made a remarkably similar assertion. The hope for a better world, however, which in 1945 must have resonated with contemporary audiences as an uplifting yet bitter statement, was now, in the context of 1959, void of expectation. Far from endorsing the Italy of the Economic Miracle as this new, better world they had fought for, the statement of Rossellini's Fabrizio is an indictment, full of disappointment rather than anger. That is the difference that the fourteen years between Rossellini's 1945 neo-realist milestone and *General della Rovere* had brought about.

Even the ultimate sacrifice, where one would expect martyrdom to lend itself to triumphal overtones, is strangely subdued. Walking with military pace in front of a German firing squad, surprised at the sight of an unexpected eleventh man, Bardone-Grimaldi della Rovere stands proud and addresses the victims: 'Gentlemen, in this supreme moment let us turn our thoughts to our families, to the Fatherland, to the majesty of the King. Viva l'Italia!' Then the Italian army firing squad, which in *Rome, Open City* had refused to shoot Don Pietro, carries out its duty.

Bardone's bravery could be interpreted as part of a patriotic discourse, in celebration of the glorious Resistance. That is exactly what it would be if, for example, it had been the morally unshakeable Fabrizio, who died. Similarly, if Bardone had confessed his deceit before offering himself to the slaughter, his catharsis would have produced an even more mythical nationalistic finale. Instead, this ending is willingly hollow, in particular because Bardone's newly found strength, morality and awareness are not his own: they belong to a persona he has adopted. Even in death, this Neapolitan drifter impersonates someone else. An artist of survival, having lived a life of many names, he dies an anonymous death.

THE RECEPTION OF *GENERAL DELLA ROVERE*

The reception of Rossellini's film reveals how much influence the concept of neo-realism still held in Italy in 1959. Moreover, this influence seems to have affected not just the left, as one might expect, but also the more conservative centre, Catholic as well as lay. This, in turn, testifies to the political difficulties of the Communist Party which, at the time, was impressive in its support yet incapable of dislodging the Christian Democrats' hold on government. The 1950s had been a hard decade for the PCI: its wartime hopes had been dashed by consecutive electoral defeats; and its credibility had been hit by the revelations of Stalinist atrocities, as well as by the Soviet repression in Hungary in 1956. Left-wing reaction to the film showed a disconcerting lack of direction, which made it unable to look at *General della Rovere* from any other perspective than that of the Resistance. Furthermore, by effectively decontextualising this film and placing it squarely in the first neo-realist tradition, the Italian left missed the opportunity to exploit the critique of Christian Democratic Italy contained within *General della Rovere.* While the strength of the Italian left's relation with the Resistance goes some way to explain its interpretation of *General della Rovere*, its reaction needs further analysis. The left's apparent bittersweet satisfaction smacked of personal satisfaction at the perceived redemption of Rossellini and De Sica. As principal interpreters of neo-realism, they had been hailed by the left as enlightened artists and forefathers of the country's new Marxist culture. Yet, in the 1950s, when the two moved away from neo-realist style and themes, the left had felt betrayed:

> Rossellini went to Germany, he went to France, became European; he reverted to the Middle Ages, flirted with mysticism, turned to Pantheism. Meanwhile, his art fell apart, the public deserted his films.[17]

The pretentiousness of such comments is foretold by the title of the six-column review that the Communist Party daily, *L'Unità,* devoted to the film after its Venice Film Festival debut: 'Through *General della Rovere* Rossellini and De Sica redeem themselves'.[18] The reviewer Ugo Casiraghi explained Rossellini's 'redemption' in terms of his 'having re-established contact with his, with our Italy, with the tragedy of the (German military) occupation, with the sacrifice and virility of the Resistance'.[19] This story of a 'crook', whose 'decadence' is called 'pitiful, outrageous, almost incredible',[20] and the idea that his eventual salvation is delivered by 'the patriots' moral example, [...] the mere contact with a worthy humanity',[21] seems to have hit a nerve. It certainly provided the Communist Party newspaper with a chance to link these multiple 'redemptions' – the director's, the actor's and the main character's – with almost religious élan.

L'Unità's merciless interpretation of the film's main character is perfectly matched by the absolute reverence the paper displays for the character of the barber–typographer, a member of the Resistance who dies in prison as a result of German torture. While his death is indeed a turning point in the fake-general's experience, the Communist Party's paper centres on him as the film's fundamental figure. The article described him as 'a precise portrait of a proletarian hero, of few words, high conscience and exemplary modesty'. But while undoubtedly Rossellini's film pitches this character's strength against Bardone's moral weakness, *General della Rovere* concludes by exalting the courage of those who act in spite of fear over those who feel no fear. Casiraghi's piece ignores this to interpret the barber's character as 'the proletarian hero'.[22] Interestingly, while this article extolled this minor character it entirely neglects the other stylised Resistance character in the film, that of Fabrizio, the middle-class partisan leader.

Another explanation for *L'Unità*'s hostility is provided by looking at the authorship of the original story by Indro Montanelli, who also contributed to the screenplay. Montanelli was not left wing. A writer and journalist, he was until his death in 2001 a right-wing intellectual, who never denied having been a fascist in his youth. It was to Montanelli that the legendary quote – which, for Italian communists, came to symbolise two generations of electoral defeats – about 'having to hold one's nose and vote DC' was later attributed.[23] As in *The Conformist*, in *General della Rovere,* Montanelli's concern with the individual, and the mechanisms determining his decision-making, is obvious. In the story, as in the film, Bardone's moral poverty and unconscious strength are not related to the Resistance but to the human condition. Moreover, in Montanelli's story the protagonist chooses to die not because of a newly-found political engagement, but in order not to betray his actor–character relationship – a much more interesting philosophical idea.

This was probably one of the elements of the original story that *L'Unità*'s reviewer despised. He went as far as suggesting that, but for Rossellini's steadying hand, Montanelli's final aim would be to revise completely historical truth. Casiraghi was unimpressed with the protagonist's ambiguity, as he expressed:

> [his] doubts [over] Montanelli's equivocal game, between spy and hero, fascist and anti-fascist, as if death, thanks to its irrevocable tragic quality, could erase all historical motive and rational explanation.[24]

History played a fundamental part in *L'Unità*'s review of *General della Rovere*, as Casiraghi drew repeated comparisons between this film and *Rome, Open City*. It is clear that the reviewer understood *Rome, Open City* and neo-realism as on-screen history: an accurate and truthful representation of the occupation. This proves the extent to which the Resistance had been idealised in post-war Italy, in particular by the Italian left. It also shows how neo-realism – mistakenly understood as a single coherent movement – had been equally idolised as the cultural arm of the Resistance.

The other fundamental flaw in this review is the inability to place *General della Rovere* in its own context of production: the Italy of 1958/9. In truth, Casiraghi picked up on this but did not exploit it to any significant length. He wrote: 'the character of the endearing conman – thanks to these years of substandard government and substandard cinema (*'sottogoverno e sottocinema'*) – has become part of the audience's conventions', and 'we are probably not far from the truth if we suggest that this character has been written "with hindsight", inspired by post-war practices'.[25] On both counts, he was absolutely right here, yet interesting points about 1950s Italian government, cinema, society, and the relationship between the three, were lost due to the writer's unwillingness to move the anachronistic focus of his piece away from the Resistance.

At least *L'Unità* pointed out, if only briefly, the relevance to contemporary audiences of De Sica's character, and at least it dedicated a six-column review to the film. Its Christian Democratic counterpart, *Il Popolo*, did neither. On the occasion of the film's release in Rome, on 8 October 1959, it published a short, factual and disinterested review.[26] The unsigned piece reported extensively on how the premiere was disrupted by fifteen right-wing youths shouting abuse.[27] Both *Il Popolo*'s lack of interest in the film and the fascists' violent reaction prove how the left, represented by *L'Unità* and the PCI, was not the only political faction still concerned with the Resistance.

Milan's *Il Corriere della Sera* and Turin's *La Stampa* adopted a more balanced position on the film. Politically unaligned, these newspapers were generally close to the establishment. *Il Corriere della Sera*, the oldest Italian daily, is a respectable bourgeois press which seldom has failed to support the political line of successive governments. In its review of the film's Venice premiere, on

Saturday 29 August 1959, film critic Arturo Lanocita expressed his appreciation for an excellent film, tainted only by the character's sudden 'crisis of consciousness'.[28] The reviewer referred to the discrepancy between Bardone's motivations in the film, and in Montanelli's original story.

Almost two months later, on 4 November, Lanocita again discussed *General della Rovere* in the pages of *Il Corriere della Sera.* This time he was less flattering, suggesting that the film succeeds 'until the poison of Latin films, rhetoric, transfigures everything in the final sequences'.[29] Consistent with his earlier critique, it is the cathartic finale, the redemption which *L'Unità* so loved, that attracted the reviewer's scorn. 'To accept the sacrifice was right [but] to shout indecorously or to demand it is aberrant', he wrote; and then again, 'with the intention of signifying a glorious death, a melodramatic death has been narrated, that is a false one'.[30] *General della Rovere*'s final scene is indeed melodramatic, as was *Rome, Open City* and a great part of neorealism. Yet melodrama was no obstacle to Rossellini's earlier work bearing a powerful message, or receiving positive reviews. Despite Lanocita's legitimate misgivings, his understanding of what the text offers was excellent and interesting for the purpose of this work. In defence of Rossellini, Lanocita wrote: 'He gave us a vivid, varied, lively portrait of what we were like during the regretful years, when there were a hundred ways to disguise cowardice but only one way to erase it.'[31] What is most interesting is that the reviewer matched his analysis of Italian wartime behaviour with a renewed mythology of the Resistance. In this matter *Il Corriere della Sera* resembled *L'Unità*, with a language where the abundance of terms such as 'martyrdom' and 'sacrifice' ridiculed the reviewer's own condemnation of Rossellini's 'Latin poison'. And here, too, despite an altogether more impartial approach and the absence of *L'Unità*'s dogmatism, the focus remained steadily fixed on issues of realism and truthfulness.

Turin's *La Stampa* devoted less space to the film, yet seemed to have a better understanding of it. For instance, Mario Gromo praised Bardone for being 'out of Maupassant, rather than De Amicis',[32] referring to his lack of rhetoric, while *Il Corriere della Sera* had accused him of being 'straight out of *Cuore*',[33] Edmondo De Amicis's melodramatic novel, which formed part of the school curriculum. On 5 September, *La Stampa* presented an interview with the joint winners of the Venice Film Festival: Rossellini, and Mario Monicelli, director of *La Grande Guerra*. The interviewer put to the directors his interpretation that both films were about con-artists and cowards who redeem themselves in the general 'climate of sacrifice' inspired by the struggle. 'Is that just a chance?' he asked.[34] Rossellini's answer was evasive, while Monicelli did not answer at all. Rossellini instead replied that young people did not know enough about the war, quoting an unreferenced French poll suggesting that two out of fifteen French schoolchildren thought Mussolini was a director. 'He was most of all a director', mused Monicelli.[35]

The reception of *General della Rovere* paints a picture in which the myth of the glorious popular Resistance against Nazism persists, as does the tendency not to discuss fascism in much detail, or at least not to dwell on its popularity until 1943. Equally evident is the popularity of this approach: the attention given to the film by critics and its success at the box office both suggest this. Rossellini's film earned 713,000,000 Italian lire.[36] Nonetheless, the far superior result of *La Grande Guerra*, which earned more than double the amount, suggests a public preference for comedy over drama.[37]

While Rossellini's film was popular, however, the implication that a martyr of the Resistance may not have been fully conscious of the reasons behind the struggle enraged the left. In the eyes of *L'Unità*, Bardone's catharsis only partially made up for the film's fatal lack of ideological commitment. In contrast, for a centrist newspaper like *Il Corriere della Sera* the catharsis was rhetorical and offensive. *Il Popolo*'s want of interest was in itself conspicuous. Given Rossellini's fame and the film's popular success, it is difficult not to see a political point in the indifference of the DC's daily.

All reviews also display a continued obsession with realism. The engagement with the film's historical accuracy was another shared element, yet interestingly there was disagreement over whether or not *General della Rovere*'s story was a true one. In a later review, *L'Unità* maintained it was not,[38] whereas *Il Corriere della Sera* insisted it was. Interestingly, however, the former praised the film for its accuracy while the latter criticised it as unrealistic and rhetorical.[39] Both were misguided in their interpretation of what constitutes historical accuracy, if not naive in their search for it. All in all, the considerable discrepancies that appear in the press's interpretations seem to follow broad party-political lines, but the unease in dealing with Italy's recent past remained unequivocal. Certain nuances of Rossellini's film, however, such as Bardone's motives and his anonymous death, and the overall gloomy atmosphere of the film, suggest the beginnings of a change.

RELIGION VERSUS RESISTANCE: *THE GOLD OF ROME*

A further aspect, which all contemporary reviews of *General della Rovere* shared, was the disregard of the Jews in the film's final section. This is not surprising, considering that it is only a fleeting sequence in a film that presents many more urgent matters for discussion. Yet the businessman's racist remark, the attention Rossellini gives to the shot of the Jews at prayer and the selective subtitles should have warranted some mention at least. The absence of any reference is especially baffling because the prayer scene is placed strategically between two crucial scenes, where Fabrizio first confronts the businessman and then meets the fake general, just before the film's climax.

My contention is that this omission is not simply explainable with the limited relevance and visibility of the Shoah in *General della Rovere*. On the contrary, the rest of this chapter will show that the reception of Lizzani's *The Gold of Rome* proves that Italian reviewers disregarded the Shoah because of a clear Italian tendency to absorb the genocide into the Resistance struggle. In understanding the Shoah as just another German crime against humanity, the Italian press shows distinct similarities with the attitude displayed by French reviewers of *Night and Fog* only a few years earlier.

One *L'Unità* reviewer opened his piece: 'Carlo Lizzani returns, with this film, to the theme of the Resistance'.[40] Yet the Resistance is to *The Gold of Rome* what the Shoah was to *General della Rovere*. As we shall see, the only episode of partisan guerrilla shown in Lizzani's film relates not to the Resistance but to the religious identity of one of the characters, David. In fact, the film's main theme is a very specific event in the persecution of Rome's Jewry: the Nazi blackmail of that community in late September 1943. On 26 September 1943, Herbert Kappler, head of the German police in Rome, called Dante Almansi and Ugo Foà, presidents respectively of the Union of Italian Jewish

Communities and the Jewish Community of Rome, to demand the collection of fifty kilos of gold, threatening the deportation of 200 men. The film begins with the Kappler's blackmail and ends with the mass-deportation of 1,007 Roman Jews on 16 October 1943.[41] In between, it follows the frenetic and eventually successful efforts to meet German demands and win a brief, misguided relief. Lizzani's film, flawed in many respects, remains today one of barely a handful of Italian films dealing with the Shoah in Italy.

The Gold of Rome is a largely collective film, which makes the community its protagonist and well describes the life of the old Roman ghetto, populated by Jews since ancient Rome (Figure 2.1). Lizzani makes full use of stereotype to paint a moving sketch of a wide range of traditional characters: tough Jewish matrons ruling the household; working-class men employed as itinerant peddlers, ragpickers, salesmen, artisans; wealthy shopkeepers and middle-class professionals. Among these, two young characters stand out: Giulia and David. Lizzani uses them to symbolise two opposite approaches to the fate their community will shortly face.

On the one hand, Giulia is a middle-class university student who falls in love with a Catholic friend, Massimo. Intermarriage may give her a better chance of avoiding deportation, but the man's wealthy conservative parents demand her conversion. She converts, marries and abandons the faith of her ancestors, but when she witnesses the SS take away her father and the other Jews, she willingly joins them. David is a shoemaker also living in the old ghetto. He is clearly in love with Giulia, so that he – and through him the audience – perceives her conversion as a double betrayal. Alone among his own people, David does not trust the Germans' promises and argues against paying a ransom. Although he has to yield to the majority's short-sighted response, he secretly contacts a partisan brigade south of Rome, which provides him with weapons. After the 'gold of Rome' has been successfully collected, David's few comrades betray him, disclosing to worried Jewish mothers the whereabouts of the weapons. In a scene made even more dramatic by hindsight, the women throw the guns into the River Tiber. David is left with no choice but to leave his house and join the Resistance. When faced with the necessity to kill another man, however, his forefathers' commandments stay his hand. David hesitates almost fatally but eventually shoots, suppressing the voice of his Jewish identity. Giulia does not shoot; she runs, then returns: she cannot turn her back on her Judaism. Giulia dies; David survives.

Lizzani favours David's heroism over Giulia's martyrdom. At the root of his stance is the deep-seated misunderstanding that atavistic, religiously-motivated passivity stopped Jews from actively resisting. The director's representation of the dilemma is naive but certainly neither isolated nor malicious. It seems fair to say that the many generalisations of this film are the result of sketchy narrative and stereotyped characters, rather than of prejudice. Lizzani's somewhat biased reading of the events was mainly the result of his political affiliation. His critique of religion was not anti-Semitic but Marxist, and his film remains, at all times, respectful and aware of Jewish identity. *The Gold of Rome* was the product of a concept of art that wanted to educate the people, and Lizzani's David – like Rossellini's Fabrizio – is a two-dimensional working-class hero. Nevertheless, there is no real disapproval of Giulia's choice, except inasmuch as armed resistance against fascism is the only option the communist film-maker can truly accept. Yet *The Gold of Rome*, unlike some of those who reviewed it, did not pass judgment on the Jewish community.

'The wandering Jew is tired now', wrote Giacomo Debenedetti in his magnificent essay on the deportation Roman Jews, *16 Ottobre 1943*.[42] Tired of running from exile to exile, from pogrom to pogrom, looking for some non-existent safe haven, Roman Jews in particular had set roots deep into the soil beside the Tiber, and were afraid to run. There were also other reasons: some Jews did not have enough money to hide; others were too wealthy to leave everything behind them, or too well established to believe they would have been persecuted. Often, hiding required the separation of families and the abandonment of elderly or sick relatives. Many in Rome believed that Rome, the Holy See of the Vatican, would be spared mass deportations; some even believed that Mussolini, restored as head of the phoney Social Italian Republic, would 'protect' Italian Jews. The majority believed what they wanted to believe: each day without arrests fed the delusion that the German malice would be satisfied by gold, then by books, then by foreign Jews, then by anti-fascist Italian Jews.[43]

They were mistaken. Neither Mussolini nor Pope Pius XII

officially criticised the deportations. The silence of Pius XII, in particular, has come under scrutiny of late, with a veritable deluge of theses and counter-theses that have attempted to shed light on this most sensitive aspect of Judeo-Christian relations. Scholars such Daniel Goldhagen, Susan Zuccotti and John Cornwell have comprehensively examined the actions and inactions of Pius XII and convincingly concluded that his silence was at least morally guilty, even though the potential effects of his taking a clearer stance against the deportations remain in the realm of speculation. Much has been made of this uncertainty by those seeking to defend the memory of the soon-to-be Saint Pius XII.[44]

In 1961, of course, the wartime actions of Pius XII were neither questioned nor questionable. Yet the potential reasons for the Jews' tentativeness also escaped Lizzani's contemporaries. The left was particularly forceful in its refusal of any justification for what it perceived as an unforgivable deficiency in political consciousness. *L'Unità*, in particular, charged the Jews with, at best, lack of foresight, at worst, by cowardliness:

> Lizzani attempts to apportion clearly the moral responsibilities of the passive behaviour and political weakness demonstrated by the Roman Jewish community (and we believe its example to be valid for all other Jews too). [The director] even imagines the possibility of cowardliness, of betrayal by those wealthy Jews who behave more or less like all rich people around the world.[45]

The hypocrisy and ignorance of pieces such as this is blatant. The writer decided to score a cheap and highly dubious political point with disturbing echoes of recurring anti-Jewish prejudices. The article suggested some sort of atavistic Jewish dejection, which David 'sacrifices [...] to the only ideal worth dying for: that of all free and anti-fascist men regardless of race and religion'.[46] The critic did not discuss the circumstances of the time. Moreover, he failed to question the behaviour of just about everyone else – of other Italians, whether fascists, indifferent, outraged but impotent, or 'free and anti-fascist'.

What was certainly new here was the writer's acknowledgement of the 'immense Jewish tragedy'. Other elements were less original, however: first, the persistence in disregarding the racial laws of 1938 and considering anti-Jewish measures as a German

Figure 2.1. *The Gold of Rome*: in one of many group scenes, the notables of Rome's Jewish community ponder how to meet German demands. (© Movietime.)

import; second, the continued failure to question the attitudes and responsibilities of the Italian police forces and population during the occupation; third, the persistent belief that the Resistance was all-important. This is exemplified by Ellebi's conclusion that 'above and beyond the Jewish tragedy, however immense, this is Lizzani's message, this is the return [...] to the spirit of the Resistance'.[47]

The Gold of Rome was released amid the final stages of the Eichmann trial, which were reported in detail, particularly by *L'Unità*. The communist paper contained an unusual number of Holocaust-related stories during November and December 1961. On 24 November, it printed the report of a Polish survivor returning to Piedmont to meet his Italian saviours. Two days later, it commented on a comic play entitled *Rascel '61*, after the name of the leading man, famous Turinese comedian Renato Rascel. The newspaper remarked on how the play also featured a fascist saving a Jew. On 11 December, the day after Ellebi's review of the film, *L'Unità* opened with news of the Eichmann trial nearing its conclusion. The newspaper's attitude towards the trial further reveals a penchant for the simplification of history. For instance, it called Eichmann 'the exterminator of six million Jews'.

The fascination with the idea of resistance was also present in *L'Unità*'s attitude towards the Israeli state, to which it was sympathetic. It went as far as comparing the 1948 Arab–Israeli conflict to the 165 BC Judeo-Roman war, and described both as 'Partisan wars'.[48] This is surprising, considering that the Italian left performed a total reversal of this position after the 1967 Six-Day War with a critique of Israeli policies more than occasionally tainted by anti-Semitic overtones.[49] But, more importantly in the context of this book, the PCI's stance in 1961 serves as a further reminder of the place that armed struggles against oppressors had occupied since the war in the psyche of left-wing Italians. One cannot stress this point enough, as this doctrine would deeply affect Italian attitudes towards the Shoah, well after 1960.

Finally, on Tuesday 12 December 1961, *L'Unità* reported the guilty verdict against Eichmann.[50] In the same article, the reporter quoted the recent acquittal, by a Genoese court, of an editor whose magazine, *La Voce della Giustizia,* had referred to the Jews as 'Deicide in act and permanence, and as such lacking any possible morality'.[51] The motivations of the sentence were not reported, but the magazine's position was not far from that repeated by Catholic catechism until 28 October 1965, when it was reversed by the 'Nostra Aetate' resolution of the Second Vatican Council.[52] *L'Unità*'s aim in mentioning the incident within the Eichmann affair was to criticise the persistence of anti-Semitism in Italian society, as well the obtuseness of a justice system that still condoned it. It was a political point aimed at linking the Christian Democratic establishment with these residues of fascism.

The left-wing newspaper's position was inevitably affected by a degree of ideological entrenchment. It was also accompanied by more generalised misunderstandings regarding the Shoah. Yet the fact that *L'Unità* talked so extensively of the Eichmann trial, and the Shoah in general, was a considerable novelty. And, interestingly, it was a development rarely shared by the rest of the Italian press. *Il Popolo,* for example, acknowledged the fate of Roman Jews but completely failed to place it in the wider European picture. The main concern of the unsigned author was that 'the generous contribution by the Vatican does not seem sufficiently highlighted'.[53] The comment is baffling as the film shows Vatican envoys offering assurances that a loan would be made available should it be necessary.

L'Osservatore Romano itself did not contravene its tradition of ignoring entertainment to comment on *The Gold of Rome*. On 27 November, however, three days after the film's release, *L'Osservatore Romano* awarded it a censorship rating of 'adult material presenting dangerous elements' (Ar), which was more a reflection of its stance on cinema than on the film's treatment of the Vatican, or its theme. Considering the judgment of 'morally unacceptable' (E) bestowed upon some of its contemporaries – such as Pier Paolo Pasolini's *Accattone*, and Louis Malle *Zazie dans le Metro* – the film was not treated harshly. What is more interesting is that, on 30 November, the rating of Lizzani's film was downgraded to an unqualified 'adult material' (A). A malicious mind could suggest that the Vatican censors realised that all the 'dangerous elements' disappear at the end of the film. The most likely explanation, however, is that the Vatican had initially rated the film before viewing it.

The film was not released in Milan, at least not in 1961 or early 1962, although it may have been distributed at a later date. Hence *Il Corriere della Sera* did not review it. The fact that the film was not shown in Milan was probably because it was perceived to be concerned with distinctly Roman matters. It may also have been a commercial decision, since the film was very unpopular, grossing only 167,000,000 Italian lire.[54] Since at the time films were not released nationwide simultaneously, it is arguable that *The Gold of Rome*'s poor showing in Rome persuaded distributors not to release it in Milan. In Rome, however, the film was favourably reviewed. The popular centrist daily, *Il Messaggero*, found the true message of Lizzani's work in David's character: 'obtaining not gold but weapons, and joining the partisans'.[55] Once again, the association of gold and Jews proved too powerful for the review's author, going under the acronym Bir., to resist a lapse into ancient stereotypes. In his opinion, Lizzani explores:

> the different psychological reactions of this people [sic], conditioned partly – by their traditional persuasion – to believe that gold could truly stop the Germans, and partly – by the no less traditional resignation to persecution – to

> consider useless any attempt to save themselves, by escaping or reacting at the appropriate moment.[56]

A history of persecution may well have played a part in some Jews' underestimation of the threat. The film itself hammers this point home by showing a rabbi reassuring the faithful by recounting stories of past papal persecutions, humiliating and avaricious, but seldom fatal. However, the article naively, perhaps even hypocritically, suggests that there was indeed an opportune moment to escape en masse, or even to fight back. Once again, five years of home-grown discrimination and persecution were ignored. Once again, Italian Jews were effectively criticised for not reacting: something that few Italians did – and fewer still before 1943 – despite having few or none of the constrictions and difficulties the Jews were under. Moreover, Bir.'s dubbing of Roman Jews as 'this people', shows a remarkable failure to understand the essence of past and modern prejudice.

CONCLUSION

These Italian films are helpful in our investigation of the relationship between Holocaust films and popular attitudes towards the Shoah. Though in neither case can we realistically suggest that the films affected Italian historical memory, through their representational choices and, indirectly, through the reception accorded to them, both films are telling examples of Italian attitudes of the time. In stylistic terms, all three films owe much of their inspiration to Italian neo-realism. Their significance, however, is not in their aesthetics but in their thematic representational choices. The choice of representing specifically the persecution of the Jews is evident in *The Gold of Rome*, and both films contain highly unusual scenes of Jewish people praying.

As the 1950s gave way to a new decade, the plight of Italian Jews was still considered only in so far as it confirmed Nazi–fascist barbarity and, hence, the righteousness of the glorious struggle against it. The Resistance remained the mythologised paradigm against which to judge all anti-fascist activities, or the lack thereof. Notwithstanding this, by 1961 reviewers recognised that Jews were persecuted in a way that differed from the Nazi–fascist repression of the partisan guerrilla. Yet this renewed awareness, for which the Eichmann trial seems only partly responsible, did not assuage the telling unease with which Italian newspapers covered Jewish identity. Reviewers acknowledged and pitied the fate of the Jews, but also criticised them as passive, occasionally flirting with stereotype. Popular response may also reinforce this argument: in particular the poor box office showing of *The Gold of Rome*, the first film to concentrate specifically on Italian Jews, is indicative though not conclusive evidence of popular uninterest or uneasiness with the subject.

NOTES

1. Myriam Anissimov, *Primo Levi: Tragedy of an Optimist* (London: Aurum Press, 1998), p.261.
2. Among Levi's 'commandments' regarding writing are: 'You will write concisely and clearly' and 'You will avoid embellishments and convolutions.' In Anissimov, *Tragedy of an Optimist*, p.252.
3. Primo Levi, *La Tregua*.
4. Giorgio Bassani, *Il Giardino dei Finzi-Contini* (Turin: Einaudi, 1962).
5. On neo-realism see, in English, Millicent Marcus, *Italian Film in the Light of Neo-Realism* (Princeton: Princeton University Press, 1986) and Peter Bondanella, *Italian Cinema from Neo-Realism to the Present* (New York: F. Ungar, 1983).
6. Lino Micciché, *Il Cinema Italiano degli Anni '60 e Oltre* (Venice: Marsilio, 1995), p.35.
7. 'La lettera di Rossellini', *L'Unità*, 9 September 1959, p.1.
8. See David Forgacs, Sarah Lutton and Geoffrey Lowell-Smith (eds), *Roberto Rossellini: Magician of the Real* (London: British Film Institute, 2000); Peter Bondanella, *The Films of Roberto Rossellini* (Cambridge: Cambridge University Press, 1993); and Peter Brunette, *Roberto Rossellini* (Oxford: Oxford University Press, 1987).
9. Micciché, *Il Cinema Italiano*, p.33.
10. Ibid.
11. Micciché convincingly compares these to Italy's cinematography at the end of the 1950s: Micciché, *Il Cinema Italiano*, pp.31–2.
12. Ibid., pp.37–76, offers a convincing, if very critical, analysis of the neo-realist renaissance. Brunetta is much kinder to the films made in this period. Disregarding the weaker works, he clearly sees the reintroduction of the theme of the Resistance in Italian cinema as a considerable credit. See Gian Piero Brunetta, *Storia del Cinema Italiano*, vol. 3 (Roma: Editori Riuniti, 2001), pp.425–7.
13. Somewhat tellingly the poster of *Tunisi Top Secret* does not advertise the director's name (Bruno Paolinelli) but promises 'Chelo Alonso's exotic and provocative dances'.
14. Micciché, *Cinema Italiano*, p.33.
15. The explanations of the CEI's censorship ratings are drawn from the *L'Osservatore Romano*'s own legend, 1959.
16. Annette Insdorf, *Indelible Shadows: Film and the Holocaust*, second edition (Cambridge: Cambridge University Press, 1989), p.180.
17. Ugo Casiraghi, 'Con il *Generale della Rovere* Rossellini e De Sica si riabilitano', *L'Unità*, 30 August 1959, p.12.
18. Ibid.
19. Ibid.

20. Ibid.
21. Ibid.
22. Ibid.
23. In fact, towards the very end of his life Montanelli became respected by the Italian left, in particular when, in 1994, he resigned as the editor of the Milanese newspaper *Il Giornale* because of interference by the paper's owner, Silvio Berlusconi.
24. Casiraghi, 'Rossellini e De Sica si riabilitano'.
25. Ibid.
26. *Il Popolo*, 8 October 1959, p.13.
27. These young thugs belonged to three separate neo-fascist organisations, a testament perhaps to right and left-wing Italy's love for political organisations and acronyms. In a commendable move towards greater privacy rights, *Il Popolo* provided names and addresses of seven of the arrested!
28. Arturo Lanocita, *Il Corriere della Sera*, 3 September 1959, p.16.
29. Arturo Lanocita, 'Un film che onora la città di Milano', *Il Corriere della Sera*, 4 November 1959, p.16.
30. Ibid.
31. Ibid.
32. Mario Gromo, 'Intervista a Rossellini e Monicelli.'
33. Lanocita, 'Un film che onora la città di Milano.'
34. Gromo, 'Intervista a Rossellini e Monicelli.'
35. Ibid.
36. R. Chiti and M. Pecorari (eds), *Dizionario del Cinema Italiano*, vol. 2 (Roma: Gremese, 1991).
37. *La Grande Guerra* grossed 1,750,000,000 Italian lire. Chiti and Pecorari (eds), *Dizionario*, vol. 2.
38. *L'Unità*, 31 October 1959, p.13.
39. Lanocita, 'Un film che onora la città di Milano.'
40. Ellebi, '*L'Oro di Roma*', *L'Unità*, 10 December 1961, p.13.
41. Susan Zuccotti, *L'Olocausto in Italia* (Milano: TEA Storica, 1995), p.149.
42. Giacomo Debenedetti, *16 Ottobre 1943* (Palermo: Sellerio, 1993), p.36. Debenedetti was also a Roman Jew who had escaped the raid. Written less than a year after the events, *16 Ottobre 1943* is extraordinary, particularly in the way it manages to reconcile a necessarily emotional tone with the clarity and sobriety the subject matter demands.
43. Susan Zuccotti, *The Italians and the Holocaust* (New York: Basic Books, 1987).
44. On Pope Pius XII and the Shoah see Daniel Goldhagen, *A Moral Reckoning* (London: Little, Brown, 2002); Susan Zuccotti, *Under His Very Windows: The Vatican and the Holocaust in Italy* (New Haven, CT: Yale University Press, 2000); and John Cornwell, *Hitler's Pope: The Secret History of Pius XII* (London: Viking, 1999).
45. Ellebi, *L'Unità*, 10 December 1961, p.13.
46. Ibid.
47. Ibid.
48. 'Il processo ad Eichmann si avvicina alla conclusione', *L'Unità*, 11 December 1961, p.1.
49. Italian journalist Fiamma Nierenstein remembers being a young communist in 1967, working in an Israeli kibbutz when war broke off. She recalls returning to Italy to find a sudden change in the way her party comrades looked at Israel and at her: "some looked at me as though I was not the same person as before, but an enemy, an imperialist *in pectore*'. Fiamma Nierenstein, *Gli Antisemiti Progressisti: La Forma Nuova di un Odio Antico* (Milano: Rizzoli, 2004), p.12.
50. 'Eichmann colpevole', *L'Unità*, 12 December 1961, p.1.
51. Ibid.
52. As David Kertzer and others have pointed out, the history of Catholic anti-Semitism neither began nor ended with the papacy of Pius XII. The recent obsession with the latter runs the risk of downplaying a much more deeply-rooted

problem in the history of relations between the Vatican and the Jews. David Kertzer, *The Popes against the Jews* (New York: Vintage Books, 2001).

53. Unsigned, *Il Popolo*, 25 November 1961.
54. M. Poppi and M. Pecoraro (eds), *Dizionario del Cinema Italiano*, vol. 3. (Roma: Gremese, 1992).
55. Bir., *Il Messaggero*, 25 November 1961, p.14.
56. Ibid.

3

The Struggle, Not the Man: *Kapò* and *L'Enclos*

'*Enclosure* makes *Kapo* look laughable, even indecent.'[1]

Released within weeks of each other in Paris during the trial of Adolf Eichmann, Gillo Pontecorvo's *Kapò* (*Kapo*, Italy, 1960) and Armand Gatti's *L'Enclos* (*The Enclosure*, France, 1961) are the product of a very specific, political interpretation of the Shoah. As shown in the previous two chapters, in the 1950s and early 1960s the idealised view of the Resistance converged with a Manichean misinterpretation of the Shoah, a generalised ignorance of its history and a polarised ideological framework to misrepresent or conceal the specific identity of Jewish victims. By analysing comparatively *Enclosure* and *Kapo*, this chapter has the aim of further testing these findings and of drawing a closer parallel between France and Italy than has yet been possible.

The works of Pontecorvo and Gatti are perfectly suited to this kind of comparative case study. Fictional stories shot in a reconstructed concentration camp in Yugoslavia, each film was, in its own country, the first fictional film to be set entirely in a Nazi lager; furthermore, both films set their action in a particular kind of concentration camp: a work camp which, in each case, contains only one Jewish inmate. As well as these remarkable representational similarities, their contemporaneous release in France provides an excellent opportunity to compare press reaction to two similarly-themed films. In fact, although *Kapo* was first released in Italy a year earlier, in 1960, the French press often directly compared these films, as in the case of the *Le Monde* uncompromising statement reproduced above.

On the one hand, *Kapo* is quite well known amongst scholars, at least partly because of Jacques Rivette's oft-cited tirade against it.[2] In fact Rivette's piece, 'De l'Abjection', is only a small if rhetorically extraordinary portion of French reaction to the film.

On the other hand, *Enclosure* is little known and has not been accorded by scholars the attention it deserves. This adds a further element of interest to the comparative analysis of their aesthetics, content and reception. The last, in particular, will allow us to draw a few conclusions about French attitudes towards the Shoah and its representation, and how these differed from contemporary Italian views. The two films suggest a link between the societies of Italy and France in the shared representation of Judaism as a hindrance to rebellion, particularly when considered in contrast with the unquestionable righteousness of the communist struggle. The emphasis given to Marxism and the Resistance is consistent with the ideological and political allegiance of the two film-makers. Furthermore, it represents a degree of continuity with the hegemonic interpretation, representation and commemoration of the Second World War in the late 1940s and 1950s.

Nevertheless, the works of Gatti and Pontecorvo are significant not only for their continuity with the past but also for the many new elements they seem to introduce in Holocaust representation. This chapter will argue that *Kapo* and *Enclosure* signalled the beginning of a change in perspective through a number of thematic and stylistic choices unimaginable in *The Gold of Rome* or even *Night and Fog*. Moreover, the parallel analysis of the reception of *Kapo* in Italy, and both films in France, will also demonstrate that – while both countries continued to struggle to accept and represent Jewish identity – by 1961 the two societies attributed different relevance to the Shoah, as an historical event and as a cinematic subject. It is on this common combination of conventional and innovative elements that this chapter will focus.

THE HOLOCAUST AS MORAL BATTLEGROUND: *KAPO*

Kapo needs to be understood within the wider wave of Italian historical films discussed in the previous chapter and yet, in many ways, *Kapo* looked different from its contemporaries. A joint French–Italian–Yugoslav production, shot in Yugoslavia with an international cast, Pontecorvo's contribution to the new Resistance genre was unusual in terms of both theme and technique. From its cast to its title, the film was pervaded by a sense of foreignness. While in this successful period for the Italian film industry and Rome's Cinecittà studios, it was common for Italian films to include foreign stars, *Kapo* featured mostly French and German actors with the American Susan Strasberg as the added star factor. Furthermore, although the word *kapò* obviously derived from the Italian *capo*, the film's producers marketed the film as *Kapò*, with a stress on the second syllable. Pontecorvo's work undoubtedly helped convey to a popular audience the French pronunciation of the word, which is still dominant.

Similarly, while Pontecorvo had learnt his trade as a film-maker in neo-realism, acting in Aldo Vergano's 1946 *Il Sole Sorge Ancora* (*Outcry*), his artistic maturity had taken him beyond it. A committed communist, he was attracted towards the more uncompromising styles of short films and documentary film-making. Thus, if his work has echoes of neo-realism, his use of colour and contrast, lighting, camera movement and music in *Kapo* was radically different from the admittedly loose conventions of realist film-making. Thematically, too, this film differed from others of the time. Its concern with the individual struggle between morality and survival, acknowledging the moral dilemmas faced even by innocent individuals, anticipated themes that belong to the 1970s more than the 1960s. In fact, as we have shown, the mere suggestion of similar concerns in *General della Rovere* infuriated left-wing Italian reviewers. With the character of Edith, the central figure of the film, *Kapo* pushed the issue of moral compromise much further than any Italian film before it, although it provided the respite of a cathartic ending. Until the final section, however, Pontecorvo's film was relentless in its pursuit of the story of a victim turned oppressor.

The victim is Edith, the teenage French Jewess, who witnesses her parents being taken away on a truck and decides to go with them. Once in Auschwitz, she sees them being herded towards the gas chambers, naked, shamefully covering their genitals in a striking yet disturbing scene. The oppressor is Nicole, the criminal whom Edith has to impersonate in order to survive. Taught to forget her name, her Judaism, her family and beliefs, Edith becomes Nicole: a daughter of the lager. To strengthen the point of her dehumanisation further, as if what she had witnessed was not sufficient, we are shown how hunger and desperation lead her to prostitution and, eventually, to becoming a ruthless kapo. Pontecorvo's choice of a young middle-class girl was significant:

firstly, his deliberately gendered representation of the moral dilemma amplified the tension between innocence and guilt; secondly, the class element denied the audience any chance of an uplifting sociocultural justification.

In opposition to Edith–Nicole is another female character, Terèse, a mature political prisoner played by Emmanuelle Riva. Terèse comforts Edith in their transport from Auschwitz to the work camp, and maintains throughout the need to remain true to one's beliefs. She is utterly distraught at Nicole's gradual decadence, but eventually, assailed by chronic hunger, she too steals a potato from a fellow inmate. Chastised, ridiculed and humiliated by Nicole, Riva's character cannot bear the collapse of her own rigid set of moral values and commits suicide by touching the electric fence. Her death highlights the moral monstrosity of the camp system.

Nevertheless, the film soon seeks to comfort the viewer with a more uplifting ending. Thus Nicole, having met and witnessed the ideological, moral and physical strength of Sasha, a young Russian prisoner of war, decides to sacrifice herself for a mass escape. She becomes victim once more, reciting the prayer of the *Shema* while dying. To the audience, who has seen this young girl gradually forget ideas of solidarity and humanity to devote herself to the task of survival, this rushed repentance provides irritation rather than relief. According to unreferenced sources quoted by Lino Micciché, the film's producers imposed a cathartic ending on Pontecorvo.[3] A couple of contemporary French reviews also had reported this news. Michalczyk disproved this theory, however, pointing to the fact that in 1982 Pontecorvo and the scriptwriter Franco Solinas had taken full responsibility for the ending of *Kapo*, which they adopted because they thought the film would be too stark.[4]

It is possible that economic concerns played their part in the genesis of this ending, but this could equally have been brought about by Pontecorvo's own proximity to the Communist Party. This view is supported by the conduct of the character of Sasha, who provides the sort of ideological paradigm, which appealed to left-wing directors at the time. A working-class hero, Sasha is symbolically and literally unflinching, as we see him being forced to spend a night standing by the electric fence, unable to move or sleep. It is his ability to accomplish this task which induces Nicole to redeem herself. Yet Sasha is a complex character, who knowingly asks Edith to commit suicide for the greater good of the camp prisoners. The final scene, accompanied by the pounding atonal score for which *Kapo* has become infamous, shows him amongst hundreds of dead prisoners, after a successful but costly escape attempt. Thus the film's conclusive shot seems to dampen Sasha's moral certitude and the straightforward righteousness of the cause, or at least question its price. This fact makes Sasha quite different from the moral certitude of communist heroes such as Fabrizio and the barber in *General della Rovere* and David in *The Gold of Rome*.

Kapo's strength is that, despite appearances, it refused to exploit the Holocaust for romantic, adventurous or pathetic means. Pontecorvo managed to ask important questions about identity and the solidity of its foundations. As well as being original in the way it tried to reverse the usual heroic scheme of Resistance movies by creating a negative heroine, *Kapo* is maybe the first Italian film to show how the Nazi persecution of the Jews sought to achieve their humiliation and complete loss of dignity, even before their physical annihilation.[5] The way it acknowledged the collective fate of the Jews was unprecedented at the time. And last, but not least, the humane and complex character of Karl, the mutilated SS who exploits and then befriends Edith, signalled a considerable shift from the orthodox demonisation of the Germans fostered by post-war Italian films.

THE RECEPTION OF *KAPO*

Kapo forced the Italian press to discuss the matter of the persecution of the Jews like no other film before it. The result revealed the low level of awareness of the scope, systematic nature and details of the Nazi Final Solution among Italian critics. For example, writing in Italy's most popular daily, the centrist *Il Corriere della Sera* printed in Milan, Arturo Lanocita stated: 'Perhaps there was still something to say' about the persecution of the Jews.[6] The piece's introduction shows that he was under the clear impression that everything had been said on the matter. On the other hand, on 8 September 1960, after the film's screening at the Venice Film Festival, Ugo Casiraghi of the Communist Party daily, *L'Unità*, was of a radically different opinion. 'After more than fifteen years, *Kapo* is the first film Italy has dedicated to the Nazi death camps', he wrote.[7] Also, after *Kapo*'s release in Turin on 11 November, another article in *L'Unità*, this time signed 'Vice', agreed that the film treated 'a subject until now far too neglected'.[8]

Critics also disagreed in their interpretation of the film's content. Different newspapers highlighted different aspects of the film, giving priority to one issue over another, raising the profile of a character or ignoring another. On the one hand, the Christian Democrats' official paper, *Il Popolo*, profusely praised what it interpreted as the film's concept of redeeming love, but completely disregarded the nationality and ideology of the character to whose love it attributed such power.[9] On the other hand, *L'Unità* rejected the idea of 'a rhetorical struggle between love and duty', while awarding particular praise to the film's realism and perceived accuracy.[10]

Il Corriere della Sera criticised the film's 'lack of subtlety in the psychological shifts', suggesting that 'it may have been less reassuring, but more realistic, to leave Edith to her moral obtuseness without resorting to the ultimate crisis'.[11] *L'Unità*, however, was of opposite opinion, suggesting that 'the psychological transformation' was 'credible',[12] but maintaining the criticism of the cathartic death.[13] *Il Popolo*, while praising the film's 'high moral value and great *engagement* and sobriety', steered clear of the characters' ethical struggle.[14] It was far more concerned with expressing regret for the fact that 'often the characters indulge in romantic excesses with unwarranted ostentation of their feelings'.[15] Considering the setting of the film and the murders, starvation and humiliation present therein, and given the rapidly changing moral standards of the time, *Il Popolo*'s concern with rather subdued displays of affection is frankly baffling. Perhaps this ostentatiousness warranted the Italian Episcopal Conference's rating of 'adult themes with dangerous elements'.[16]

L'Unità, on 12 November 1960, sported a picture of the crowd at the Turin premiere of the film with a comment on its excellent public success, but there is no real evidence that this success extended past the first couple of weeks. *Kapo* enjoyed average financial gains, earning 558,000,000 Italian lire.[17] The impression is that while popular at first, interest fizzled out rather rapidly. Similarly, the quantity, quality and length of the reviews in contemporary papers suggest that *Kapo*, while raising immediate interest, failed to impress critics.

Astonishingly, one aspect of the film that all the reviewers missed was Edith's Judaism as a fundamental part of her identity, exemplified by her deathbed prayer. Edith recites the *Shema*, which is not just any prayer, but the fundamental statement of faith of Jewish theology. The way contemporary commentators considered her Judaism as unimportant, almost incidental, reinforces the feeling that Italian society had an incomplete perception of the persecution of the Jews. This misconception is proved further by the insistence on the film's realism and historical accuracy. Interestingly this praise was shared by all reviewers, whatever their political background. Thus, critics suggested the film 'merges documentary and chronicle',[18] praising its 'meticulous closeness' to the Nazi extermination camps.[19] Yet no one noticed that, apart from a few minutes, the film is not actually set in a death camp, but in a work camp, populated exclusively by non-Jewish prisoners.

This is particularly interesting as in France, where the film came out on 26 April 1961, commentators had an utterly contrasting impression. The film was received mercilessly by many, and one of the criticisms regarded its perceived lack of realism. A critic, in *France-Observateur*'s entertainment section, *Aux Écoutes*, called *Kapo* 'nothing but a cruel, atrocious melodrama, scarcely tolerable'.[20] He pointed out two factual mistakes: the contemporary advertisements appearing in the background of an early scene (which was supposed to be set in Paris in 1943), and Sasha's spoken French, which was far too 'pure' to resemble that of a Soviet prisoner of war. Less narrow-minded and more crucial was *France-Observateur*'s comment: '*Kapo* is a commercial enterprise' without 'absolute integrity'.[21] *L'Humanité*, too, called the film 'less a testimony than a dramatic action unfolding around the *univers concentrationnaire*'.[22]

Paris-Presse provided a more or less solitary voice in suggesting that aesthetic considerations should not cloud the judgement of a work intended as 'testimony, document, acknowledgement'.[23] Almost unanimous in their criticism of the film's cathartic ending, no French reviewer saw this film as a documentary or a chronicle. Instead, the vast majority of reviewers focused on the key issues regarding *Kapo*: the duty of remembrance and testimony; the moral and spiritual cost of the camps; the issue of Holocaust representation in its own right.

The Eichmann trial, unfolding in Jerusalem during those months, seems to have influenced many commentators' interpretation of the film as a warning not to forget. A review in

Dernières Nouvelles d'Alsace quoted the court case,[24] and the communist *L'Humanité* referred to it in a subheading.[25] Most critiques, whether negative or positive, acknowledged *Kapo*'s good faith and its value as an honest and moving contribution. They unequivocally praised the film's aims, even when they disapproved of its tactics. Unlike in Italy, no one had the presumptuousness to dismiss Edith's choices as 'moral obtuseness'.

The French reviewers' understanding of the phenomenon that would later be called 'the grey area' is impressive when compared to the lack of interest demonstrated by their Italian counterparts. 'Pontecorvo has been able to evoke with pity and emotion, the moral vilification that turns a victim into an oppressor, one of the Nazis' most unforgivable crimes', wrote Michel Aubriant in *Paris-Presse*.[26] *L'Express* described the main character's condition as 'physical survival, moral murder'.[27] *Télérama* praised the film's interest in finding the responsibilities behind 'the moral degradation of a child'.[28] Henri Marc in the socialist *Populaire* also called the film 'necessary', comparing it to Alain Resnais's *Nuit et Brouillard* (*Night and Fog*) and Wanda Jakubowska's *Ostatni Etap* (*The Last Stage*, Poland, 1948),[29] suggesting – quite unlike his Italian counterparts – some knowledge of foreign Holocaust films.

Several reviewers directly asked the question of the possibility of representing the Shoah on film. Many critics, such as Vera Volmane in *Aux Écoutes*, were clear in condemning the very idea of representing the Shoah in film, 'no matter how laudable the author's aims'.[30] Others, such as an unnamed reviewer in *L'Express*, suggested that the attempt was legitimate, since even a fictionalised story can 'awake the consciences'. She also praised Pontecorvo's choice to set the action in a work camp, deeming it an understandable 'hesitation in front of the worst, which cannot be told'.[31]

The critic, theorist and Nouvelle Vague director, Jacques Rivette, weighed in on the debate with a ruthless critique of *Kapo* in *Les Cahiers du Cinéma*. Interestingly, Rivette's position was different from both the Italian and French reviews of *Kapo*. Whereas the former praised the film for its realism and the latter criticised it for its lack of it, Rivette censured the film because of its realistic facade. He criticised not so much what Pontecorvo said, but the fashion in which he said it. In particular, he singled out the director's travelling shot over Emmanuelle Riva's dead body after her character's suicide. In this sequence, the camera moves forward to linger on the inmate's corpse, earning the critic's 'most profound contempt'.[32] Rivette made the travelling shot the symbol of all traditional cinematic language and, effectively, of cinema's artifice. This language, and the conventions which apply to it, cannot, he suggested, be used to represent the concentration camps: 'any attempt to reconstruct or make up [is] derisory and grotesque, any traditional "entertainment" approach appears voyeuristic and pornographic'.[33]

In this matter, according to Rivette, realism could only be as realistic as an audience can physically tolerate: that is, realism would never be entirely truthful and would undoubtedly mislead the viewers. Moreover, in his view, by presenting the horror in a bearable fashion, realist Holocaust films effectively desensitised the viewers. 'You do not get used to *Night and Fog*', he wrote. The logical consequence of Rivette's argument is that 'the film-maker judges what he will show, and is judged by the fashion in which he has shown it'.[34] In this framework the critic praised Resnais and damned Pontecorvo. In questioning the wisdom of applying conventional cinematic language to the representation of the Shoah, Rivette's argument anticipated much of what the ongoing debate over Holocaust representation is about, and 'le travelling de *Kapo*' has deservedly become a byword for this issue: the French press referred to it both in 1992, in a piece on Steven Spielberg's *Schindler's List*,[35] and in 1998, during the controversy over Roberto Benigni's *La Vita é Bella* (*Life is Beautiful*, Italy, 1997).[36]

The analysis of the reception of *Kapo* suggests that, in Italy, the film was misunderstood: critics neglected the originality of its approach only to depict it as yet another late neo-realist work on the Resistance. In France, however, thanks to the example of *Night and Fog* and to an altogether less provincial outlook, film critics were already discussing the possibility, legitimacy and nature of Holocaust representation. *Kapo* thus inserted itself within a debate which was destined to be long-lived. Another remarkable difference is in the reviewers' understanding of the historical details. Pontecorvo's choice of setting the film in an unnamed work camp, rather than in Auschwitz, did not go unnoticed in France. On the contrary, in Italy, critics failed to see any difference between the two. Similarly, Italian reviewers made nothing of Edith's religion, the very reason for her deportation, while

French critics invariably devoted some attention to it. *France-Observateur* even commented on Edith's final prayer, which it called a 'profession of Jewish faith'.[37]

Both in terms of quantity and quality, the French reception of *Kapo* is more impressive than the Italian one. This dichotomy suggests that the film was more controversial in France than in Italy. In France, the film attracted interest for various reasons: first, *Kapo*'s French stars made it of interest to public and critics alike; second, in France the film was released in 1961, and the unfolding Eichmann trial played a part in generating interest around it. The reception of *Kapo* in France suggests that French society was able to view the persecution and attempted genocide of the Jews as a quite separate issue from the repression of domestic anti-German Resistance. A strong element in support of this argument is the way in which Resnais's *Night and Fog*, which had initially suffered because of that very confusion, had, by 1960, become the term of comparison for all Holocaust films. In Italy, instead, *Kapo* suffered in popularity partly because it coincided with Luchino Visconti's *Rocco e i suoi Fratelli* (*Rocco and his Brothers*, 1960), which absorbed much of the limelight.[38] Yet this explains the relative lack of debate around it, not the lack of understanding of it. This has to be imputed to the fact that to all intents and purposes *Kapo* was to Italians a foreign film just as the Shoah was to them a foreign event. Only this conclusion can make sense of the reception of Pontecorvo's film and explain why – as we have seen – in reviewing *The Gold of Rome* only a year later, *L'Unità* believed Lizzani's film to be first Italian effort about the Shoah.

THE SHOAH AS IDEOLOGICAL BATTLEGROUND: *ENCLOSURE*

The difference between France and Italy is further evidenced by *Enclosure*, the 1961 film realised by anarchist, publisher and Oranienburg survivor, Armand Gatti. Part memoir and part ideological treatise, *Enclosure* is a remarkable film on the nature of oppression and political commitment. Rejected by the official selection of the Cannes Film Festival, Gatti's film, like *Night and Fog* in 1956, was screened anyway outside of the *kermesse*. A film of remarkable interest both aesthetically and conceptually, *Enclosure* has been all but ignored by scholars so far.[39] In part, this is because Gatti's was a rather obscure and unpopular film, which has only become readily available in 2003. Nonetheless, the film was widely reviewed in France in 1961: the critics were almost unanimously enthusiastic of the politics of *Enclosure*. Alone, *Le Figaro*'s film critic, Louis Chauvet, criticised the film, yet not for its message but for its 'excessively theatrical' aesthetics.[40]

Enclosure needs to be understood in the context of France in 1961, in the midst of what Henry Rousso has convincingly and famously dubbed the 'Vichy Syndrome'.[41] Notwithstanding that Gatti's film is not primarily about France, the political, moral and ideological issues it raises should be considered relevant to the domestic political situation of those years. The film is undoubtedly informed by Gatti's personal experiences in the Second World War, but also by the unfolding Algerian War and the return to power of General Charles de Gaulle. In fact, through its representation of the concentration camp, *Enclosure* well suits the second phase of the Vichy Syndrome, the period Rousso calls 'repression of memory'. Yet, at the same time, Gatti's work signalled the emergence of a new French interest in the war, in Vichy and the Shoah, which would take full form in the 1970s, perhaps highlighting a limitation in Rousso's rather rigid subdivision.

In short, *Enclosure* is the story of the Nazi attempt to humiliate a German communist prisoner, Karl, by forcing him to commit murder in return for his life. Karl is locked in an enclosure within the camp with a French Jew, David – a watchmaker and the only Jew left in the camp – to whom the same offer has been made. While David mistrusts Karl, the latter's awareness and faith in the struggle is absolute and unwavering: he at no point considers murdering David. Instead, after Karl is rescued by the camp's underground resistance; David learns the lesson of collectivism by sacrificing his life to keep Karl's secret. The very last shot of the film is an extreme close-up of Karl's eye, revealing his guilt for David's necessary sacrifice, just as the final sequence of *Kapo* had seen Sasha's despair at the human cost of the tragedy. There are other similarities in the treatment of the Shoah in *Enclosure* and *Kapo*. First, Gatti's acknowledgment of the extermination of the Jews, not dissimilar from *Kapo*'s, confirms a growing knowledge about and sensitivity towards the subject. Just as Pontecorvo felt he had to justify Edith's survival as extraordinary, Gatti constructs a fictional reason for David's existence as the only surviving Jew in the concentration camp.

As the audience is informed that David survives because of his skills in repairing watches, it also learns that all other Jews were immediately exterminated. Just as *Kapo* tackles the genocide, with explicit and implicit images of the extermination of women, children and the elderly, David's reminiscence of systematic persecution in France reinforces the recognition of the specific anti-Jewish policies of the Nazis.

Second, the representation of camp life is similar to, if altogether more accomplished than that in Pontecorvo's film. Aesthetically, both films abandon somewhat the realist conventions of neo-realism. *Enclosure* does so by using the enclosure itself, in which most of the action takes place, as a straightforward allegory of the camp. This allows Gatti to discuss the *univers concentrationnaire* in depth while not being forced to attempt an ultra-realist representation of camp existence. Thematically, Gatti, like Pontecorvo, privileges the issues of dehumanisation and what Primo Levi called 'the grey zone', the ambiguous boundary between good and evil, survival and morality. The film opens with an extraordinary three-minute sequence of prisoners working in the camp quarry. The camera shows only their feet, an endless line of clogs and makeshift shoes which reveals symbolically the anonymity of the victims and the constant pervasiveness of the dehumanisation process (Figure 3.1). Immediately afterwards, we see two inmates carrying a rat on a stretcher and giving it a solemn burial while human corpses lie unattended to on the ground (Figure 3.2). In the following scene, two inmates are forced to fight to the death before the winner is himself murdered, for 'damaging Reich property'. Thus, the first few minutes relentlessly and shockingly, if not necessarily realistically, convey the atmosphere of loss of dignity and constant threat of the Nazi concentration camps.

In another remarkable similarity with *Kapo*, Gatti employs the character of Anna to further the analysis of the corrupting influences of fascism. Anna is a young prisoner who, humiliated by imprisonment and weakened by hardship, turns to prostitution to survive. The collective effort to save Karl will lead her to redemption. And, although, unlike Edith in *Kapo*, she is never violent towards her fellow inmates, her passive compliance with the Nazis is enough to require yet another a cathartic death. Thus, both films choose to use sexual exploitation as a physical symbol of dehumanisation and to single out women as particularly

Figure 3.1 and 3.2. *Enclosure*: Images of de-humanisation. (© 1961.)

vulnerable to the moral and physical degradation of the Nazi system. Both these aspects of the films represent a significant break with the way French and Italian society, ever since the war, had failed to distinguish between the Nazi persecution of political opponents and their attempted genocide of the Jews. Indeed, as we have shown thus far, they had consistently privileged the former over the latter.

The attention to detail demonstrated by French critics in the reception of both *Enclosure* and *Kapo* proves that this increased awareness was not solely the result of two particularly sensitive or knowledgeable film-makers. Rather, in France the films were symptoms of an already changing attitude. Conversely, the lack of insight of Italian reviewers of *Kapo*, and in particular their disregard of Edith's Jewishness, shows that Italian perceptions had not followed a similar shift. Here, *Kapo*'s more innovative elements were left unrecognised.

However, if in the ways discussed above *Kapo* and *Enclosure* shared some breakthroughs in the representation of the Shoah, in other ways they contained significant elements of continuity with early post-war perception. First, both films offered an openly Marxist interpretation of the anti-fascist struggle revealing a vision still heavily affected by ideological polarisation. There is no doubt that Karl is the hero in *Enclosure*, just as Sasha is in *Kapo*. David learns his lesson from Karl just as Edith learns hers from Sasha. The Soviet is not only communist but a fighting communist: it is his readiness for action that makes him the redeemer, rather than Riva's equally idealistic but ultimately weak character. Karl is just as forceful if a much more complex character than Sasha. Long voice-overs establish him as a veteran of the concentration camp, in his tenth year of imprisonment. Instead of Sasha's innocence, he has the understanding of a German who has experienced the rise of the Nazi system from the beginning, and the awareness that, even if he survives the war, he will not survive the peace.

This is where Gatti is at his strongest, where his clarity of thought and expression allow him to convey the lessons of his personal experience. It is not incidental that he devotes powerful long sequences to prisoners whispering information to one another, using tracking shots to highlight the collective effort of the camp's Resistance movement. In comparison, Pontecorvo's hurried discussion of the camp's underground movement is sketchy and naive, lacking the first-hand knowledge Gatti's film implies. On the one hand, *Kapo* suggests that resistance could be organised relatively easily, over a short time, merely with the initiative of a homogeneous group of motivated people; on the other hand, *Enclosure* portrays the camp underground infinitely more accurately, as an organisation which relied on prominent prisoners employed in the camp's bureaucracy, involved a complex way of relaying information and was geared primarily towards the protection of its members.

The explicit ideological interpretation of the concentration camps offered by *Enclosure*, like that of *Kapo*, confirms a primarily political interpretation of the Shoah and in some ways contradicts the film's point on the murder of the Jews. Over the night they spend in the enclosure under the watchful and derisory eye of the SS, Karl confronts David with the assuredness of the justice of his cause. In the night's climax, Karl tells David: 'What counts here is not the man, but his struggle: you are nothing and that's why you are going to die.' Similarly, the overwhelmingly positive reception of the film shows that this interpretation was seen favourably by the vast majority of the French press, less starkly ideologically divided than its Italian counterpart. The left-wing and centre-left press – comprising *Le Combat*, *Libération*, *L'Humanité* and *Le Monde* among others – were utterly fascinated by a film whose explicit message was the inevitable victory of collectivism over individualism. Moreover, the film's message, reinterpreted in a humanist vein, also appealed to the conservative press, from *Le Figaro* to *La Croix*.

Another aspect common to both films, and another element of continuity with the past, concerns the representation of Jewish identity. In criticising individualism, both *Enclosure* and *Kapo* seem to advocate the need to sacrifice non-political aspects of individual identities in order to defeat fascism. Religious, ethnic and national identity are simply an obstruction to a full and unconditional acceptance of the anti-fascist, and specifically communist cause. Indeed, *Enclosure*. particularly suggests an interpretation of Europe's Jewry in the 1940s as passive, apolitical and exclusivist, and therefore as complicit in their own destruction. The Jew, in both films, is only an agent in choosing death.

The two films, however, differ in one crucial aspect. While both Edith and David experience cathartic deaths, Edith's sacrifice is accompanied by a reappropriation of her Judaism; David's is accompanied only by his acceptance into the communist fold. Edith recites the *Shema*; David receives the dedication of a revolutionary song by the camp orchestra while marching to his death. While neither film is accusatory, both present the Jewish characters as in need of redemption, and both choose death to enact it. Yet Pontecorvo suggests that a religious identity is compatible with a political one, while Gatti suggests the latter requires the rejection of the former. Religion carries with it ignorance in *Enclosure*: David is suspicious, paranoid, morally and physically weak, while Karl is exactly the opposite: aware, strong, self-confident, sure of the righteousness of his cause.

Reviewers of *Enclosure* picked up on this aspect, noting David's passivity and individualism, and approving his belated catharsis. The words they employed in doing so reveal at the very least a continued misunderstanding of Jewish identity, if not a degree of persistence of certain atavistic prejudices. Expressions such as 'petit horologer juif' (little Jewish watchmaker), or simply 'petit juif', recur in most reviews.[42] These words imply an inherent weakness of David's character and, through him, of Jewish victims in general. Perhaps most tellingly of all, *Combat* assumed the Nazis had put 'a Jew and a German political prisoner' together in such a situation to see 'whether the former will betray the latter to save his skin'.[43] This suggests the opposite would be inconceivable. Thus, the contemporary reception of *Enclosure* suggests that the French critics were still unable to reconcile a greater knowledge of historical detail with a closer understanding of the Jewish perspective. If one matches this French attitude with the Italian reviewers' disregard of Edith's prayer, one can see clearly that Italy and France were still, by 1961, unable to understand the Shoah as a Jewish tragedy or relate to the perspective of Jewish victims.

CONCLUSION

If one considers *Kapo* and *Enclosure* in the context of the representation of the Shoah in France and Italy before 1960, it is clear that they present many elements of significant innovation: the acknowledgment of a specific anti-Jewish extermination programme; the interest in the social structure and functioning of the concentration camps; the fascination with dehumanisation and the fragility of individual morality; the move away from realism to convey more appropriately aspects of life of the *univers concentrationnaire*, which defy realist representation. These issues already contain the seeds of the shift in perception which would take place – especially in France – from 1968 onwards, with memorable films such as Marcel Ophuls's *Le Chagrin et la Pitié* (*The Sorrow and the Pity*).

Nevertheless these novel elements did not signal a new overall approach to the Shoah and its representation and, in particular, to Jewish experiences in the Shoah. In fact, both Pontecorvo and Gatti continued to understand the Shoah primarily as one battlefield in the ideological war between fascism and anti-fascism. Within this framework – and because of this framework – the Resistance remained the mythologised paradigm against which to judge all anti-fascist activities, or the lack thereof. Marxism was the only possible answer for both directors, at the expense of the understanding of the specific circumstances of many deportees. In both films the representation of Jewish identity remains confused and the search for a Jewish perspective frustrated; in *Enclosure*, though not in *Kapo*, this rationale also seems to imply the necessity to reject Jewish identity as inherently individualistic and inhibiting. This confirms early post-war attitudes towards the Shoah and suggests that France and Italy followed, to some extent, parallel paths until this stage.

Furthermore, the reception of the films confirms that the interpretation of the Shoah offered by Gatti and Pontecorvo was not far from the dominant view. Often bordering on stereotype, the overall reception of *Kapo* and *Enclosure* reveals the films' misunderstandings to be part of a wider social and historical problem in accepting the Shoah as a Jewish tragedy, and specifically as a trauma of each country's Jewish community. Nonetheless, it is important to stress that most reviewers in both countries recognised that Jews were persecuted in a way that differed from the Nazi-fascist repression of the partisan guerrilla. That is a significant change from what appeared to be the case only a few years earlier, on the occasion of the release of *Night and Fog*. Further evidence of this was the role of *Night and Fog*, which was constantly referred to by French reviewers of *Kapo* and *Enclosure*. Resnais's film, having survived censorship, had already become the paradigmatic work on Holocaust representation, the theoretical and practical manifestations of which French critics were alone in debating.

In contrast, Italian reviewers seemed to dismiss the Shoah as a foreign tragedy. Despite having experienced twenty years of fascism, a regime which in full independence had passed anti-Semitic laws as early as 1938, and despite having witnessed the deportation and murder of as many as 6,800 of its Jews,[44] Italians clearly believed the Shoah was an essentially foreign event. However, the 1960s' increasing distance between French and Italian understanding of the Holocaust is also explained by the beginnings of France's process of reappraisal of its recent past. This was a process which Italy had not yet undertaken; a process which the Algerian War had catalysed by brutally confronting France with the collapse of its self-proclaimed civilising mission. As we will see in the rest of this book, it is in the events of those years that we find one of the most convincing explanations of the striking difference in how Italy and France have since related to and represented the Shoah.

NOTES

1. Jean de Baroncelli, *Le Monde*, 16 May 1961.
2. Jacques Rivette, 'De l'Abjection', *Les Cahiers du Cinéma*, 120 (1961), pp.54–5.
3. The producers' intervention is reported in Lino Micciché, *Il Cinema Italiano degli Anni '60 e Oltre* (Venezia: Marsilio, 1995), p.114.
4. John Michalczyk, *The Italian Political Filmmakers* (Cranbury, NJ: Associated University Presses, 1986), pp.188–9.
5. Joseph Stangl, head of Treblinka, in Gitta Sereny, *In Quelle Tenebre* (Milano: Adelphi, 1975), p.135.
6. Arturo Lanocita, *Il Corriere della Sera*, 30 September 1960.
7. Ugo Casiraghi, *L'Unità*, 8 September 1960.
8. Vice, *L'Unità*, 11 November 1960.
9. Paolo Valmarana, *Il Popolo*, 8 September 1960.
10. Casiraghi, *L'Unità*, 8 September 1960.
11. Lanocita, *Il Corriere*, 30 September 1960.
12. Casiraghi, *L'Unità*, 8 September 1960.
13. Vice, *L'Unità*, 11 November 1960.
14. Valmarana, *Il Popolo*, 8 September 1960.
15. Ibid.
16. The Vatican censorship rating is reported in both *Il Popolo* and *L'Osservatore Romano*, for a fortnight from 8 September 1960.
17. Roberto Poppi and Mario Pecoraro (eds), *Dizionario del Cinema Italiano*, vol. 3 (Roma: Gremese, 1992).
18. Vice, *L'Unità*, 11 November 1960.
19. Casiraghi, *L'Unità*, 8 September 1960.
20. Vera Volmane, *Aux Écoutes*, 5 May 1961.
21. *France-Observateur*, 4 May 1961.
22. Samuel Lachize, *L'Humanité*, 26 April 1961.
23. Michel Aubriant, *Paris-Presse*, 3 May 1961.

24. R. K., *Dèrnieres Nouvelles d'Alsace*, 19 May 1961.
25. Lachize, *L'Humanité*, 26 April 1961.
26. Aubriant, *Paris-Presse*, 3 May 1961.
27. *L'Express*, 27 April 1961.
28. R.D.M., *Télérama*, 14 March 1961.
29. Henri Marc, *Populaire*, 4 May 1961.
30. Volmane, *Aux Écoutes*, 5 May 1961.
31. Ibid.
32. Jacques Rivette, *Les Cahiers du Cinéma*, 120 (1961), pp.54–5.
33. Ibid.
34. Ibid.
35. Serge Daney, 'Le Travelling de *Kapo*', *Trafic*, 4 (Autumn 1992).
36. Pascal Merigeau, 'Oublier l'Holocauste: de *Kapo* à *La Vie est Belle*', *Le Nouvel Observateur*, 15 October 1998.
37. *France-Observateur*, 4 May 1961.
38. John Foot, 'Cinema and the City: Milan and Luchino Visconti's *Rocco and his Brothers* (1960)', *Journal of Modern Italian Studies*, 4, 2 (1999).
39. The only reference to the film is a brief mention in Ilan Avisar, *Screening the Holocaust: Cinema's Images of the Unimaginable* (Bloomington, IN: Indiana University Press, 1988), p.29.
40. Louis Chauvet, *Le Figaro*, 30 October 1961.
41. Henry Rousso, *The Vichy Syndrome: History and Memory in France since 1944* (Cambridge, MA: Harvard University Press, 1991).
42. G.S., *Les Lettres Françaises*, 8 November 1961; Jean Rochereau, *La Croix*, 8 November 1961.
43. *Combat*, 15 May 1961.
44. Susan Zuccotti, *L'Olocausto in Italia* (Milano: Tea Storica, 1995), p. 25.

4

Unveiling the Mirror: *Le Chagrin et La Pitié*

In the 1960s, French commentators showed a clearer understanding of the Shoah than their Italian counterparts. As the contrast between the two countries' reception of *Kapo* proves, this difference in appreciation derived primarily from a greater public and historiographical interest in the topic. In both countries, a strong Marxist influence on film-making and film criticism helped to continue to delay the acknowledgment of the Shoah as a historical event distinct from the conflict between fascism and anti-fascism in wartime Europe. Nevertheless, during this period, France had at least begun to consider the Jewish specificity of the Nazi persecutions. The publication of historical studies and other literature on the Holocaust gained new momentum. Jewish historians, mostly working under the aegis of the Centre de Documentation Juive Contemporaine (CDJC), were instrumental in this effort. These included studies on the deportations of Jews from France,[1] memoirs,[2] works of analysis of French Jewish deportees,[3] works on French institutional anti-Semitism,[4] and the scholarship of historians such as Léon Poliakov.[5]

This process, however, had little impact on popular and academic interest in French anti-Semitism and national involvement in the persecution of the Jews. Throughout the 1960s, the memory of Jews deported from France continued to be sacrificed to a sanitised memory of the wartime nation. In 1962 a memorial on the Île de la Cité was dedicated to 200,000 'martyrs of the deportation'.[6] Symbolically, the plaque is located in the heart of Paris and near the Marais, but, perhaps also symbolically, Nôtre Dame turns its back to it and even today it can seem almost hidden. By not mentioning the Jews directly, the French authorities assumed possession of the identities of tens of thousands of foreign or denaturalised Jews deported from France by the Germans, often with the help of French police.[7] Moreover, after the 1967 Six-Day War between Israel and its Arab neighbours, President de Gaulle declared that 'the Jews [...] who had always been an elite people, self-confident and domineering, would, once gathered in the land of their former greatness, transform the very moving desires they had formed for nineteen centuries into a burning and conquering ambition'.[8] Prejudice was alive and well, even in unexpected and influential quarters of 1960s France.

Rousso has ably described the uneasy silence that surrounded the Vichy years in French society, culture and historiography, between the end of the war and the late 1960s.[9] Even the Comité d'Histoire de la Deuxième Guerre Mondiale (CHDGM), the body that was meant to initiate investigation in these matters, deliberately reinforced this vision through historiography and also, as described in Chapter One, through film.[10] Rousso convincingly identifies the emergence of a different phase in French memory of Vichy – what he calls 'the broken mirror' – as coinciding with the release of Marcel Ophuls's *Le Chagrin et la Pitié* (*The Sorrow and the Pity*, 1971). Although the French historian remains wisely shy of suggesting that Ophuls's four-and-a-half-hour documentary single-handedly broke the mirror, he is in no doubt that the film was a well-aimed brick thrown at it. In actual fact, the events of May 1968, followed by the departure and later the death of Charles de Gaulle, had already significantly weakened the French perception of France's recent past.[11] The generational confrontation invoked by the 1968 movement, with its sometimes patricidal overtones, combined with the loss of France's most striking father figure, certainly provided a preamble highly charged with symbolism as well as historical significance.

In 1969, Stanley Hoffmann had written: 'Collaborationism, whether servile or ideological, could not have developed so readily in a country that remained fundamentally deaf to its appeal had there been no state collaboration.'[12] The following year a conference organised by the Fondation Nationale des Sciences Politiques (National Foundation for the Political Sciences) began a new type of debate on Vichy. Yet the conference's coverage extended only to 1942, and discussed neither the policy of collaboration nor the persecution of the Jews. Nonetheless, this is evidence that at least the academic climate was changing: the process of scaling 'the impregnable walls that

Aron, Siegfried, and many others had erected between the Pétainists in Vichy and the fascists in Paris' had started.[13]

Granted that the change in French perceptions of Vichy was a gradual process rather than a sudden realisation, *The Sorrow and the Pity* nonetheless seems a useful and significant landmark. Certainly the film proved to be an appropriate tool to move discussion from conference halls to daily papers and the streets. Its importance is further justified by the shock value of its thesis, the scandal it provoked, the new approach it took with regards to both documentary film-making and historical analysis and, finally, by the legendary status it went on to acquire. This chapter will argue that *The Sorrow and the Pity* is one of those rare examples of films which anticipate changes in the collective memory of their time and shape it in a long-lasting manner. As we will see, the film spoke openly for the first time of Vichy's racial laws, French anti-Semitism and France's active role in assisting the German persecution. But most importantly, Ophuls's film exposed French attitudes to Vichy during the war in a revolutionary way. Far from concentrating only on anti-Semitism or even Vichy, this was a French film about France: this explains its success and the controversy which surrounded it.

The film has something of a legendary status, and most modern histories of France accord it some mention. Nevertheless, *The Sorrow and the Pity* has been discussed widely but not always in as much depth as it deserves. André-Pierre Colombat has produced a comprehensive textual analysis of the film, which nonetheless disregards its reception.[14] Rousso's analysis of the film is more concise but effective, highlighting many of its main points.[15] He has also given some attention to the film's reception, arguing that the significant impact of a film seen by relatively few people – about 700,000 – was helped by the urgency of *The Sorrow and the Pity*'s discussion of memory and its abuses.[16] Stanley Hoffman, in the essay that accompanied the published script in 1972, placed the film in its historical context, thus stressing its significance as a contribution to the politics of the late 1960s, as much as to the debates over memory and history popular in those years.[17] As Margaret Atack has pointed out, many analyses of the film play down its links with 1968 just because it was released in 1971. On the contrary, Atack has argued that *The Sorrow and the Pity* must be considered in the context of 1968, in order to understand the way Ophuls simultaneously 'repoliticises the Resistance for a new generation, but depoliticises narration'.[18]

Despite these and other studies on *The Sorrow and the Pity*,[19] there has been a tendency to separate the film from its reception. In the light of this, it is worth returning once more to this fundamental text, both to reassert its centrality to French collective memory of the Second World War, and to link it to a comprehensive analysis of its reception. By looking not only at the oft-cited immediate controversy that surrounded the film's release, but also at its long-term reception – up to its maiden television broadcast in 1981 – this chapter will highlight the shifts occurred in the perception of the issues raised by the film.

MEANINGFUL MANIPULATION

Marcel Ophuls and producers Alain de Sédouy and André Harris, who also conducted some of the interviews for the film, realised this 251-minute documentary in 1969. Until 1968, Ophuls, Harris and de Sédouy had all been employed by the Office de la Radio et de la Télévision Française (ORTF), for whom they had made *Munich ou la Paix pour Cents Ans*, in 1966. *Munich* possessed much of the revisionist fervour which animate their later work, intending to 'provide an opposition to and deliver an alternative to that collapse of self-satisfaction, which seemed to us to dominate the national networks'. Originally conceived in the same mould, as a television documentary, *The Sorrow and the Pity: Chronicle of a French Town under the Occupation* followed a thematic narrative structure within a broadly chronological framework which sees the film divided into two parts: 'The Defeat' and 'The Choice'. The material used consisted of a mixture of wartime French, German and Allied footage and post-war testimonies, the latter being privileged over the former. This composition was a remarkable innovation of the traditional documentary style, which, as we have seen in the case of *Nuit et Brouillard (Night and Fog)*, favoured footage and a running explanatory voice-over. Instead, it is only very occasionally that Ophuls provides a commentary. This features more prominently at the beginning of the film, particularly in order to introduce new witnesses, but gradually disappears later on.

Instead of using voice-over, Ophuls relied heavily on the selection, shooting, editing and setting of the interviews in order

Figure 4.1. *The Sorrow and the Pity*: Marcel Verdier and his family. (© Milestone.)

Figure 4.2: *The Sorrow and the Pity*: the Grave brothers. (© Milestone.)

to put across his argument. The witnesses, all men but one, included twenty-four French people, five Germans and as many British ones but, both in qualitative and quantitative terms, these testimonies carry different weights within the film. Both Henry Rousso and Annette Insdorf have attempted a quantitative analysis of the witnesses' political positions.[20] Rousso has also introduced a partial qualitative distinction, particularly by singling out Mendès-France's testimony. On both counts, Rousso suggested a degree of bias towards the Resistance, although he also acknowledged Ophuls's own view that the film is evenly split, with 20 per cent of the script devoted respectively to Resistance and collaboration, and 55 per cent to neither specifically.[21] The difference between the two is to be explained by the fact that Rousso considered only testimonies, while Ophuls referred to the whole script, including the archival footage.

All these analytic methods, however, are flawed. The first problem is that *The Sorrow and the Pity* is less interested in collaborators or *résistants* than in exploring the motives of the vast majority of indifferent or apolitical Frenchmen. The Pétainists and partisans Ophuls interviews are people motivated by ambition, self-preservation or a general discontent rather than by ideology. Furthermore, he seems intrigued by those people who remained neutral or indifferent. Not by chance the film's title mimics words pronounced by Marcel Verdier, a Clermont chemist, 'whose characteristic perch, firmly on the fence, is almost a caricature'.[22] Hence, to analyse the film's contents in terms of 'Resistance versus collaboration' risks missing the point. The second, related problem is that neither analysis allowed for silent testimonies, or shots of individuals who are not being interviewed. These may seem mere details and may add nothing to the script, yet they are often meaningful contributions to the overall feel of the film. Thus an analysis of the witnesses, such as the ones suggested by Rousso, does not allow for the wife of retired Wehrmacht Colonel Helmut Tausend, the children of Marcel Verdier, Geminiani's dice-playing partner, or the wives of the Grave brothers, who silently walk in and out of the interview room. The camera pauses on all these people, examining their body language, their expressions, their behaviour, all of which combine to provide a silent answer to Ophuls's questions. In fact, in his 1980 edition of the full script, Ophuls included a description of witnesses' facial expressions and of camera movement.[23] A different type of silent witness, equally misrepresented by an analysis either of the interviewees or of the script, is the one that appears in footage. The French crowds hailing Pétain on a visit to Clermont-Ferrand for example, or the solitary Parisian gendarmes saluting the parading German army, are almost as important as modern-day testimonies. Caught in the act by a camera, the complexities of their actions are lost in a rather pitiless editing technique that permitted no reply.

If the selection of the interviewees was in itself part of Ophuls's argument, his management of the interviews was his main means to strengthen it. Ophuls skilfully employed suggestive surroundings to comment on the witness and the testimony. When the audience sees the middle-class chemist Verdier in the comfort of his sitting room, surrounded by well-groomed children and sporting the mannerisms of the French professional bourgeoisie, it immediately classifies him as a man devoted to his family and its success (Figure 4.1). In *The Sorrow and the Pity* this method of setting the context was the rule, not the exception. The partisan Grave brothers were first filmed in their fields to emphasise the fact that they are working class, then in their wine cellar to recreate the conspiratorial mood of wartime underground meetings (Figure 4.2). Similarly, reformed French fascist Christian de La Mazière is interviewed in the Castle of Sigmaringen, residence of the Vichy government after its flight from France.[24] Some – like Helmut Tausend, who is interviewed at a family wedding and allowed to speak freely and with pride of his days in the German army – are allowed to feel at ease and unthreatened; others, such as Clermont shopkeeper Marius Klein, are approached by surprise and in a confrontational manner. Thus, by the use of specific techniques and settings loaded with symbolism, Ophuls guides the testimony and the audience's reaction to it.

On several occasions, Ophuls also uses the soundtrack to reinforce his point. This is not the ever-present musical score of *Night and Fog*; in *The Sorrow and the Pity*, non-original soundtrack appears on only five occasions and is intended to qualify the interview, rather than manipulate viewer emotions. On three occasions, Ophuls used popular songs of the 1940s sung by Maurice Chevalier. Their lyrics and positioning in the film are telling, as is their singer. Maurice Chevalier was one of France's most popular entertainers throughout the occupation. His success and his outspoken praise of Pétain saw his name included in a list of collaborators published by *Life* magazine in 1942. Later, in 1946, he was arrested for the same reason, though he was released shortly afterwards.[25] Ophuls uses Chevalier as the embodiment of a French popular culture intent on making the best of defeat and occupation. In the film, his songs, obsessed with escapism, become a symbol of the shallow survivalism that is Ophuls's primary target: thus, Chevalier's 'Ça Sent Si Bon La France' ('France Feels So Good') accompanies images of Pétain's official visit to Clermont-Ferrand, met by bowing clergymen and officials, and cheering crowds – some performing the fascist salute; and his words, 'Let it rain, let it snow/ I'll be up in the rainbow/ Sweeping the clouds away', complement footage of de Gaulle's triumphant homecoming parade, met by similar acclaim. Soundtrack is also employed meaningfully as a clear condemnation of a page that ranks among the least glorious in the history of the French Resistance: 'La Tondue', by Georges Brassens, accompanies American images of young French women being shaven in public following the liberation.[26] Though brief, this is a crucial episode in the film: when Brassens sings, 'I should have said a word to save her mane', his self-accusation is extended to the film-maker and to the audience.

Finally, the film-makers selectively employed archival footage to comment on the points made by the interviewees. On some occasions this is a straightforward procedure of illustration, such as when images of Vichy's anti-Jewish propaganda match Pierre Mendès-France's recollections. At other times, Ophuls employs montage more innovatively, silently to challenge the interviewee's statements. Thus, as Georges Lamirand, Vichy Minister of Youth, dismisses the National Revolution as 'just a word', Ophuls cuts to a 1942 public address where Lamirand had hailed Vichy's social policies. The same objective was reached by cross-editing testimonies of two or more interviewees with contrasting or complementary recollections. Through this cross-editing technique, Ophuls manages to render the complexity of historical events, thus dealing with the medium's inability to examine contrasting theories and explain or link events happening simultaneously.

Ophuls's manipulative techniques came under scrutiny and attracted considerable criticism. Indeed, it is arguable that the technical ability and personal style of Marcel Ophuls, his use of freeze-frame, suggestive camera angles and evocative surroundings for his interviews, do not marry particularly well with the detachment one associates with historical research. There is no trace of dishonesty, however, in the film-maker's manipulation, which instead has to be read as an attempt to use the rules of film to achieve a synthesis between investigative journalism and historiography. Nonetheless, there is no doubt that Ophuls intended to prove a particular thesis and that his film is, in the healthiest sense of the word, a revisionist work.

REDRESSING THE BALANCE: ELEMENTS OF DISCONTINUITY WITH THE PAST

The Sorrow and the Pity challenged not only the way in which history was told, but also what it said. Most of all, the film confronted 'the linearity and total unreality of historical programs [which propounded] the notion that History is something to be nailed to the wall for people to look at'.[27] This was the attitude which had brought ORTF to ask the Ophuls–Harris–de Sédouy partnership to leave, as what they 'envisioned more and more as a history of the Occupation continued to be labelled a history of the Resistance by the bureaucrats'.[28] *The Sorrow and the Pity* took history off the nail and shattered the orthodoxy of the time. For the first time, a French film tackled the extent of German influence over Vichy; the role of the Resistance, the Vichy government, the collaborators and the so-called 'average' Frenchmen; the proportions and origins of French anti-Semitism. These were aspects of that period of French history which hitherto had either been ignored, or subjected to only partial and simplistic investigation.

The film-makers' choice to focus their analysis on Clermont-Ferrand was essential for them to confront each of these elements. Inspired by the film, in 1986 John Sweets dedicated a meticulous study to Clermont-Ferrand, which he saw as an ideal location on which to test the responses of French men and women to the challenges of war, dictatorship and occupation.[29] The regional capital of Auvergne was ideal for several reasons. It was a medium-sized city in the heart of France, not too distant from Paris and less than fifty miles from Vichy, and it had itself been capital of France for forty-eight hours during the debacle of June–July 1940.[30] Clermont-Ferrand's proximity to the wartime capital of France had increased its political significance, so that it provided Ophuls, Harris and de Sédouy with sufficient material to cover many facets of the relationship between French and occupiers. Moreover, the Auvergne had been both the centre of one of the largest and most successful Resistance groups, and the birthplace of Pierre Laval.

Clermont-Ferrand had also been the stage of trials for treason of significant Third Republic politicians such as Pierre Mendès-France, who features prominently in the film,[31] and Jean Zay.[32] The former prime minister's remarkable talent for storytelling and his considerable political nous made him one of the stars of the film. Tried as a deserter by Clermont-Ferrand's military court, Mendès-France opened the proceedings by stating: 'My colonel [the judge, Colonel Perret], gentlemen, I am a Jew, I am a Freemason, but I am not a deserter. And now let the trial begin'.[33] Found guilty, he escaped from the local prison, then reached London via Switzerland and re-joined active service as a bomber pilot in the Free French air force. Skilfully related and punctuated with amusing anecdotes, his story would have featured well in a Hollywood epic, yet the importance of the role he fulfils in the film goes beyond his fascinating story or his admittedly deep understanding of French history and politics.

Pierre Mendès-France and Clermont-Ferrand thus acted as the connection between those who lived the reality of the occupation and those whose political and military decisions affected their lives. Intending to move away from the *grande histoire* favoured by de Gaulle and the post-war French establishment, Ophuls managed to strike a balance between it and micro-history, alternating interviews of lesser-known protagonists in Clermont-Ferrand's history with those of key national and international players. The latter included Anthony Eden, Major-General Spears, Jacques Duclos, Georges Bidault and General Warlimont of the Wehrmacht. Yet in contrast with documentary film-making up to that point these powerful men are not the focus of *The Sorrow and the Pity*; rather they are there to allow the viewer to insert the opinions and choices of the less famous people featured in the film into the larger context of the war.

THE GERMANS

The choice of Clermont-Ferrand was crucial because it allowed Ophuls to break with the collective self-image of the time. Being placed in the Southern zone, the Auvergne district capital was not occupied by German forces until November 1942. The absence of the enemy permits the film-makers to focus for large parts of the film on Vichy politics. This choice represented a remarkable challenge to the dominant thinking, which attributed the horrors of the war to the German forces, aided by only a handful of 'bad' Frenchmen. As Rousso has pointed out, Ophuls ignored what General de Gaulle called 'the thirty years' war', and successfully revealed internecine divisions to have affected the French more deeply than the occupation.[34] The second part of the film opens with the interview of the Clermont-born former French cycling ace, Raphaël Geminiani, who hesitantly mumbles: 'The Germans, [...] we saw them in the outskirts [...] as they arrived, but in the end we were not occupied'.[35] The director reinforces this passing statement, cutting to a black-and-white shot of a cyclist racing, and superimposing Geminiani's misquoted words in capital letters: 'The Germans, we did not see them.' In his trademark style, he then immediately cuts to Verdier, who proclaims:

> I have seen too many. I would see them during the day and, when I slept, I would see them at night. [...] I would see them everywhere. I would see nothing but helmets and nothing but Germans.[36]

With Geminiani, Ophuls examines those people who chose not to see or later preferred to forget what they saw, while Verdier epitomises those who, in the comfort of their present, liked to pretend they did, saw or knew more than they did. The director then follows both interviews with the testimony of Helmut Tausend, a captain of the Wehrmacht stationed in Clermont-Ferrand from 1942. Thus Ophuls establishes the presence of German troops in Clermont-Ferrand and assesses the reliability of his witnesses without having to confront them. Tausend, and Matheus Bleibinger, a Bavarian mason and former Wehrmacht private also stationed in Clermont-Ferrand, are the only two Germans interviewed with specific reference to Clermont-Ferrand. In a further confirmation of the film-maker's predilection for less well-known figures, they are also the most visible German contributors. The other three appear but briefly to clarify broader historical points: General Warlimont, formerly of the Wehrmacht supreme command, was interviewed about the rapid French defeat and the armistice; Dr Paul Schmidt, Hitler's interpreter between 1934 and 1944, recalled briefly Hitler's encounters with Pétain and his private thoughts on the French people; and Dr Elmar Michel, a high-ranking economic advisor attached to the German military command in occupied France, was able to comment on what the French newsreels of 1942 euphemistically termed 'Franco-German economic collaboration'.[37]

Ophuls found Elmar Michel in a French propaganda newsreel. He was filmed at the Gare du Nord in Paris, shaking the hand of the ten-thousandth man to leave for Germany as part of the *Réléve* scheme to exchange prisoners of war for skilled workers.[38] Then an immediate cut to Michel in 1969 shows him prosperous and successful, at the head of a large Stuttgart shoemaking factory. Michel seems a little uncomfortable about his role, quickly trying to establish that his appointment to Paris in 1940 was an attempt to keep the post away from a member of the Nazi Party. Asked whether he was not himself enrolled in the same party, he hesitates, then replies: 'we tried to conciliate the reasonable with the possible'.[39]

Ophuls's main concern is not 'the alibis of senile Nazis, the arguments of Generals embittered by defeat, the lies of old spent politicians',[40] but Michel's recollections about French attitudes towards the occupiers. When asked, Michel recalls that in September 1940 he received a petition to resume horse racing in Paris. The request was backed by Vichy's Transport Minister, and Michel agreed to it. Without delay, Ophuls's editing shows us 1942 footage of the Longchamps racecourse crammed with Parisians and German officers alike. Similarly, 1940 footage of Strauss being played at the Paris Opera House is followed by Michel's comment that 'the theatres too resumed their activities thanks to us'.[41] What Michel is attempting to do is to claim credit for making life easier for the French people, yet what he achieves, through Ophuls's filter, is to paint a picture of occupied Paris where life continued more or less as normal, and where Parisian people, particularly the elites who sported their fine outfits at the theatre or the races, were determined and able to make the most out of an undoubtedly regrettable situation. Ophuls keenly pursues this line of questioning:

Ophuls: 'Surely you do not ignore that since the war the

habits of thought in France are such that it is often attempted to deny that these contacts existed?'

Dr. Michel: 'Yes ... but they existed.' [42]

Michel's impression of Paris matches Tausend's and Bleibinger's recollections of Clermont-Ferrand. Their undoubtedly partisan testimonies suggest that the French population was at least not entirely hostile to the occupying forces. This is true despite the fact that Bleibinger was wounded and taken prisoner by the Maquis in October 1944, and Tausend is questioned at length about the partisan struggle – what the Germans called 'anti-terrorist activities'. Interviewed in a beer-parlour wearing the traditional Bavarian costume, Bleibinger has fond memories of Clermont-Ferrand and he recalls having a girlfriend in the town. The little French he learnt there was fresh in his memory in 1969: 'S'il vous plaît mademoiselle, voulez vous un petit peu promener avec moi?'[43] Tausend is entirely different from Bleibinger. Utterly confident and repeatedly arrogant about the past, he sports several medals earned during the war, claims Alsace to be a rightfully German region and expresses regret at losing the war. Ophuls interviews him at his daughter's wedding, giving him importance and allowing him to feel comfortable. Well fuelled by wine and cigars, he has very clear memories of partisan warfare, including details of actions, but somehow has no memory whatsoever of German reprisals, which he imagines may have been enforced by the Gestapo. To a direct enquiry about persecutions, he replies: 'No, I have seen nothing and I have heard nothing.'[44] The arrogance of this former officer borders on the caricature. Except, of course, it is absolutely real. The only time in which he seems to lose, for a moment, his distasteful self-assurance is when he is asked directly about the persecution of the Jews. First, he pretends to misunderstand, playing on the assonance of the German words *juden*, Jews, and *jugend*, young people; then, once the confusion has been cleared up, he dismisses the issue:

Ah! As far as the Jews are concerned, we could not know to what extent they had infiltrated the partisan gangs. In any case, it was not up to us, the army, to take charge of the Jews.[45]

His memories match Bleibinger's, however, in one crucial aspect. Like Bleibinger, Tausend remembers his time in Clermont-Ferrand as hardly unpleasant. Both make a temporal distinction, Tausend placing the change in popular attitude towards the Germans around the beginning of 1943 and, in particular, the Allied bombing of the Michelin plant.[46] Before that, however, Tausend narrates the occupation of Clermont-Ferrand almost as a holiday: 'The people of Clermont liked us. The link was good and for them French and Germans were the same.'[47] In this respect, as in his memory of an abundance of food, his recollections may well differ from that of many Frenchmen, yet the message that the inhabitants of the French town were not hostile comes across clearly. As he had done with Bleibinger, Ophuls presses the point home:

> Ophuls: 'Did you have the impression that the people who had dealings with you, let us say the shop-owners, the hoteliers, that because of those dealings all those people were a little corrupted in the eyes of the other Frenchmen?'
>
> Tausend: 'Oh no! In any case not in 1942!'

The direct testimony of the two German soldiers, perhaps gently steered but not substantially manipulated by the interviewer, contradicts several common assumptions. First, the film dispels the idea that, had it not been for the German occupation, there would not have been any inkling of collaboration within the Vichy regime. Second, *The Sorrow and the Pity* quashes the belief that German soldiers were the sort of inhuman monsters we have grown accustomed to through countless war films: Bleibinger comes across as a simple but not unpleasant man; even Tausend, despite his despicable comments, posture and beliefs, displays the very human prerogatives of arrogance and ignorance. Third, Ophuls's work challenges the idea that the Resistance was a spontaneous expression of dissent by which the French people, as a whole, reacted to the occupation.

THE RESISTANCE

What soon becomes evident is that in the dynamics of *The Sorrow and the Pity*, the testimony of German eyewitnesses serves almost exclusively the purpose of qualifying French attitudes towards the occupation and the political and ideological conflicts of the time. The picture that emerges from this investigation is mixed, and it would probably not have been considered as demystifying a work, had the myth not been so widely and deeply rooted into

French culture in the first place. Looking at it closely, *The Sorrow and the Pity* treats the French Resistance with much of the respect and admiration to which it had been accustomed, and indeed deserved. Despite some of the reactions to the film, the target of Ophuls's revisionism is not the Resistance, but the orthodoxy that had been built around it. The Resistance not only appears in the documentary, but it does so in a prominent role. Ophuls's revisionism does not concern the concept of Resistance, but its political nature, formation, size and role. Ophuls does not deny the existence of the Resistance or downplay its significance, rather he seeks to wrest the Resistance from the hands of political ownership, nationalist or communist.

The communists are chiefly represented by their charismatic wartime and post-war leader, Jacques Duclos. He was for two decades the number two of Maurice Thorez, secretary general of the PCF. As Thorez sought refuge in Moscow in 1939, following the government's persecution of the communists, Jacques Duclos became the acting leader of the clandestine party. In this role, he negotiated 'the dark years', embodying the embarrassing contradiction of all communists: first, he confirmed the party's neutrality in line with the 1939 Nazi–Soviet pact, writing: 'we must bear no hatred for the German troops. We are against de Gaulle and the capitalist clan whose interest are tied to Vichy';[48] then – after the Nazi invasion of the USSR – he led the party into active resistance.

Duclos, a former confectionary worker and veteran of Verdun who, in 1969, ran for the presidency of the Republic and achieved 21 per cent of the votes, speaks with pride of the courage shown by the communists. An excellent raconteur, with the looks, accent and charm of a working-class hero, he narrates with flair several anecdotes of communist martyrs. At the same time, he attributes little recognition to non-communist partisan formations, suggesting rather that they often were *salonards*, armchair *résistants*, playing on the assonance with *salopards*. In Duclos's mind, one of these may well have been Colonel du Jonchay, a conservative former army *résistant* with whom Ophuls cross-edits Duclos's testimony. As a Catholic and a Frenchman, Du Jonchay explains, he could not cooperate with godless internationalists. Ophuls makes no comment, perhaps leaving the viewer to ponder on the actual cohesiveness of the Resistance camp.

The little space accorded to the communist Resistance is matched by that left to General de Gaulle. De Gaulle appears in person twice, in wartime footage, and several times he is evoked in conversation with other witnesses, with varying meaningfulness. The first appearance of de Gaulle, therefore, has the immediate effect of diminishing the proportions of his involvement and influence: in discussing the armistice, the film-makers dwell on the fact that de Gaulle's famous radio appeal on 18 June 1940 went mostly unheard or unnoticed.[49] This is one of only two mentions of de Gaulle in the entire first half and the only one with any political significance. In other words, the defeat, the establishment of the Vichy government and early responses to it – including British ones – unfold without the leader of the Free French being accorded more than a brief, and dismissive, mention.

In the second half of the film, too, references to de Gaulle are both infrequent and unflattering. Even the lengthy discussion of the Resistance, which occupies the middle part of the second half, manages to avoid an in-depth discussion of the general's role. Asked about the PCF's disregard of London's wartime orders to suspend military actions, Jacques Duclos replies mischievously: 'In fact, we took advantage of a slogan of de Gaulle's, to turn it against him somewhat: "The national insurrection is inseparable from the liberation." '[50] Through the extensive use of cross-editing, Duclos's statement eases in further comments about the general in what is the closest the film ever gets to a proper discussion of his character. A cut takes the viewer to an elegant Parisian flat where André Harris is interviewing Emmanuel d'Astier de la Vigerie, a leader of the Libération–Sud Resistance organisation, founder of the clandestine left-wing periodical *Libération* and Internal Affairs Minister in the first post-war government:[51]

> Harris: 'Is it your impression that today's France has been marked, affected somewhat by what it was during the war, in fact between 1939 and '44?'
>
> D'Astier: 'Certainly, certainly, because de Gaulle started his life, his political life, by means of an abuse of confidence. [...] I think that if, in 1940, one had held a referendum much like the one we have just had [...],[52] 90% of the French people would have voted for Pétain and for a wise German occupation.'[53]

His words introduce BBC footage showing a call to arms by General de Gaulle, then D'Astier continues by relating his first meeting with him:

> D'Astier: 'I found myself in front of a man who astonished me because he was already the King of France.'
>
> Harris: 'A King of France unknown by his own subjects.'
>
> D'Astier: '[His subjects] did not exist! [They] did not exist.'[54]

D'Astier's personal recollections are followed by those of two more people acquainted with de Gaulle. First, Anthony Eden expresses the peculiar nature of de Gaulle's Free France which, unlike the Polish, Norwegian or Belgian governments in exile, was not a democratically elected Cabinet. Eden himself, otherwise explicitly and consistently unwilling to pass judgment, had to concede that this was the strongest possible indictment of Pétain's government.[55] Then, Mendès-France relates his own first meeting with the general, which he recalls as both moving and pleasant:

> Mendès-France: 'It is true that de Gaulle, exactly because he did not have means, because his army was insignificant, because the territories loyal to him were of secondary importance [...], had no other possibility but to remain inflexible about the respect of the rights of which he had become guarantor.'
>
> Ophuls: 'His pride became a weapon?'
>
> Mendès-France: 'Of course, his pride, his rigidity, in fact his character, often unbearable ... All that did not help things. [...] Having said that, I do not want there to be any misunderstanding. Politically, he was right.'[56]

These two testimonies, punctuated by relevant footage from British newsreel, effectively conclude all references to de Gaulle in the film, until the closing credits, which run footage of his victory parade on the Champs Elysées. In total, Charles de Gaulle occupies fewer than four pages of the script.

This descriptive textual analysis allows us to draw a few conclusions concerning the treatment of de Gaulle. First, the film does not ignore de Gaulle completely. The general plays a part in the film despite – perhaps even because of – the fact that the two interviewers only ever mention his name once. A close analysis of his historical role, however, is unquestionably absent. His character is recalled but anecdotally, and while these recollections can be close to the mark, they hardly provide a comprehensive critical consideration of his role. If one adds to this the fact that the film almost completely overlooks the Gaullist Resistance forces, such neglect becomes even more obvious. There can be little doubt that the underestimation of Gaullist and communist Resistance was a deliberate and integral part of Ophuls's thesis. As Rousso suggests, 'the Resistance lost its status as a purely patriotic movement and came to be seen instead as a form of commitment'.[57] Ophuls, however, did not achieve this through the relative neglect of individual political sides, but through the utter disregard of all those institutions which, by institutionalising and nationalising the Resistance, gave it the structure of a clandestine state. The Comité Français de Libération Nationale (CFLN) – later Gouvernement Provisoire de la République Française (GPRF) – based in Algiers and the Conseil National de la Résistance (CNR) hardly deserve a mention. Indeed, through the testimony of Colonel du Jonchay, the CNR is referred to only so as to assert its impotence.

Finally, the question remains as to why the film-makers chose this path. One plausible but partial explanation is that *The Sorrow and the Pity* is a film about occupied France. In the life of France under the occupation, de Gaulle played little part, particularly until 1942/3, perhaps with the exception of the annexed or permanently occupied regions of northern France, such as Normandy and the Pas de Calais where a residual Anglophilia matched deep resentment at the German presence.[58] It seems no coincidence, in fact, that the witnesses who talk about de Gaulle are those who spent at least part of the war in London, or who were involved at the very highest level in the Resistance. In particular, de Gaulle held little significance in the France Ophuls describes: the one hypothesised in d'Astier's imaginary referendum. But perhaps the most plausible explanation is that Ophuls, like many of his generation, was tired of de Gaulle's hegemony in the 1960s. The context of 1968 and the formidable opposition to the general undoubtedly played a part in Ophuls's choice to snub de Gaulle. Here, reasons of structural cohesiveness and political intent become blurred, and there is no doubt that the desire to address the myth of the forty million *résistants* affected the film-makers' decision in this matter. If the end result may well have gone too far in the opposite direction, then we may judge the general not to be absent from *The Sorrow and the Pity* but, on the contrary, to have weighed heavily on its conception, its reception, even its content.

THE COLLABORATION: 'DONNE-MOI TA MONTRE, JE TE DIRAI L'HEURE'[59]

'I knew what an armistice was, but I had not grasped quite what a Marshal was.'[60] Roger Tounze, a Clermont-Ferrand journalist working for *La Montagne*, was among those who did not understand the armistice and were undoubtedly saddened by the defeat, but who, in 1940, still regarded Pétain as the hero of Verdun and, in his own words, 'the last Marshal we had left'. After the Montoire summit between Pétain and Hitler of 24 October 1940, however, Roger Tounze began to understand the nature of collaboration, which he summarised in the phrase: 'Give me your watch, I'll give you the time.' *The Sorrow and the Pity* seems to identify in the Montoire meeting the beginning of a time of choice for the French people. However, Ophuls also puts across how, even long after Montoire, it was possible not to make a choice between collaboration and Resistance. Tounze, like the Grave brothers, Emile Coulaudon and several other characters of the film, was among those who chose to resist, but one of the novelties of Ophuls's documentary was a close look at those who chose the other side.

Ophuls employed footage of French fascists such as Doriot ranting against Great Britain and Chateaubriand's racist lecture on the New Order. These were well-known figures at the extreme fringes of France's wartime politics. Ophuls, however, also introduced a character virtually unknown to the French public, with the interview of Christian de la Mazière. A young volunteer in the Charlemagne Division of the Waffen SS, de la Mazière speaks candidly about his youthful fascist ardour. Moreover, he recalls the roots of that ideology in a certain type of conservative French bourgeoisie, Catholic and nationalistic. He narrates a childhood steeped in militarism and xenophobia, against the backdrop of the fierce social struggles of the 1930s. In 1971 de la Mazière represented a skeleton in the wardrobe of French collective memory: he was a collaborator and a collaborationist, a self-proclaimed fascist, yet he was neither a brute nor a sadist; his position had been generated from neither cowardice nor greed, and he sported a well-spoken and charming, if somewhat affected, persona.

'With de la Mazière suddenly a reassuring image collapses', writes Rousso.[61] The choice between Resistance and collaboration could no longer be dismissed as a struggle between morality and immorality, but had to be comprehended as a much more complex clash between conflicting sets of values and opposite visions of social and political structure. Moreover, this ideological conflict was revealed to be internal to French society, rather than simply one with a foreign, barbaric invader. However, both as an active collaborator and as someone who wore the German uniform, de la Mazière belonged to a tiny minority. Even though Ophuls did not specify this fact – leaving himself exposed to right-wing critics wishing to exploit the film's revisionism for their own apologetic purposes – it is arguable that de la Maziére, as a French SS, is still only partially responsible for the collapse of the 'reassuring image' to which Rousso refers.

Instead, it is with its representation of less committed collaborators and indifferent masses that *The Sorrow and the Pity* challenged the very meaning of collaboration, truly rocking French collective memory. Indeed, Ophuls treats indifference and apathy with more contempt than he does outright collaborationism. In *The Sorrow and the Pity*, indifference is collaboration, and the indifferent are charged with allowing Vichy to seize and maintain power, permitting the emergence of all types of collaboration. In this respect, characters such as Marcel Verdier, Marius Klein, or the schoolteachers Danton and Dionnet, come across bearing more responsibility for the rise of Vichy than de la Mazière, who fought alongside the Germans.

They provide a picture of wartime France that does indeed induce sorrow, but little pity, where popular discontent was not moral but merely material. Danton and Dionnet oscillate between recalling episodes of resistance in their school and hiding their own inertia behind a short memory. Marius Klein had posted an announcement in Pierre Laval's Clermont-Ferrand-based *Le Moniteur* to claim his Aryan race:[62]

> 'I have the honour to inform my loyal clientele that, contrary to [what has been suggested by] anonymous information, I come from an old French family of the Northern

> Department. I was born in Dunkerque in 1893 and I have fought in the war of 1914–1918, as have my three brothers.'[63]

When confronted aggressively and by surprise, he mumbles apologetically: his wartime actions tell us as much about his clientele as they do of himself.

Verdier himself plays a far greater role in the film. He recalls the widespread shortages and rationing, and consequently the reopening of the hunting season in the autumn of 1942 as a great event. He says, revealingly, that to him losing the war was like losing a rugby match. He almost brags about having known every detail of the persecution and planned murder of the Jews without realising that his supposed acumen, when matched by his inaction, is anything but flattering. Verdier's own words were adopted as the film's title, and it would be no exaggeration to describe him as the central character of a work which seems fascinated with those who do not fall into a clear political category: *résistants*, Gaullists, communists, fascists, collaborators. Ophuls mistrusts these categorisations, perhaps considering them the building blocks of collective myths.

The link between these people and de la Mazière is provided by former Vichy officials and regime apologists, who present a mixture of the historical justifications built around Pétain's government. In *The Sorrow and the Pity*, these are represented by Georges Lamirand,[64] whom we have already encountered, and Count René de Chambrun, Pierre Laval's son-in-law, who has dedicated a life to rehabilitating his father-in-law.[65] Lamirand defends Pétain's actions with the well-worn excuse that he spared France the fate of Poland, while blaming the excesses of the regime either on bad counsellors or on German coercion. In particular, he claims the existence of a conflict between the Marshal and Laval, consisting of both personal and ideological differences. The former Vichy Minister of Youth has, for Pétain, the lasting devotion of a man touched by a celebrity.[66]

The same complex seems to afflict the entire population of the village of Chateldon, Laval's birthplace in the Auvergne, not far from Clermont-Ferrand. André Harris is taken on a grand tour of the village by de Chambrun, who questions several locals about the late Vichy prime minister. What we see is an inventory of deferential workers of a local factory expressing undying gratitude to Laval. 'We were privileged',[67] says one former POW with misplaced pride. To de Chambrun these testimonies seem enough to rehabilitate Laval's political choices:

> I am convinced that today, in their vast majority, the French people know that Pierre Laval did everything to defend them; [...] you have walked around the village today, you have interviewed people who saw Pierre Laval at work, and not one of them would have subscribed to any accusation which would bring him discredit.[68]

Not unlike Lamirand, de Chambrun suggests that Pétain was surrounded by right-wing advisors but, unlike Lamirand, he maintains that Laval 'was a man whom today we would call a centrist'. This passage of the film once again implicitly challenges the concept and extent of collaboration. It also sheds macabre light on post-war France's process of sanitisation of its wartime memories. In accordance with the interviewing style of the film, Harris refrains from confronting de Chambrun, or questioning either his ideas or his rather inadequate sample group of French public opinion. Ophuls is less charitable when de Chambrun attempts to use the small percentage of French Jews who perished in the Shoah to prove further Laval's enlightened statesmanship. De Chambrun's attempted distinction between French and foreign Jews brings Ophuls to an uncustomary angry reaction: 'does a statesman [...] have the right to choose matters of that nature between two groups of people?'[69]

FRENCH ANTI-SEMITISM AND THE SHOAH

The final key aspect of *The Sorrow and the Pity*'s challenge to the post-war amnesia is the persecution of French Jews. Arguably, Ophuls's aim was never to explain the Shoah or the extermination camps, but rather to clarify the role of the Vichy government in the deportations of Jews from France. Given the film's premise, it is interesting that anti-Semitism is given remarkable space despite the fact that the persecution of Clermont-Ferrand's Jews is not treated in any detail. This suggests that Ophuls, himself a Jewish wartime exile, also meant to raise consciousness of the Shoah in France. Indeed, his work was among the catalysts of a widespread resurfacing of Jewish consciousness in the 1970s.

Two sections in particular deal with this topic, one in each half of the film. The first one is instigated by the unfolding of

Mendès-France's trial, at which his race seems to have played an unspoken but important role. The second one is a slight digression from the main thread of the documentary, inspired by the aforementioned exchange between de Chambrun and Ophuls. This digression focuses on the *rafle du Vél' d'Hiv*, the rounding up of Parisian Jews. This relies almost entirely on a lengthy conversation with the French biologist Dr Claude Lévy, a survivor of Dachau and author of a book on *Vél' d'Hiv*.[70]

Pierre Mendès-France escaped Clermont-Ferrand's prison in June 1941 and reached London in March 1942, via Switzerland. The months in between he spent hiding in Clermont-Ferrand in self-imposed isolation, while around him the Vichy propaganda machine publicised and extolled the regime's racial laws. Ophuls utilises footage of the time to attempt to reconstruct the anti-Semitic atmosphere. French newsreels show a plaque dedicated to Edouard Drumont, 'immortal author of *La France Juive*', and an exhibition teaching 'how to distinguish a Jew from a Frenchman'. Spending much of his time hiding in cinemas, the former French premier had a privileged view of the worst type of propaganda. He recalls how the names of Jewish actors had been erased from the credits of pre-war French films, while German propaganda films were presented as entirely French productions, dubbed by French actors whose names replaced those of the original German ones in the credits. Ophuls reinforces this by inserting a short extract from the Nazi historical film *Jud Süß* (Veit Harlan, *Jew Suss*, 1940), including the French opening credits. This was propaganda dressed up as melodrama, and both Mendès-France and cinema owner Pierre Le Calvez remember how it could be quite successful, though its effectiveness in France should not be overstressed.

In the same section of the film are several other testimonies of anti-Semitic incidents, and one of solidarity towards Jews. The latter is narrated by Verdier, who boasts the employment of two young Jewish girls from Alsace. Ophuls could have given further echo to this episode by accompanying it with a discussion of Clermont-Ferrand's solidarity with the Strasbourg Polytechnic, which included many Jewish members. A long sequence about this had been shot by Ophuls, but was omitted in post-production. This wholesale omission is regrettable, and it is one of few instances where Ophuls sacrifices nuance and accuracy for the pursuit of his argument. In other words, in order finally to tell the truth about French anti-Semitism, Ophuls is prepared to risk obscuring acts of solidarity, even though by doing so his image of France may well be as partial as the one he wished to dispel.

Notwithstanding this, there is no dampening the images and recollections of spontaneous French anti-Semitism presented by *The Sorrow and the Pity*. In this regard, the first section is more remarkable, because it shows hostility towards Jews in the Unoccupied Zone, and therefore reveals feelings independent of German interference. However, the second section too, despite being devoted to events in the Occupied Zone, says much about French attitudes. Dr Lévy remembers clearly French participation in the persecution: from anti-Semitic insults by fellow students at his Parisian school to being arrested by French police. The story of his ordeal is a French story. Lévy points out how French police carried out the arrests of 12,884 mostly foreign Parisian Jews on 16 and 17 July 1942, who were held in Paris's indoor racing track before being shipped en masse to Auschwitz via Drancy. In an excess of zeal, the French police also seized 4,051 children whom the SS had not yet planned to liquidate. In obsequious observance of their original plans, the German authorities moved the adults to Drancy while awaiting instructions with regards to the children. A telegram sent by Danneker, the representative of SS Security Service – the Sicherheitsdienst – reports Laval's remonstration that 'the children must be deported too'.[71] As further evidence, Lévy quotes a Protestant minister, Pastor Boegner, who pleaded with Laval to explore the possibility of evacuating the children abroad, only to be told: 'It does not matter, [...] I am doing some prophylaxis.'[72]

Lévy does not mince words: he clearly states that France collaborated in carrying out the Final Solution, and his list of specific charges is a terrible indictment on the Vichy government, French police and French civilians. Examining this now, in full awareness of the home-grown anti-Semitism which afflicted all European countries to different extents, Ophuls's denunciation seems underwhelming. Yet, in 1971, its novelty was striking: much of what the film says must have come as a revelation to the younger generations and as a reminder to the older one. The reaction to this revelation was bound to be mixed, and indeed *The Sorrow and the Pity* caused rejoicing and outrage, as well as introspection. The notoriety of the film, as in the case of *Night and Fog*, was undoubtedly helped by the decision of the public television service, ORTF, not to broadcast it. But, in contrast with 1956, this was an all-French affair.[73] The film's content stirred and divided all political factions, gaining both enemies and admirers and indelibly changing France's memory.

THE RECEPTION OF *THE SORROW AND THE PITY*: 'THE PITILESS MIRROR', 1971

By 1971, two years after the completion of the film, ORTF had failed to purchase the television rights of *The Sorrow and the Pity*. On 15 April 1971, the film-makers released the film at the Studio Saint Séverin, a small art cinema in Rue Xavier-Privas in Paris's Quartier Latin. Not far from the Sorbonne, the theatre was perfectly placed to attract the generation of May '68, still in search of answers regarding their past and their present. By no means limited to young students, the screenings were an immediate public success, drawing crowds from all generations and classes. Many reviewers at the time noted the long queues outside the cinema. Although thirteen days later the much larger Paramount-Elysées cinema also followed suit, the Studio Saint-Séverin became closely associated with *The Sorrow and the Pity*, which it continued to show twice a day for eighty-seven weeks. At the end of this impressive run, 232,000 people had seen the film in that cinema alone, averaging 190 people a showing in a cinema that could seat just 200. Overall, 600,000 people had seen it.[74] The controversy that surrounded the film undoubtedly helped its box office success. Nonetheless, controversy alone is not a sufficient explanation. The enthusiasm with which audiences queued up for the film suggests a true yearning for debate of the issues it raised. Moreover, the bulk of reviews of *The Sorrow and the Pity* appeared after the film's release in the more mainstream theatre on the Champs Elysées, so for once it would seem that public demand inspired press coverage rather than vice versa. This is also suggested by the fact that the showings and the crowds persisted long after the summer of 1971, when the worst of the controversy had been played out.

Unlike in the case of most films with political implications, the reception of *The Sorrow and the Pity* lacked any political consistency: the film was hailed and condemned in the strongest terms, but for completely different reasons, by both the left and the right. Right-wing commentators either attacked the film for being anti-Vichyite or praised it for demystifying the resistancialist myth; left-wing critics either hailed it as a celebration of the Resistance or shunned it for its questioning the accepted version of the facts. Most people lamented omissions or inaccuracies, but many struggled to understand or accept the film's complexity, opting instead to ignore part of its argument. A review by Claude Mauriac for the conservative *Le Figaro* of 23 April 1971 pointed out the absence of de Gaulle from the film in rather a theatrical way: 'The heart is missing. Ours suffers.'[75] Yet only three days later in the same newspaper, film critic Pierre Mazars raved about how Ophuls would revolutionise not just film-making but also historical research.

On 29 April, *Le Monde* published short comments by viewers outside the cinema, a sort of exit poll with just as little statistical reliability. Out of seven people interviewed, between 24 and 65 years of age, only one was negative. What was striking was the recurring statement, particularly by the younger interviewees, of how shocking, original and informative they had found the film. A 25-year-old office worker said: 'The occupation? I did not realise what it was. In any case, I did not imagine it to be like that. It is sad!' Another young girl declared: 'I had been told about that period, but deep down I did not know that much. [...] Watching this film I tell myself that really there is nothing to boast about.'[76] All the young people consulted seemed to agree that there was insufficient debate, and therefore insufficient knowledge of the period. Older interviewees presented a different approach, because they could compare what they saw on the film with their own memories of the occupation. A chemist, 58 years of age, left the screening after just forty-five of the film's 251 minutes: 'I cannot stand Mendès-France, and the occupation had nothing to do with his little trial', he stated, confirming the politically-charged atmosphere surrounding Ophuls's work. A 65-year-old accountant said that he was outraged by ORTF's censorship of the film, dubbing it 'a cowardice as shameful as that of many Frenchmen during the war'. A 34-year-old researcher, for example, remembered her father being a supporter of Pétain, before adding: 'I notice that he was [a Pétainist] no more than all French people.' This was just the sort of generalisation that some critics accused the film of encouraging.

The other charge concerned the ammunition many felt the

film gave to right-wing revisionists, keen to exploit the weakening of the resistancialist myth for their own purposes. The response of extreme right-wing paper *Rivarol* justified this apprehension: it voiced its hope that 'the viewers [...] will understand that the 'collaboration' – so often misrepresented – was the least of the occupation's ills'.[77] The article's author, Jean Langlois, praised the film's representation of German soldiers and despicably took advantage of a remark by Louis Grave – who had remembered there being a cinema in Buchenwald – to minimise the hardships suffered by deportees. This type of critique, however, was very much the exception. The majority of reviews by left-wing and centrist papers gave *The Sorrow and the Pity* credit for its powerful images, its work of demythologisation, the honesty of its testimonies. Albert Cervoni, in *France-Nouvelle*, praised 'the degree of organisation and thoughtfulness' of the film; Jean-Louis Bory writing in *Le Nouvel Observateur* commended its human dimension; Michel Capdenac on the left-wing *Les Lettres Françaises* wrote: '[*The Sorrow and the Pity* is] a coherent and rigorous overall study which allows the new generations to decipher and understand the phenomena of collaboration and resistance'; finally Henri Chapier of the Socialist *Combat* saw himself, his contemporaries and their past in the film:

> This pitiless mirror held out at each one of us shows us a fierce reflection, which many will dislike but which has the gift of smashing lies to pieces. It was high time that the gaze at our past ceased to be dependent on electoral mythologies or interests of the time.[78]

Many reviewers pointed out gaps in the film's treatment of certain issues. Albert Cervoni's article in *France-Nouvelle* lamented the film's failure to discuss the behaviour of the Catholic hierarchy.[79] Many noticed how little attention was paid to de Gaulle and some, in particular communist reviewers, rejoiced at the snubbing of the general, despite the fact that the PCF had been equally overlooked. Writing in *L'Humanité*, André Gisselbrecht pointed out this shortcoming, but still hailed the film as 'a political act not depressing but purifying'.[80]

Few reviewers of *The Sorrow and the Pity* were altogether negative, showing how the myth had already started to crack. Those critics who disliked the film, however, did so intensely. *Le Monde* hosted two such critiques. On the left, former *résistant* Germaine

Tillion lamented that Ophuls had emphasised 'a scandalous quarter truth' at the expense of 'the timeworn version that tells the other three quarters'.[81] The result, she suggested, was the 'profile of a hideous country'. Like other former resistance fighters, Tillion not unjustifiably feared that a general disillusionment with wartime France would spell a specific disillusionment with the Resistance. On the right, Alfred Fabre-Luce, the right-wing intellectual and author who had published extensively under Vichy and in praise of Pétain, accused the film of challenging the conformism of the time only to fall into the opposite excess, presenting 'an ignoble France'.[82] In a piece entitled 'Morale et Cinéma', Fabre-Luce accused Ophuls's work of telling 'lies by means of true images, [employing] tricks, omissions and deliberate falsifications'.[83] Insisting on a political and historical distinction between Pétainists and collaborators, he charged Ophuls with exonerating Germany, teaching children 'to despise their parents', and even reawakening a latent anti-Semitism. Some of this may well have been on display when Fabre-Luce resented Jews such as Ophuls 'condemning the man [Pétain] to whom they owe their life'.[84]

Le Monde, which had rapidly become one of the centre stages of the debate, also hosted a reply by historian Pozzo di Borgo, who acknowledged that Ophuls's choices of what to exclude or include in the film were arbitrary, but asked whether the picture of Vichy that he painted was not true. Focusing in particular on what he called 'macabre accounting' – the debate over the percentage of French Jews killed – he systematically challenged every point raised by Fabre-Luce.[85] Thus the debate extended beyond film critics to include historians, politicians, intellectuals, former *résistants* and former Vichy supporters. Soon, they ceased to argue over a film, and confronted issues of historical truth and how this truth should be remembered. The fact that the film gave origin to this debate was a sign of the sensitivity of the issues it raised. This was perhaps Ophuls's greatest achievement.

The Sorrow and the Pity did not suddenly reveal to French public opinion the existence of a 'resistancialist' myth, but uncovered its fragility by forcing public opinion to confront it. Most commentators, in fact, acknowledged the mythology, though some were unwilling to see it dismissed. Interviewed by the Senate's Committee for Cultural Affairs, Jean-Jacques de

Bressons, general director of the French state television channel, denied ever having been offered the broadcasting rights for *The Sorrow and the Pity*. In a way he was not lying, since between 1970 and 1971 he repeatedly refused to meet the film-makers, or even watch the film;[86] it was not censorship, as ORTF had neither commissioned the film nor been forbidden to show it. Rather, it was a sort of boycott characterised by Ophuls as 'censorship by inertia'.[87] Perhaps because, as de Bressons put it to the committee, 'the film destroys myths the people of France still need'.[88]

THE RE-RELEASE OF 1979

De Bressons' attitude seems typical of institutional responses to *The Sorrow and the Pity* by the successive governments of Pompidou and Giscard d'Estaing: the institutions seemed absent. In 1956, during the controversy around the censorship of *Night and Fog,* ministers had repeatedly intervened to explain the situation and reassure those worried about state censorship and German meddling; nothing of the sort happened for *The Sorrow and the Pity*, which involved the government of France more than Resnais's documentary had done. In 1972, Arthur Conte replaced de Bressons as head of ORTF and announced that the film would be aired,[89] but it still was not purchased. Eventually the film would be shown on the state network FR3 over two nights, on 28 and 29 October 1981, ten-and-a-half years after its release.

By then, the myth had long been buried. In 1972 Robert Paxton's *Vichy France: Old Guard and New Order* had been published in the USA. The following year, its translation in France caused a heated controversy of its own. As Rousso has successfully argued, the mid-1970s were a time of almost obsessive research into the Vichy regime and the phenomenon of collaboration, with many important works being published between 1974 and 1977.[90] On the other hand, the late 1970s saw the emergence of a new type of denial of the Shoah. Already in 1964, the former *résistant* and Buchenwald internee Paul Rassinier had suggested that the gas chambers had not existed, since he had not seen any during his time in the concentration camp. Rassinier's *Le Véritable Procès Eichmann* (1962) and *Le Drame des Juifs Européens* (1964) became the forebears of the 1970s *négationisme*, or Holocaust denial.[91]

Watched in 1979, or 1981, *The Sorrow and the Pity* certainly did not have the same revelatory effect as in 1971, but it should have been a valuable reminder. For this reason, too, and following the 1978 television screening of the controversial American mini-series *Holocaust*, in 1979 the issue of broadcasting *The Sorrow and the Pity* was raised once again. Ophuls's film had by then been shown in Switzerland, West Germany, Belgium, Britain and the United States, and in Italy, where a revised and abridged version of *The Sorrow and the Pity* was screened on 19 and 26 September 1972,[92] as an homage to the 'vast movement [...] which represented the genuine forces of France in the partisan struggle'.[93]

Rousso reports that the conservative Minister for Health, Simone Veil, a Jewish survivor of Auschwitz who in 1971 had been on the board of ORTF, may have used her influence to prevent a showing.[94] In reaction to this continued censorship, on 11 April 1979 *The Sorrow and the Pity* was distributed to three Parisian screens.[95] Both popular and critical reactions to it, however, were entirely different from those on its first release eight years earlier. The public deserted the film, which attracted only 30,000 viewers. The critics treated it like an old classic which had once had some punch but whose power had been diluted by familiarity. As Claire Devarrieux noted, 'at present the painful demystification that the film started, and in truth brought about, is assimilated'.[96] As a result, a film that in 1971 had been thought to prove the collective culpability of the French people, in 1979 came across as a more balanced work. By 1979, it would seem, the taste of the French public had already shifted somewhat towards the less troubling individual tales of courage or turpitude, which remain popular today. Moreover, in 1979, the new generation felt disaffected with their past, whereas their 1971 equivalent had clashed violently with it. In that, too, it is possible to see the start of a long-term trend.

THE TELEVISION BROADCAST: 1981

Whether or not the fall of the myth had indeed been 'assimilated', as suggested by Devarrieux, opinions about the film remained polarised. In August 1981, three months after Mitterrand's election, French television finally gave news that it would broadcast *The Sorrow and the Pity* on 28 October 1981. The controversy was reignited for one final time. On 27 October 1981, Fabre-Luce once again went on the attack: there was nothing cathartic in this film, which 'should have been called *The Hate and the Delight*'.[97] This time writing in *Le Figaro*, the right-wing author reiterated that Ophuls's work gave German viewers the chance to feel that, during the war, the French had been 'as guilty' as the invader. He concluded by suggesting that the ratings of the television showing would prove whether the film's 1979 flop was due to people's lack of interest in history, or the awareness that this was 'a false history'.

Three days later, in the same newspaper, Michel Mohrt recommended yet another alternative title for Ophuls's film: '*The Trap and the Mockery*'. 'We have no right to pity', he wrote, 'and as for the sorrow, it is expressed through derision and sarcasm'.[98] Accusing the film-makers of selecting interviewees who were not representative of the nation, he dismissed the documentary as a lie built on omissions and a crafty misleading of witnesses by means of loaded question and dishonest editing. Ophuls's aim, Mohrt suggested, was to show all Frenchmen as 'cowardly, or reckless, or bastards'.[99] Simone Veil, by then President of the European Parliament, also accused the film of illustrating 'a cowardly, selfish, evil France', blaming Ophuls for a 'psychologically pernicious' generalisation.[100] In Veil's view, the film, by placing all French people in the collaborationist camp, offended those who resisted, judged unfairly those who did nothing, and diminished the culpability of those who actively collaborated with the Germans.

Veil's powerful and well-argued criticism would make perfect sense if *The Sorrow and the Pity* had indeed suggested that all French people had been 'cowardly, selfish and evil'. As my analysis of the film has shown, however, its thesis is more complex than that. Perhaps its complexity was the reason many of the film's admirers also seemed to misinterpret it. For example, Claude Serraute commended Ophuls for showing how the communists were the only ones to respond to de Gaulle's 18 June appeal. In a politically charged review, Serraute quoted Dennis Rake's statements about the 'magnificent French working classes', to conclude: 'do not watch this documentary with the eyes of the past but with those of the future'.[101] At the same time, a review by Jean-Pierre Rouger shied away from a critique of the film to concentrate on the characters of Roger Tounze and Louis Grave, two of the unsung heroes described by *The Sorrow and the Pity*:

Rouger's piece effectively suggested the film focused almost exclusively on the Resistance.

CONCLUSION

What is most remarkable about the reception of *The Sorrow and the Pity*'s television showing is the contrast with that of its first release ten years earlier. The difference is not in the controversy it stirred but in the approach of French commentators. 1971 – when the myth was still in place – should have seen a marked opposition between two distinctive, ideologically-motivated interpretations of French history. Instead, it is in 1981, at the end of a decade of debate, that one finds the least introspective and most entrenched reviews. The fact that, in 1981, not a single reviewer was able dispassionately to discuss the film's flaws and its considerable merits is baffling. This failure becomes even more surprising if one considers that, compared to their 1971 counterparts, these critics had advantages such as hindsight, emotional distance from the original release and a more developed historiographical debate around the facts. The reviewers' main critiques were that the film had generalised and simplified, according to some deliberately and maliciously, the history of those years. In fact, *The Sorrow and the Pity* never claimed nor attempted to be a definitive account of French attitudes during the war. It certainly was not simplistic, as it showed the French people neither as all *résistants* nor all collaborators, but as deeply divided.

All in all, however, the 1981 reviews seem to disregard the film's powerful message well beyond the loss of urgency and shock value which one would associate with the natural ageing of its material. Why? If we look closer, we discover that many supporters and detractors of *The Sorrow and the Pity* were effectively upholding the same uplifting image of the past: the former, did so by attacking what they saw as a revisionist work; the latter, by closing their eyes to the film's revisionism. If, alongside this fact, we consider also the lukewarm reception of the film during the 1979 spell in cinemas, it is possible to suggest that, although by 1981 French public opinion could acknowledge the darker aspects of the *Guerre Franco-Française*, it still consciously chose not to draw attention to them.

There is also an element of political allegiance to the later reception of *The Sorrow and the Pity*, which was less evident around its original release. In 1971, in fact, the film seemed to attract both praise and criticism from both left and right, while ten years later the opinions seemed more polarised. Although some criticism remained on the left, conservative public opinion was now merciless, as shown by *Le Figaro*'s publication of two extremely negative reviews accusing Ophuls of bringing the nation into disrepute. In an interview published in *Le Monde* on 18 August 1981, Ophuls complained of a 'deliberate misunderstanding regarding the film's political impact. It is not anti-Gaullist but inasmuch as it questions the myth of "French grandeur" – just as [it questions] the communist myth of "the people on the march".'[102] Ophuls was right, yet the political importance of his film should not have been hard to envisage. The reason it caused more criticism from the Gaullist camp than the communist one was that to argue against de Gaulle's mythology of the war was to dismantle his persona, which had repercussions for his post-war legacy as well. By contrast, Ophuls's argument against the communist wartime mythology was not a personal attack against Duclos or Thorez or Marchais or any other individual, and had a less marked effect on what the PCF had stood for in the post-war era. Moreover, the film did not, at any point, suggest that communist militants did not take part in the Resistance. In comparison, Ophuls's criticism of de Gaulle's role was much more serious: the general's influence was shown as minor, neither active on the ground nor institutional, almost ceremonial.

In this sense, the timing of *The Sorrow and the Pity* was essential: it came at a crucial moment just after the death of de Gaulle but before anyone else had openly challenged the myth of a *résistant* France associated with him. The younger generation was particularly eager to know more about the occupation: in challenging the agreed history of that period they rejected both their parents and the post-war political establishment, two crucial elements of the repressive authority they had attacked in 1968. As Rousso has pointed out, a resulting generational difference appears, in the reception of *The Sorrow and the Pity*, between those who had lived the experience of the war and those who had not.[103] In general, those who had experienced the occupation disliked the film, while those who had been born after the war appreciated its work of demythologisation. The young of the 1960s, having grown up in the relative wealth of the *trentes glorieuses*, were less affected in their reaction to the film by painful memories of the war and the occupation. But this dichotomy was also caused by the content of the film: in fact, as well as tackling historical issues – such as the extent of collaboration or the nature of French anti-Semitism – the film also raised questions about memory and the uses of history: how should memory be passed on? How should history be taught? What version of history should be taught? These were all issues with which the youth of 1971 could identify.[104]

Films rarely affect collective memory; sometimes they anticipate a trend in popular understanding of history; often, they are excellent expressions of such a trend already in action. *The Sorrow and the Pity* did not single-handedly explode the 'resistancialist' myth or create the appropriate atmosphere for it to be challenged, yet it did embody this challenge in a way that was groundbreaking both in content and style. It also worked as a catalyst for further debate on Vichy and the Shoah in France, and influenced much of the academic work which followed it. To analyse the Shoah in France involves an analysis of Vichy, collaboration and popular indifference. In that sense, *The Sorrow and the Pity* changed French popular perceptions of the Shoah by encouraging a shift in the popular memory of Vichy. Although *The Sorrow and the Pity* is less directly concerned with the Shoah than other films explored in this book, Ophuls's contribution was crucial, as his work recreated a link between Vichy and the Shoah which had been severed by the dynamics of memory in post-war France. In the words of Henri Chapier, Ophuls's chronicle of a French town during the occupation was a 'pitiless mirror'. Finally placed in front of the French people, this mirror changed forever France's collective memory. Yet still it remained all too easy to avert one's eyes.

NOTES

1. Claude Lévy and André Tillard, *La Grande Rafle du Vél d'Hiv* (Paris: Laffront, 1967).
2. Rachel Minc, *L'Enfer des Innocents* (Paris: Centurion, 1966).
3. Fred Sedel, *Habiter les Ténèbres* (Paris: CDJC, 1962).
4. Joseph Billig, *Le Commissariat Général aux Questions Juives*, 3 vols (Paris: CDJC, 1955–60).
5. Leon Poliakov, *Histoire de l'Antisémitisme*, 3 vols (Paris: Calmann-Lévy, 1961–67). Also by Poliakov in the 1960s, *Bréviaire de la Haine* (Paris: Calmann-Lévy, 1960) and *Auschwitz* (Paris: Archives Juillard, 1964).
6. Robert Gildea, *France Since 1945* (Oxford: Oxford University Press, 1996), p.67.
7. Serge Klarsfeld indicates the figures of deportees to Auschwitz from France to be around 47,000 foreign Jews and 23,000 French Jews. He also points out the deportation of 5,000 Jews (4,000 foreign and 1,000 French) to other camps: Serge Klarsfeld, *Le Mémorial de la Deportation des Juifs de France*, published in Paris by the author, 1978. Quoted in Gildea, *France*, p.68; the figures are also confirmed by Serge Klarsfeld, *La Shoah en France* (Paris: Fayard, 2001).
8. Charles de Gaulle quoted in Gildea, *France*, p.67.
9. Henry Rousso, *The Vichy Syndrome: History and Memory in France since 1944* (Cambridge, MA: Harvard University Press, 1991), pp.15–97.
10. The work of Henri Michel, in particular, added historiographical substance to the Gaullist vision. Among his works of the 1960s were *Histoire de la France Libre* (Paris: PUF, 1963) and *Vichy: Année '40* (Paris: Robert Laffront, 1967).
11. Richard J. Golsan, *Vichy's Afterlife: History and Counter-History in Postwar France* (Lincoln, NE: University of Nebraska Press, 2000), pp.9, 72–87.
12. Quoted in Rousso, *Vichy Syndrome*, p.252.
13. Ibid.
14. André Pierre Colombat, *The Holocaust in French Film* (Metuchen, NJ: Scarecrow Press, 1993), pp.167–211.
15. Rousso, *Vichy Syndrome*, pp.101–14.
16. Ibid., pp.111–12.
17. Stanley Hoffman, 'Introduction', in Marcel Ophuls, *The Sorrow and the Pity: A Film* (New York: Outerbridge & Lazard, 1972), pp.i–xxxix.
12. Margaret Atack, *May '68 in French Fiction and Film* (Oxford: Oxford University Press, 1999).
19. An accessible guide to *The Sorrow and the Pity* is provided by Milestone Films, who released the film on DVD: www.milestonefilms.com/pdf/SorrowPity.pdf.
20. Rousso, *Vichy Syndrome*, p.103, and Annette Insdorf, *Indelible Shadows: Film and the Holocaust*, second edition (Cambridge: Cambridge University Press, 1989), pp.237–43.
21. Ibid.
22. Rousso, *Vichy Syndrome*, p.101.
23. Marcel Ophuls, *Le Chagrin et la Pitié* (Paris: Alain Moreau, 1980).
24. The standard work on Sigmaringen was, for two decades, Henry Rousso, *Un Château en Allemagne: La France de Pe?tain en Exil, Sigmaringen 1944–1945* (Paris: Ramsay, 1980). Recently, this has been updated by Jean-Paul Cointet, *Sigmaringen: Une France en Allemagne (Septembre 1944 – Avril 1945)* (Paris: Perrin, 2003).
25. See Edward Behr, *Thank Heaven for Little Girls: The True Story of Maurice Chevalier's Life and Times* (London: Hutchinson, 1993), cited in Julian Jackson, *France: The Dark Years 1940–1944* (Oxford: Oxford University Press, 2001), pp.313 and 589.
26. The treatment of women during the purge has attracted much recent interest. The most comprehensive study to date is Fabrice Virgili, *Shorn Women: Gender and Punishment in Liberation France* (Oxford: Berg, 2002). See also Alain Brossat, *Les Tondues: Un Carnaval Moche* (Paris: Hachette, 1994).
27. André Harris quoted in Rousso, *Vichy Syndrome*, p.109.
28. Ibid., p.110. Ophuls's quote comes from *Téléciné*, 21, special issue on *The Sorrow and the Pity* (July 1971), p.31.
29. John Sweets, *Choices in Vichy France* (Oxford: Oxford University Press, 1986).
30. In fact, Clermont-Ferrand itself had been capital between 1 and 2 July 1940. Ibid., p.4.

31. A vast literature in French exists of the former prime minister. Among these are Jean-Louis Rizzo, *Mendès-France ou la Rénovation en Politique* (Paris: Presses de la Fondation Nationale des Sciences Politiques, 1993) and Jean Lacouture, *Pierre Mendès-France* (New York: Holmes & Meier, 1984).
32. Jean Zay was a precocious and successful politician of the 1930s, Radical MP at 27 and Minister of Education with Blum at 31. He was murdered by the French Milice on 20 June 1944. Zay's memoirs were published posthumously: Jean Zay, *Souvenirs et Solitude* (Paris: Juillard, 1946). See also Marcel Ruby, *Jean Zay* (Paris: Corsaire, 1994).
33. Statement reported by Mendès-France's lawyer, Mons. Rochat: Marcel Ophuls, *Le Chagrin*, p.82.
34. Rousso, *Vichy Syndrome*, p.104.
35. Ophuls, *Le Chagrin*, p.118.
36. Ibid., p.119.
37. Ibid., p.68.
38. Nicholas Atkin, *The French at War, 1934–44* (London: Pearson Education, 2001), pp.67 and 122.
39. Ophuls, *Le Chagrin*, p.69.
40. Ibid., p.18.
41. Ibid., p.71.
42. Ibid.
43. Ibid., p.116.
44. Ibid., p.162.
45. Ibid.
46. Ibid., p.120: 'At the end of 1942 things were still very calm in Clermont.'
47. Ibid., p.120.
48. *La Vie du Partí*, 9 (September 1940).
49. Ibid., p.51.
50. Ibid., p.148.
51. See Laurent Douzou, *La Désobéissance: Histoire d'un Mouvement et d'un Journal Clandestins: Libération-Sud (1940–1944)* (Paris: Odile Jacob, 1995).
52. D'Astier is referring to the constitutional referendum held on 27 April 1969, which eventually resulted in de Gaulle's departure from office.
53. Ophuls, *Le Chagrin*, p.149.
54. Ibid., p.150.
55. See Lord Eden's memoirs: Anthony Eden, *The Memoirs of the Rt Hon. Sir Anthony Eden, KG, PC*, 3 vols (London: Cassell, 2002). On the issue of the legitimacy of de Gaulle's outfit, see R.T. Thomas, *Britain and Vichy* (London: Macmillan, 1979).
56. Ophuls, *Le Chagrin*, p.151.
57. Rousso, *Vichy Syndrome*, p.106.
58. On perceptions of de Gaulle in France see his biographies: Jackson, *De Gaulle*; Lacouture, *De Gaulle*; and Shennan, *De Gaulle*. On public opinion under Vichy see Pierre Laborie, *L'Opinion Française sous Vichy* (Paris: Seuil, 1990).
59. 'To us the collaboration meant, "give me your watch and I'll give you the time".' Roger Tounze in Ophuls, *Le Chagrin*, p.64. Here Tounze borrows a phrase first used in Jean Galtier-Boissière, *Mon Journal pendant l'Occupation* (Paris: La Jeune Parque, 1944).
60. Ibid., p.45.
61. Ibid., p.105.
62. Laval and *Le Moniteur* obtained considerable financial gains by the forced relocation to the Occupied Zone of other organs formerly active in Clermont. Sweets, *Choices*, pp.10 and 150.
63. *Le Moniteur* on 19 October 1940.
64. On the educational and cultural policies of Vichy see Wilfred Douglas Halls, *The Youth of Vichy France* (Oxford: Clarendon Press, 1981) and Halls, *Politics, Society and Christianity in Vichy France* (Oxford: Berg, 1995).
65. Among his more than forty books, his vision of Vichy France is outlined in René de Chambrun, *Les 2,600,000 Otages Français de Hitler: La France Puissance Protectrice*

de ses Prisonniers (Paris: France-Empire, 1988) and de Chambrun, *René de Chambrun, Mes Combats pour Pierre Laval* (Paris: Perrin, 1993).

66. On *le Maréchal*'s personality cult see Pierre Servant, *Le Mythe Pétain: Verdun ou les Tranchées de la Mémoire* (Paris: Payot, 1992); Harry Roderick Kedward, 'Patriots and Patriotism in Vichy France', *Transactions of the Royal Historical Society*, 32 (1982) and Richard Vinen, 'Pétain's Hollow Crown', *History Today* (June 1994). Three key biographies of the French dictator are also useful in placing Pétain's personality in context: Nicholas Atkin, *Pétain* (London: Addison Wesley Longman, 1997); Marc Ferro, *Pétain* (Paris: Fayard, 1987); and Richard Griffiths, *Marshal Pétain* (London: Constable, 1970).
67. Ophuls, *Le Chagrin*, p.158.
68. Ibid., p.157.
69. Ibid., p.163.
70. Lévy and Tillard, *Vél d'Hiv*. On the Vél d'Hiv and the Shoah in France see, among others, Klarsfeld, *La Shoah*; Michael Marrus and Robert Paxton, *Vichy France and the Jews* (New York: Basic Books, 1981); and Susan Zuccotti, *The Holocaust, the French and the Jews* (New York: Basic Books, 1993).
71. The original document is held by the CDJC in Paris. For a detailed treatment of the days after the round-up, including the issue of the children, see Klarsfeld, *La Shoah*, pp.130–5.
72. Ophuls, *Le Chagrin*, p.167.
73. On censorship under de Gaulle see Alain Peyrefitte, *C'était de Gaulle*, 3 vols (Paris: Éditions de Fallois, 1994–2000). On ORTF's response to May 1968 see Comité? d'Histoire de la Télévision, Fondation Nationale des Sciences Politiques, *Mai '68 à l'ORTF* (Paris: DF/Radio-France/INA, 1987).
74. The source for these figures is Claire Devarrieux, *Le Monde*, 14 April 1974. Rousso reports a figure of 700,000 viewers, but does not refer to a specific source. It is likely that his figures relate to the whole of France, while Devarrieux's statistics may well be limited to Paris.
75. Quoted in Rousso, *Vichy Syndrome*, p.108.
77. *Le Monde*, 29 April 1971.
78. Jacques Langlois, *Rivarol*, 23 April 1971.
79. These opinions were reported in a review of the press's response to the film, *Le Monde*, 29 April 1971.
80. Ibid.
81. André Gisselbrecht, *L'Humanité*, 20 September 1971.
82. Germaine Tillion, *Le Monde*, 8 June 1971, quoted in Rousso, *Vichy Syndrome*, p.108.
83. Alfred Fabre-Luce, 'Morale et Cinéma', *Le Monde*, 13 May 1971.
84. Ibid.
85. Ibid.
86. Pozzo di Borgo, *Le Monde*, 8 June 1971
87. A detailed account of the exchange is told by Ophuls and Harris in 'Le Film et l'ORTF', *Le Monde*, 8 June 1971.
88. Interview by Colette Godard, *Le Monde*, 18 August 1981.
89. Quoted in Rousso, *Vichy Syndrome*, p.110.
90. Claire Devernieux, *Le Monde*, 14 April 1979.
91. For a detailed account of the reception of Paxton's work in France and the following scholarship on Vichy, see Rousso, *Vichy Syndrome*, pp.251–8.
92. Paul Rassinier, *Le Véritable Procès Eichmann ou les Vainqueurs Incorrigibles* (Paris: La Vielle Taupe, 1962) and Rassinier, *Le Drame des Juifs Européens* (Paris: La Vieille Taupe, 1964). On Rassinier see R. Lewin, 'Paul Rassinier ou la Conjonction des Extrêmes', *Silex*, 36 (1984).
93. The Italian version of the film, *Il Dolore e la Pietá*, was edited by Ezio Pecora and Stefano Munafó.
94. *Il Corriere della Sera*, 19 September 1972.
95. Rousso, *Vichy Syndrome*, p.111.
96. These cinemas were the Publicis Saint-Germain, Publicis Matignon and Paramount Marivaux.

97. Claire Devarrieux, *Le Monde*, 14 April 1979.
98. Alfred Fabre-Luce, *Le Figaro*, 27 October 1981.
99. Michel Mohrt, *Le Figaro*, 30 October 1981.
100. Ibid.
101. Simone Veil, interviewed by Europe1 radio station; reported in *Le Monde*, 30 October 1981.
102. Claude Serraute, *Le Monde*, 28 October 1981.
103. Marcel Ophuls interviewed by Colette Godard, *Le Monde*, 18 August 1981.
104. Rousso, *Vichy Syndrome*, pp.110–12.

5

Blurred Boundaries, 1970 to 1974: *Il Giardino dei Finzi-Contini*, *Il Portiere di Notte* and *Lacombe, Lucien*

'There has never been anti-Semitism in Italy.'
(Vittorio De Sica)

SORROW-LESS ITALY

The 1970s were the decade in which Italian and French perceptions of the Shoah most dramatically parted company. The themes, and sometimes the style, developed along broadly parallel paths, and the long-standing unease at representing Jewish identity persisted, yet the understanding of the historical context changed. French and Italian Holocaust-related fiction films of the 1970s showed similar concerns, yet the interpretation of those concerns by both artists and critics differed. As in the 1960s, French commentators continued to approach the subject in a way that was better informed, and generally more successful in placing artistic licence and individual directorial choices in the appropriate historical context. This disparity was intensified, however, by the impact of *The Sorrow and the Pity*. Subsequently France became more self-critical, while Italy continued to maintain that the Shoah was not an Italian matter.

French Holocaust films of the 1970s were almost invariably set in France, dealt with French heroes and villains, and with French Jews. Michel Drach's *Les Violons du Bal* (*Violins at the Ball*, 1973) and Louis Malle's *Lacombe, Lucien* (1974), as well as *Monsieur Klein* (1976) by American director Joseph Losey, all clearly addressed the persecution of French Jews at the hands of French collaborators. They also all discussed the questions of collaboration and civil cowardliness, presenting a morally bankrupt nation. With perhaps one notable exception, Italian films insisted on adopting a foreign setting for their stories. In the concentration camps represented in Liliana Cavani's *Il Portiere di Notte* (*The Night Porter*, 1974) and Lina Wertmüller's *Pasqualino Settebellezze* (*Seven Beauties*, 1975), Jews are either absent or mute background figures identified exclusively by the Star of David on their clothes. In both films, the lager itself is an unspecified and amorphous one: in the former it is almost a place of the subconscious; in the latter it is a blue-tinted surrealist vision in which the inmates literally march underground along a Dantesque downward spiral.

It is not my contention that Italian film-makers in the 1970s purposely disregarded Italy as a setting for Holocaust narratives to preserve a pristine image of an anti-fascist Italy. This chapter argues, however, that this trend demonstrates the resilience of the view encountered in the late neo-realist films analysed in previous chapters: Italy continued to maintain that, although a small number of Italian Jews had been murdered by the Nazis, an Italian dimension to the Shoah had simply not existed. Furthermore, this chapter shows that all political sides and classes shared this conviction.

Undoubtedly, the difference with France had much to do with Italy's lack of a film of the calibre of Ophuls's work. By first stimulating the discussion, and by then acting as a catalyst for the multiplication of scholarly and popular works on collaborationism, *The Sorrow and the Pity* played a fundamental role in challenging and changing French memory of both Vichy and the Shoah in France. As shown in the introduction, in Italy this particular process simply did not take place, or at least not until much later. The fact itself that such a film was not thought of or produced in the Italian environment is emblematic of Italy's immobile perception of its past. The question remains whether it was the absence of a film such as *The Sorrow and the Pity* which meant Italians were not forced to confront their role in the Shoah, or whether no similar film was made precisely because Italians were so reluctant to confront their recent past.

There are a number of reasons why a film like that of Ophuls could be made in France rather than in Italy, and why the debate that engulfed France was not matched south of the Alps. The role of neo-realism is perhaps surprisingly important. Innovative though it was in the beginning, neo-realism had soon become in some ways the cinematic arm of Italy's orthodoxy of memory. The over-exploitation of the style, and the industry's inability to transcend it, contributed to neo-realism's institutionalisation. Consequently, in the second half of the 1960s, the new generation of film-makers and audiences aimed its cultural challenge at neo-realism's style, not at its representation of the country's history. Nonetheless, the resulting interest in degrees of guilt; ambiguous behaviours; the fragility of the ego; individual and collective morality; and the psychological toll of dealing with war and survival, are not entirely different from the issues raised or alluded to by *The Sorrow and the Pity*. A developing understanding of the history of the Second World War and the effect of totalitarianism on the individual seems to be manifest in the filmic production of both countries.

The challenge to the hegemonic political and historiographical view of the time divides Italy from France, and the post-war political histories of these two countries provide one explanation of this division. In Italy, the post-war economic boom was not marred by the process of decolonisation undergone by France. As a result, the necessary work of redefinition of national identity was much easier in Italy. In Italy, the unstable consistency of Christian Democrat rule since 1948, as well as the systematic but sterile strength of the communist opposition, had not forced the country to deal with the memory of fascism. The official version of this history was acceptable to both main parties, as the communists could proudly state their predominant role in the Resistance while the Christian Democrats, by embracing the rhetoric of the partisan war, effectively suffocated its socially-progressive potential. With the far right relegated to the margins of politics, there existed neither the need nor the will to reassess the respective roles of fascism, the Resistance, and Italian wartime activity in general. Of course, the 1968 Movement, which in Italy was powerful and prolonged, challenged mainstream politics, questioned bourgeois values and probed the so-called sins of the fathers at least as much as in France. Rather than demanding an historical reassessment of the Resistance, however, the Movement criticised what it felt had been the betrayal of loosely-defined Resistance values by the dominant political parties.

This chapter considers two key Italian Holocaust films of the first half of the 1970s: Vittorio De Sica's *Il Giardino dei Finzi-Contini*

(*The Garden of the Finzi-Contini*, 1970), and Liliana Cavani's *The Night Porter* (1974). Other Italian films of this period are more or less loosely related to the Shoah. Among these, Wertmuller's *Pasqualino Settebellezze* (*Seven Beauties*, 1975), while set against a backdrop of the Second World War, and in part located in a grotesque lager, is not really about the Shoah. Instead, it is concerned principally with national, even regional, identity. Similarly, Visconti's two related films, *Vaghe Stelle dell'Orsa* (*Sandra*, 1965), and *La Caduta degli Dei* (*The Damned*, 1969), are only marginally connected to the Shoah; they are much more concerned with the mechanisms linking individuals, families and power.[1] In contrast, *The Garden* and *The Night Porter* are more representative of the distinctive representational trends of the period. At the same time, their reception illustrates the long-term tendency of Italian critics, already encountered in the analysis of other films, to ignore the Shoah even when it is at the centre of the text being assessed. Both were reviewed extensively in France; a fact which adds a comparative aspect crucial to this work. Cavani's film in particular lends itself to a direct comparison with its contemporary, Louis Malle's *Lacombe, Lucien*, as the two films were reviewed together by French critics.

Malle's 1974 work is itself a central work on the representation of the collaboration in France. Of the films treated in this book, *Lacombe, Lucien* is perhaps the one which has commanded most attention by academics. Besides film specialists, it has interested historians and literary scholars who have examined in depth the screenwriting role of novelist Patrick Modiano.[2] However, the lacuna in existing work on the film is a detailed study of its reception. It is crucial to look at the film's reception in order to understand the society that produced it and received it, to draw some conclusions regarding the visible shift in Holocaust representation between 1970 and 1974, and to demonstrate how the origins of this change can be traced back to Ophuls's *The Sorrow and the Pity*.

DISOWNED ADAPTATION: *THE GARDEN OF THE FINZI-CONTINI*: RANK, RELIGION, REGION AND RACE

Elie Wiesel said of De Sica's *The Garden* that 'it succeeds in moving us without falling into sentimentality'.[3] An adaptation of Giorgio Bassani's autobiographical novel, *The Garden* relies greatly upon symbolism and metaphor to portray the decadence of a class, and to investigate collective behaviour. Set in Ferrara, in the Po river plains, between 1938 and 1944, it is the story of a young middle-class Jewish university student, Giorgio, who is in love with an aristocratic girl. Micòl Finzi-Contini belongs to an exclusive and exclusivist Jewish family who lead a lifestyle which De Sica himself has described as 'a bourgeois and aristocratic climate of egoism and comfort'.[4] The love story is not destined to enjoy a happy ending, both because Micòl prefers the gentile Milanese worker, Malnate, and because she will be deported and murdered. Hints of incest between Micòl and her brother, Alberto, questions over Alberto's own sexuality, and the Giorgio–Micòl–Malnate triangle, at times come across as pretentiously provocative in their rhetorical morbidity. In this, they are, of course, perfectly in keeping with the cultural concerns and artistic productions of that time; yet they also explain Bassani's rejection of De Sica's adaptation of his book, an issue to be discussed later in this chapter.

Despite its romanticism and aestheticism, which sometimes spill into oversimplification and rhetoric, the film succeeds in addressing the historical events that constitute the unique context to this story of adolescence and love. The personal relationships are played out against the background of fascist Italy: the 1938 anti-Semitic laws, the start of the war and Italy's first defeats, ending with the deportation of the Jews of Ferrara. The recreation of the historical setting, though by no means free of contemporary interpretations, is what separates *The Garden* from other films of the period. In this fact, according to Insdorf, the director's neo-realist roots are evident, as 'De Sica is in a sense as true to the subject here – the crème de la crème of Italian Jewry – as he was to the impoverished Italians that he depicted in post-war classics like *Bicycle Thieves* and *Shoeshine*'.[5]

De Sica directly attacks Italian complacency over the rise of fascism, and the later Nazi persecution of the Jews. The apathy of both gentiles and Jews comes under scrutiny. The gentile bourgeoisie is epitomised by the director of Ferrara's public library, who regretfully expels Giorgio, defending his position with the fact that he has 'a family [to feed]'; Giorgio remonstrates that 'the whole of Italy has a family [to feed]'. The Jewish middle class is represented by Giorgio's father, a card-carrying member of the Fascist Party who, even after the racial laws, excuses Mussolini's actions with the confidence that 'Mussolini is not Hitler'. Significantly, Giorgio accuses his father of 'not having raised a finger', when fascism persecuted other people. De Sica was fascinated by these characters, though he may have understood their situation as bourgeoisie better than their predicament as Jews: 'This is what drew me to the book. Italian Jews were completely unaware. They could not bring themselves to believe what was threatening them.'[6] Perhaps unfairly, he criticises them for this lack of foresight, but his main critique of them remains as members of a class, the bourgeoisie, which had welcomed Mussolini's law and order.

The Garden is as much about the decadence of a social class as it is about the persecution of Italian Jews. De Sica centres his film around Finzi-Contini's magnificent garden – quiet, green and luxurious. Their walled private grounds, their extensive library where Giorgio is symbolically imprisoned, their tennis courts where a fictitious harmony reigns, are all at once a defence, a hiding place and a prison. The Finzi-Contini may well have chosen a deliberate alienation, but it is one motivated by class, not religion or political discrimination.

Their Judaism is therefore passive, and it seems to be for them little more than the reason for which they are persecuted. They are Italians before being Jews; they feel closer to members of their class or profession than to those of their religious community; they respect their religion out of convention rather than devotion. With occasional scenes of domestic and public religiosity, however, De Sica manages to capture these people's own way of being Jews. In this respect, too, his film has scant company in the history of Italian Holocaust films.

Furthermore, it also needs to be stressed that De Sica's characterisation is loyal both to history and Bassani's memoirs. Most Northern Italian middle-class Jews of the 1930s were indeed completely integrated in Italian society. Bassani wrote:

> That we were Jews [...] still counted fairly little in our case. For what on earth did the word Jew mean? [...] It derived from the fact that our families, not through choice, but thanks to tradition [...] belonged to the same religious rite.[7]

Significantly, other Northern Italian Jewish authors such as Primo Levi and Natalia Ginzburg have also expressed their memory of a well-assimilated Italian Jewry along similar lines.[8]

Figure 5.1. *The Garden of the Finzi-Contini*: 'The film's Jewish characters can only achieve a collective Jewish identity when the class distinction is removed by their arrest.' (© Arthur Cohn.)

The relations between characters are inserted and played by the rules of a class system. Giorgio's father tells him to forget about Micòl because she is '*di un'altra classe*', which can be interpreted either as 'a class apart' or as 'of a different social class'. In this case, she is probably both. At the same time, he also suggests that this was the very reason his son was attracted to her: she was different and unreachable. In a similar way, Micòl despises and at the same time is attracted by Malnate, the gentile Milanese factory worker. Her interest is strongly determined by his being a member of the working class: 'too industrial, too communist and too hairy'. Insdorf suggests that his class is even in his name: 'Malnate, badly or lowly born'.[9]

The film's Jewish characters can achieve a collective Jewish identity only when the class distinction is removed by their arrest (Figure 5.1). Still, this unity is tainted by their inability to identify themselves as a people beyond geographical boundaries: in the classroom where they are being held, Giorgio's father comforts Micòl by stating that 'at least we are together, us Jews of Ferrara'. Moreover, the idea of unity is contradicted further by the painful suggestion that Giorgio's family can survive only through its separation: his brother had left for France before the war, and Giorgio himself, warned by a friend, manages to escape with his mother and younger sister.

THERE ARE NO GERMANS IN THE GARDEN OF THE FINZI-CONTINI

While the emphasis on class and personal relations unequivocally places *The Garden* in the 1970s, the film's apparent willingness to describe the persecution of Italy's Jews as an Italian phenomenon, rather than a purely German one or a universal crime against humanity, places it well ahead of its time. Indeed, in its apparent acknowledgement of the persecution of Italian Jews as a reflection of generally accepted anti-Semitism, De Sica's film constitutes an important breakthrough within Italian filmography on the Shoah. Whether or not this was a deliberate decision, a conscious effort to 'Italianise' the Holocaust, this remains a fundamental credit to the film. Nevertheless, this is a very significant question mark over De Sica's approach, as the director's own statement to *La Croix* of 10 January 1971 testifies:

> In Italy there has never been anti-Semitism. In this domain the fascists have been merely the imitators of the Nazis. And these arrests of Jews took place without the least violence, indeed with great courtesy, which is the height of cruelty.[10]

This statement confirms the ambiguity of 1970s Italy's relation with the Shoah. On the one hand, the film portrays uncompromisingly the rise of anti-Jewish feeling in Italy and the Italian role in the genocide, specifically depicting Italian militiamen – and not German troops or SS – carrying out the arrest of the city's Jews. On the other hand, the film's own director all too easily dismissed Italian anti-Semitism as a cheap reproduction of Germany's, thus reiterating one of the most popular explanations of the Italian racial laws.

At the end of the film, the policeman arresting Micòl calls her 'Mícol', in accordance with the autarchic fascist rules for pronunciation (Figure 5.2). A significant, understated detail, it reinforces the message that the anti-Jewish persecution depended not on the actions of a single person, but on a deliberate climate of xenophobia and anti-Semitism inextricably linked to fascist

Figure 5.2. *The Garden of the Finzi-Contini*: three generations of the family leave their family home under arrest. Their attire prefigures their fate as individuals and as a class. (© Arthur Cohn.)

nationalism. This, along with several other anti-Semitic incidents in the film, suggests either that Italy was predisposed to anti-Semitic sentiment or that anti-Semitism was opportunistic – revealing that if Italians were not genuinely racist, they were at least not *brava gente*. And yet De Sica's statement invalidated this by denying the existence of Italian anti-Semitism. It is hard to make sense of this film in the light of the director's words.

It is necessary to analyse the reception of *The Garden* in both Italy and France to reconcile these apparently contradictory elements, and to understand if and how contemporaries reconciled them. It is almost impossible to establish what contemporary movie-goers thought of De Sica's representation of wartime

Italy, but we do know that this particular aspect was almost entirely ignored by Italian critics. It should be noted, however, that the film was commercially and critically successful, grossing 710,000,000 Italian lire and winning awards, including the Golden Bear at the Berlin Film Festival in 1971 and an Academy Award for Best Foreign Language Film in 1972.[11]

At the same time, however, *The Garden* was widely dismissed as a mediocre film. As a psychological portrayal of ambiguous personal relations it seemed both conceptually and artistically inferior to Visconti's works; as an interpretation of the country's history it fell short of the merciless suggestions of Bertolucci's *La Strategia del Ragno* (*The Spider's Stratagem*) and *Il Conformista* (*The Conformist*), both released in the same year. Only as the adaptation of a respected literary work did it attract much attention, though Bassani's disavowal damaged the film. De Sica's own reputation, of course, granted the film much visibility, and yet also proved a disadvantage: following a decade of many uninspired directorial and starring choices, he had come to be seen by many as not sufficiently *engagé* for the 1970s, or in any case as past his best.

Despite the fact that fourteen years had passed since De Sica's last neo-realist film, *Il Tetto* (*The Roof*, 1956), the film-maker's past particularly affected the film's reception. *L'Unità*, which in 1959 had hailed De Sica's 'rehabilitation' on the occasion of his starring role in Rossellini's *General della Rovere*, once again drew a comparison with his early works. At the release of the film in Rome, the communist daily called his effort 'a return to the dignity, if not to the coherent inspiration, of his best years'.[12] On the same day, an article in the Christian Democrat paper *Il Popolo* drew a parallel between the final sequences of the film and 'the best De Sica, his neo-realist tone'.[13]

In fact, the film's finale is also its least realist section, as the scene of the arrests is followed by slow-motion flashbacks to the Finzi-Contini siblings playing tennis, dressed in white and bathed in a striking bright light, accompanied by a lyrical voice singing the names of the extermination sites: Auschwitz, Majdanek, Treblinka. What reviewers did was pay tribute to the parts they liked by calling them 'neo-realist', even though they clearly were not. In other words, while neo-realism had long been dead and film-makers experimented with different styles, critics, in 1970, continued to use the word 'neo-realist' as a general praise, rather than in reference to the immediate post-war film school. This tendency is testament to the privileged place neo-realism held in post-war Italian culture, carrying the connotations of aesthetically beautiful, thematically important and ideologically sound. As well as the personality of the director, the controversy between De Sica and Bassani conspired to draw attention away from the film's content and tone. The author took the film's producers to court and successfully dissociated his name from it, though the judge allowed the film to continue to be distributed under its original title. On the day of the film's premiere in Milan, newspapers reported the judge's decision to add to the film a disclaimer stating the looseness of its connection with the book.[14] On the same day, *Il Corriere della Sera* reported that the film, shown at the Jerusalem Film Festival, had won Golda Meir's praise for its artistic and moral virtues. The same article, however, also reported that an Israeli paper had simultaneously published an article by Bassani entitled: 'The betrayal of my garden'.[15]

There is no doubt that De Sica's film differs from Bassani's novel both in detail and in the overall tone of the text. In the novel, the memory of the time, people and places of Bassani's youth plays as central a role as the events he recounts, the transpiring sadness of the memory of the loss making it superfluous to indulge on the circumstances of such loss. De Sica sacrificed the subtlety of the relationship between narrator, witness and character by changing the book's original narrative structure, mixing Giorgio's reminiscence with an omniscient narrator. He struggled to adapt the text to the conventional narrative structure of a film. In the novel, Micòl neither returns Giorgio's love nor betrays him, denying the film-makers all the traditional outcomes of romantic entanglements. Consequently, De Sica added, cut and changed the plot freely. He invented the secret affair between Micòl and Malnate, who are caught out by Giorgio; he transformed the closeness between the two siblings into a relationship with more than a hint of incest; he added anti-Semitic episodes and round-ups to give a sense of passing time and to allow the tension to mount to its climax; he reached this tragic climax with the arrest of the Finzi-Contini and Giorgio's father, when the latter had actually escaped capture.

Nevertheless, in the context of this book, De Sica's film is not assessed merely as an adaptation of a literary text, but rather in order to address the question of what the film says, and how. This is precisely what its contemporaries were unable or unwilling to do. Only the popular Roman daily *Il Messaggero* gave any attention to De Sica's representation of wartime Italy and the anti-Jewish legislation: it noted, for instance, that Italians take the Finzi-Contini family away. But, instead of making anything more of this significant detail, the critic simply asserted its historical accuracy. Thus, paradoxically, the part of the film praised by the article for its authenticity was an invented detail. Bassani's novel says nothing of the circumstances in which these arrests took place, and thus the film-maker's representation is at best the result of speculation.[16]

Otherwise, reviews ignored the theme of Italian history altogether, to focus on already mentioned matters of aesthetics and acting, narrative structure and judicial troubles. Discussion of the ambiguity of the relationship between Micòl and her brother Alberto, and between the latter and Malnate, outweighed that of class relations and political struggle. The renowned *Il Corriere della Sera* film critic, Giovanni Grazzini, suggested that the 'suspicion of incest and abnormal friendships' were part of the film's 'languid' atmosphere, foretelling the approaching catastrophe.[17] Much was made of the film's commercial success, and how this was achieved at the expense of loyalty to the novel, and occasionally of good taste. In particular, both French and Italian reviewers made reference to a gratuitous nude shot of Micòl.[18] Critics were also uniformly negative about the actors' performances.

Why, then, was the theme of Italian history so blatantly ignored? An initial explanation for this may be found in Italian cinema's preference for using historical settings for its stories. From its beginnings to the resurgence in the early 1960s of films about the Second World War, the historical recreation had been a successful genre. In general, these films did not require historical knowledge or curiosity on the part of the audience to be entertaining, nor did they aspire to comment on the historical period in which they set their narratives. A good example is the entire *Peplum* genre: these were immensely popular Roman-mythological films of which there were 170 between 1957 and 1964, equal to 10 per cent of the Italian film industry's total output. In these films, which did not hesitate to mix Hercules with Zorro and Genghis Khan, history was so contaminated or so remote that it became a refuge from history.[19] At other times, history was merely an excuse for a contemporary critique. Visconti's *Senso* (1954), for example, uses a historical critique of the mismanagement of the 1866 War of Independence to address the state's creation and exploitation of a nationalist mythology.[20] If Italian historical films had traditionally had an escapist or presentist flavour, then perhaps there was no reason for *The Garden* to be considered any differently.

Additionally, it is arguable that, in the politically-charged post-1968 environment, reviewers and public alike were immediately able to recognise that the film was about class more than it was about fascism. It may have been obvious to them that De Sica had filmed a romantic melodrama against a background of individual and collective tragedy without revisionist aspirations. This assumption would have been reinforced by the director's own failure to present his film as anything but an exploration of the forces at play in youth, love and class relations.

Finally, it is arguable that the orthodox version of that history, in which the persecution of Italy's Jews had been not only relatively insignificant but also almost entirely the work of the Germans, had become too deeply rooted to be shaken by a subtle, and perhaps unwitting, voice to the contrary. While all three of the aforementioned explanations played a part, this last one is the most convincing. The 1972 Italian response to the television broadcast of Ophuls's *The Sorrow and the Pity*, which I have described in the previous chapter, supports the idea that the resistancialist orthodoxy, left unchallenged for so long, affected the analysis even of those few works which dared to question it.

Several other elements confirm this explanation. In the first instance, we can point to the reviewers' inability to draw even elementary conclusions from the film's content. As mentioned, *Il Messaggero* reported the arrests by Italian personnel without asking any questions about what this signified, or attempting to place the incident within the wider Italian filmography of the war.[21] Another example is given by how many reviews identified in the film an indictment of Jewish passivity, without at any point speaking of the passivity of the Italian population at large: one of these, in *Il Messaggero*, described Giorgio's father as 'a man who naively has deluded himself that he can collaborate with the regime', but made no mention of the population's repeated acts of cowardliness or open hostility.[22] And the reviewer's criticism of conformism did not target a social class, as De Sica did, but purely the Jewish population.

A second point in support of this argument is the fact that French newspapers did comment on *The Garden*'s representation of fascist Italy, and specifically on anti-Semitism. *L'Humanité* stated that the subject of the film was 'the slow and inexorable rise, between 1938 and 1943, of the persecution of Jews in the conditions specific to Italy', and considered it 'a testimony on this phenomenon and the period in question'.[23] Jean Rochereau in *La Croix* employed similar terminology, praising De Sica's 'documentaristic rigour' in the representation of 'fascism and its corollary, anti-Semitism'.[24] Even *Le Monde*, though approaching the film from an altogether more literary point of view, saw the historical background as crucial.[25] In fact, in stark contrast with Italian reviewers, French articles uniformly touched on this subject.

Yet while French reviewers were more aware of the historical and political implications of the film, they too persisted in judging anti-Semitism as alien to Italy and Italian history. *La Croix* pointed to 'anti-Semitism, imposed by fascism onto a country which did not know the very meaning of the word'.[26] This evident contradiction further identifies the durability of this version of the events. The image of *Italiani brava gente* had spread, in France as elsewhere: two-and-a-half decades of flatteringly self-deprecating Italian war films – simultaneously mocking the Italians' lack of discipline, organisation and military courage, and glorifying their compassion, charity and human warmth – had played their part in this process.

Finally, the persistence of this particular vision of the country's history is supported by De Sica's own statement about Italian anti-Semitism, made to *La Croix* and reported in full earlier in this chapter. The apparent contradiction between the director's film and his subsequent statement can ultimately be explained by the fact that Italian self-acquittal had been so pervasive and persuasive that, in his mind, as in those of his audiences, the two visions had ceased to be incompatible.

AN UNWITTING INDICTMENT

Whatever the explanation for the short-sighted if not blind Italian reception of *The Garden*, two significant things about the film are evident. First, that it remains to this date one of only a handful of Italian films making reference to the racial laws of 1938. It was the first to hint at active and passive Italian anti-Semitism, and it continues to be the only one to show the deportation of Italian Jews by the Italian police. In this sense, at least, the film maintains its honesty with regard to history, if not to Bassani's novel. Second, that the reception of the film, particularly in Italy, ignored all this. In contrast, the French reception of *The Garden* on its release in December 1971, though equally tepid, did remark on these issues but seemed to be unable to draw the logical conclusions from them. While it is pointless to speculate over what the French would have made of the film had it been released there a year earlier, it is inevitable to see a link between their reading of it and the release of *The Sorrow and the Pity* only a few months before. Unlike the opinions of Italian reviewers in 1970, those of French reviewers in 1971 were undoubtedly informed by Ophuls's film.

The remaining sections of this chapter will enable us to test further this thesis, while also determining whether or not the far-reaching effects of *The Sorrow and the Pity* contributed also to a change in the way Italian film-makers represented the Shoah. By looking at *The Night Porter* and *Lacombe, Lucien*, an Italian and a French film both made three years after *The Sorrow and the Pity*, they will consider whether a parallel change had similarly affected the way in which Italy received and interpreted Holocaust films, and ask whether this was a direct consequence of Ophuls's film, or happened independently despite the lack of an equivalent event.

A REPLACEMENT MYTH? THE RETRO-STYLE: *THE NIGHT PORTER* AND *LACOMBE, LUCIEN*

'Cette fois De Gaulle est bien mort.'[27]

The critic Serge Daney, writing for *Les Cahiers du Cinéma*, defined 'positivity' as 'the outmoded and tedious consistency required of conscious heroes, clear messages, a precise political line'.[28] In these terms, *The Garden* is a product of the 1960s rather than the 1970s. In De Sica's film, there is no doubt that the audience is asked to identify with Giorgio. Despite the occasional unpleasantness of the often aloof Finzi-Contini family and the audience's unfulfilled desire to see Micòl return Giorgio's affections, there is no confusion between positive and negative characters. Notwithstanding De Sica's and Zavattini's socio-economic critique of the middle and upper classes, the film does not blur the boundaries between guilt and innocence.

In contrast, *Lacombe, Lucien* and *The Night Porter* contain an element of ambiguity between victim and perpetrator, which is central to their discourses. *The Garden* is a film shot entirely from the victims' perspective; the title character of *Lacombe, Lucien* is in effect, if not in essence, a perpetrator; *The Night Porter* concerns itself with the link between the two. If one considers these latter two films within the wider context of 1970s Holocaust films, they reveal a widespread interest in fascism and the 'murky underworld' of collaboration.[29]

'WE ARE ALL BOTH VICTIM AND MURDERER AND VOLUNTARILY WE ACCEPT THESE ROLES.'

The Night Porter was a co-production shot in English, with an international cast, by Liliana Cavani. Cavani was a respected *engagé* film-maker in her thirties with excellent ties in France. Her filmography up to 1974 included documentaries such as the 1965 *Primo Piano: Philippe Pétain Processo a Vichy* and several fictional dramas including a Bulgarian production entitled *Galileo* (1969) and two Italian films, *I Cannibali* (*The Cannibals*, 1970), inspired by Sophocles, and *L'Ospite* (*The Guest*, 1972). *The Night Porter* is set in Vienna in 1957, and tells the story of a survivor of the camps (Lucia), who recognises in the night porter of her hotel the SS doctor (Max) who had taken her as his protégé in the lager. Cavani employs a series of alternate flashbacks to reveal to the audience that Lucia had survived by accepting Max's attentions. Their victim–persecutor relationship is restored as the two characters attempt to recreate camp conditions. This time they are both victims, however, as Max's secret association of former SS members murders them both to protect themselves from potential witnesses.

Cavani's representation of the lager, in the lengthy flashbacks, is made entirely of seedy, smoke-filled interiors ruled by violence, alcohol, sex and voyeurism. Voyeurism exists in this film in three different ways. First, it exists in the film's narrative, particularly in two crucial episodes: a flashback reveals how the first encounter between Max and Lucia took place as he was filming the deportees; and back in the present Lucia secretly witnesses a meeting of the former Nazis. Moreover, later in the film, Max, unnoticed, watches Lucia at the opera in a clearly voyeuristic sequence.

Secondly, voyeurism is integral to the narrative structure of the film: this is omniscient narration based on the alternance of present and past expressed in flashbacks. Cavani consistently introduces her numerous flashbacks by having the camera move in and linger on a close-up of the person remembering, so that her flashbacks are almost literally peepholes into the characters' minds. Thirdly – according to a cinematic convention which is epitomised particularly well in this film – both the film-maker's camera and the audience are voyeurs: this is particularly in evidence in the final shot of the film, where Cavani's camera pans over the dead bodies of Max and Lucia, but throughout the film the camera over-invests with meaning the body – both female and male – by lingering on it.

The lack of outside spaces allows Cavani to draw a parallel between the lager-period and 1957, where also most of the sequences are shot in dark cramped rooms, either in the hotel or in Max's claustrophobic apartment. A fundamental difference, however, remains in the fact that in the post-lager environment, Lucia has a choice. Although trauma theory realistically suggests that Lucia's action are forced by the need to play out her original trauma, Cavani herself chooses to represent victimhood as a role assumed deliberately: Lucia is not blackmailed by impending death or subjected to the terrifying conditions of the camp, although she is haunted by the memory of it. Similarly, Max is aware that his relationship with her will not be tolerated by his former comrades. Nonetheless, they each choose to resume their relationship and to reproduce the sense of foreboding, without which the liaison could exist.

Though it is tempting to interpret *The Night Porter* as a disturbing yet powerful analysis of the far-reaching consequences of the concentration camp experience, such a reading would be limited at best. This film is not about the perpetuity of the Shoah unless it is so by suggesting that the psychological mechanisms ruling human relations are the same within the camp as outside it. By establishing two parallel universes, one within and one outside an unidentified concentration camp, Cavani seeks to establish that, in both these universes, Lucia and Max voluntarily choose to accept their roles respectively as victim and murderer.

Moreover, those roles soon become blurred. Cavani places the suggestion of complicity upon Lucia as she performs topless for the camp guards, wearing (half) an SS uniform, and opens

Max's gift of the severed head of another inmate. Later, Max kills a former SS informer in order to hide her identity and, finally, Lucia becomes at least partly responsible for Max's death, as it is her presence that triggers his execution. Similarly, Max is a murderer in both universes, but in the last instance also a victim. Thus, if Cavani's lager becomes a place of the mind, then tormentor and tormented also become one and the same, those roles decided by the desires of individuals rather than through external circumstances. If Lucia's sexual relationship with Max makes *The Night Porter* exceedingly uncomfortable to watch, it is Cavani's suggestion of a subconscious affinity between victim and persecutor that makes this a preposterous and extremely unpleasant film.

THE LONELINESS OF THE COLLABORATOR

In *Lacombe, Lucien*, Louis Malle, too, looks at the relationship between a young member of the French Gestapo (Lucien Lacombe) and a Jewish girl (France Horn). However, while *Lacombe, Lucien*'s plot is itself less than comforting, it nevertheless does not share *The Night Porter*'s more disturbing elements. Instead, its main concerns are the motives behind a young collaborator's choice. In short, *Lacombe, Lucien* is the story of a teenage southern French peasant working as a janitor in a hospice, who seeks to become involved in the Maquis. Refused entry by a local Resistance leader, his former schoolteacher, Lucien ends up stranded by a punctured tyre in front of the mansion of the local section of the French Gestapo. He joins the collaborators almost by default, after denouncing the schoolteacher. No formal job offer is ever made, or accepted. Increasingly enjoying the power and wealth his position bestows upon him, Lucien becomes sentimentally involved with a young Parisian Jewess, France Horn, ultimately killing a German soldier in order to save her.

The Horn family consists of three people and three different generations: the grandmother, who speaks only Yiddish; the father, Albert Horn, a tailor who has assumed Parisian elegance but retains a thick German accent; and the young, sophisticated daughter, France, whose absolute assimilation to her country of birth is hammered home not only by her name, but also by her attitude and 'Aryan' looks. France lives her Jewish identity as a

Figure 5.3. Incommunicability. Therese Giehse and Pierre Blaise take a break on the set of *Lacombe, Lucien*. Only when Lucien acknowledges the grandmother's identity, by saluting her in Yiddish, does she reply in French, revealing her refusal to assimilate to have been deliberate. (© Louis Malle's film/NEF.)

burden: 'I am fed up with being Jewish', she exclaims while abandoning herself in Lucien's arms. Similarly, Albert, when asked whether 'all the Jews are enemies of France', answers 'Not me', rejecting the collective aspect of his Judaism. Both are categorically identified as Jewish by the prejudice of others rather than by a conscious claim to that part of their identity. Malle's Jews contain an ambiguity which is also subtlety: on the one hand, this representation led Insdorf to air the possibility that 'when physical beauty or social class eclipses all other roots of identity, (...) the aesthetic can become an anaesthetic';[30] on the other hand, it finely epitomises the different traditions that form European Judaism. These two extremes of European Jewish identity, France and her Yiddish-speaking grandmother, survive by escaping with Lucien (Figure 5.3). The film ends with a long, almost dialogue-free sequence that shows them hiding in idyllic countryside, until a title informs us that Lucien was arrested and executed on 12 April 1945. This reference automatically suggests that the film was factual, which it was not.

Interestingly, the setting of the sequence made some French commentators complain that it was 'outside history', yet this date,

1945, is the only specific definition of the film's temporal space, which is otherwise indeterminate. The indefinite nature of place and time is arguably not a refusal of historical accuracy, but a reinforcement of Lucien's anonymity. Even his name suggests anonymity, presented as it is in the undistinguished manner of bureaucratic language, surname followed by first name.

Throughout the film, his actions seem pointless and his motives unclear. The film opens with Lucien, stuck at his job with nothing to do, indifferently killing birds with a slingshot. When he attempts to join the Maquis, he does so for no clear political reason, nor for nationalist sentiment, nor to seek glory. Later, he denounces his schoolteacher not out of revenge nor for personal gain, but in a casual gesture. As he does so he is drunk, yet his subsequent absence of any remorse removes drunkenness as an explanation. Then, in yet another seemingly casual gesture, he kills the German soldier and escapes with France. This is perhaps his only clear-cut choice and potentially the redemption that conventional film-making would demand. The trigger for his actions, however, is the German's theft of a watch Lucien had previously given to France's father. At no stage does he reject the evil of persecution. His final actions imply no realisation, redemption or admission of guilt.

Neither can the few hints we are given about his personal situation successfully explain these acts. His poverty, his adolescence, his immaturity, the fact that his mother is betraying his missing father with her boss, can go some way to justify his anger and his desire to fit in. They do not provide, however, a convincing explanation of his collaboration with Nazism. In fact, the audience's customary search for justification is doomed, because it assumes the presence of choice, yet Lucien does not seem to make any choice, but simply follows whichever path is laid before him either by circumstance or by the choice of others. As such, *Lacombe, Lucien* is a fine, though provocative, metaphor for the French nation in the period 1938–45.

'WITHOUT SORROW AND WITHOUT PITY': THE FRENCH REVIEW *LACOMBE, LUCIEN*

The issue of personal choice is central to this film and to *The Night Porter*, as well as to their reception. In the absence of choice, Lucien's actions are devoid of moral considerations and explained instead with an almost animal-like defence of his territory. In *The Night Porter,* however, it is the presence of choice that troubles the audience's concepts of morality. In fact, Lucia's acceptance and – the film suggests – her enjoyment of her status as victim, identifies victimisation as one of the base human desires which also govern Lucien.

Different though they are, both films seem to be fascinated with 'the other side', represented here by French collaborationism, there by Nazism. Perhaps, the specific circumstances of the Second World War were only a context for the film-makers to express their opinions. Nonetheless, the choice of that context is telling, especially as it fitted a new wave of interest in the occupation, which critics writing in *Les Cahiers du Cinéma* named 'la mode rétro', or retro-style.[31] In the aftermath of *The Sorrow and the Pity*, films such as *Lacombe, Lucien* and *The Night Porter* were identified by critics as profoundly political works. Malle's film in particular stirred emotions, because it was made by a Frenchman and focused on France, but critics easily identified in both films a growing tendency to question common assumptions about the nature of morality and political engagement.

Many saw *Lacombe, Lucien* as the attempt to replace the myth of the Resistance with the portrait of a cowardly, racist and corrupt France. *Lacombe, Lucien* was the fictional equivalent of Ophuls's documentary: it set its action in unoccupied France; it played down the role of the German forces; it approached the subject of anti-Semitism; it devoted more attention to collaboration than resistance; it even contained characters, such as the professional cyclist, who bore considerable resemblance to people interviewed in Ophuls's film. Yet, because of the fictional nature of his work, Malle could not argue for its accuracy as convincingly as Ophuls could. Instead, he and his scriptwriter, the novelist Patrick Modiano, were left to fend off accusations from both the right and the left of the political spectrum, of having insulted French history and the French people.

Le Point entitled its main critique 'Without sorrow and without pity', drawing on the legacy of Ophuls's documentary.[32] 'There is not a single image in this film where the French are not portrayed in a detestable light', wrote Delfeil de Ton.[33] In the same article he blamed five years of 'Pompidouism' for 'the first film to attempt to rehabilitate providers of the Nazis into their victims'.[34] The Gaullist historian, journalist and political commentator

Pierre Viansson-Ponté criticised Malle for having replaced the heroic, feel-good narratives of the 1950s and 1960s with the opposite extreme, a bleak France populated by 'Gestapo agents and informers'.[35] Critics referred, in particular, to a scene in which a secretary moans about the number of anonymous denunciations as she tries to sort out genuine from false ones.

Viansson-Ponté concluded by sighing: 'one must surrender to what is evident: this time De Gaulle is truly dead'.[36] In fact, five years after his death, film-makers still endeavoured to attack the general's view of wartime France, while reviewers still used this view as the benchmark against which to judge historical films. The ghost of Gaullist national reconciliation was mentioned both in favour of and against *Lacombe, Lucien*. And while those five years had seen sufficient change for de Gaulle's myth to be dubbed 'la viellie imposture' – 'the old lie of national reconciliation'[37] – the debate and emotion still commanded by the memory of the occupation belied this almost mocking assumption.

Le Nouvel Observateur criticised Malle for seeking 'a new national reconciliation, where all people are united in cowardice rather than heroism'.[38] In identifying an artistic trend to re-evaluate the Vichy period, the journalist accused retro-style writers and film-makers of replacing a black-and-white picture of historical guilt with a monochromatic one, where all individuals are equally grey. 'In virtue of this', the reviewer added, 'collaborators and *résistants* become interchangeable, the Maquis and the Gestapo two equivalent options open to an adolescent's evasion.'[39] On the same note, Gérald Suberville, former Resistance leader of the Hérault region –writing in *Libération* under his wartime pseudonym of Commander Janvier – accused Louis Malle of exchanging 'the (no less mystifying) Gaullist imagery of the Resistance' with a blurred vision that erases all responsibilities.[40]

Enraged by the suspicion that Malle was lumping together all French people into a sort of moral mediocrity, the majority of reviewers ignored the capable and subtle way in which Malle describes and condemns Pétainist France in his film. In the first nine minutes, the film addresses Vichy's own neo-revolutionary trio of values: 'work, family, country'. The first scene shows Lucien working in a hospital, where he lackadaisically sweeps the floor, listens to the radio, kills a bird. Work does not seem the elevating experience it was in the words of the right's propaganda, but a useless duty. In the second sequence, Lucien comes back home to find an adulterous mother and another family living in his house. Is this the family Pétain talked about as the basis of a healthy society? In the same scene, the landowner complains that his son has left him to join the Resistance: 'I have a patriotic son', he says sarcastically. Religion and education are also questioned early on in the film, as instruments of rhetoric or social control rather than pillars of morality.

Not all reviewers missed this. In some cases, they hailed *Lacombe, Lucien* as a painfully honest film. For example, the fortnightly literary magazine *Quinzaine Littéraire*, while agreeing with others that Lucien's France is 'a country of cowards', lamented that 'this is a truth that spares no adult'.[41] *Politique Hebdo* speculated on how present-day France would react to a reactionary drift.[42] Among the popular newspapers, opinion was also divided. *Le Nouvel Observateur*'s Jean-Louis Bory rather pompously thanked Malle for not allowing himself to be 'blinded by the cowardly complacency of a delayed patriotism'.[43] Jean de Baroncelli saluted 'a great French film, which owes nothing to fashion, or the intellectualism of this side or the other'.[44] Writing on 31 January, before the worst of the controversy, de Baroncelli was sufficiently lucid to point out that Malle's refusal to judge his protagonist is not tantamount to an absolution.

Rather than pointing this out, however, Malle and Modiano attempted to fend off their critics by suggesting the historical context of the story was coincidental. Malle complained that the emotional nature of the period in question drowned out his film's point on what one might call 'the banality of fascism'.[45] Modiano also played down the historical context: 'what fascinates me is not the occupation, but a murky underworld, an ideal climate where people reveal themselves for what they are, an exaggerated image of what happens every day'.[46] However, if statements such as this helped shift the focus from the film's representation of the past to its contemporary outlook, they did not assuage the worries of those who thought the film had gone too far, and may indeed have increased these.

The film, then, was no longer seen to be simply throwing mud at France's past, but questioning the integrity of the country regardless of the time. It is arguable that *Lacombe, Lucien* was controversial only in part because of its representation of Vichy France. Its echoes of the Algerian War, of the Harkis, the Algerian Front de Libération Nationale (National Liberation Front, FLN) and the Organisation de l'Armée Secrète (Secret Army Organisation, OAS), also unsettled public opinion. Although this angle was wilfully neglected at the time, Malle made no mystery of the fact that, while he had lived through the German occupation, the inspiration for this particular story came from his time in Algeria.[47] Once again, as with *Night and Fog*, the director of a film ostensibly about Vichy claimed instead that Algeria was the key to its interpretation. Once again, critics disregarded this perspective.

Most importantly of all, the film caused outrage for its stance on ideology. This transcended the historical setting of the story and particularly offended left-wing intellectuals. For intellectuals in France, life was about making a choice. This was especially true during the occupation when they spoke of their *engagement*. With the exception of *Tribune Socialiste*, left-wing dailies, periodicals and specialised journals such as *Les Cahiers du Cinéma* reproached the film and its authors. What the film was clearly guilty of was suggesting that political allegiance could be ruled by chance; that ideology may have little to do with choosing one side; that political commitment could in fact lack all commitment.

Charlie Hebdo chastised Louis Malle as 'a reactionary' and his work as 'extreme right-wing cinema'.[48] *Libération* refuted the idea that a difference existed between choosing collaboration and being a collaborator. It rejected the distinction between the naive Lucien and the sweaty torturers, drunken sadists, greedy cowards and self-promoting fanatics who populate Malle's house of horrors.[49] *Libération*'s critic, Gerard Lefort, saw in this the infuriating residue of a bourgeois vision of the peasant, unaware of ideology, devoid of ideas or judgment, and therefore innocent: 'scratch the fascist and you will find the man. Exasperation of that idiotic philosophy [*philosophie à la con*]!'[50]

This view could not have been further from that of Jacques Bertin and *Tribune Socialiste*, who specifically hailed the film as 'true to its working-class soul'.[51] For *Tribune Socialiste*, political struggle is not about fighting amoral individuals but an amoral system. Bertin's article seems more interested in polemicising with the critics of *Libération* and *Charlie Hebdo*, whom he clearly saw as armchair activists and bourgeois intellectuals, than in analysing the film. A similar interpretation was also given by Michel Flacon, who condemned 'the vestals of political cinema' who are not willing to accept that ideological commitment can be ruled by chance.[52]

RETRO-STYLE STEREOTYPES: MALLE, CAVANI AND *LES CAHIERS DU CINÉMA*

If left-wing critics were 'vestals of political cinema', then *Les Cahiers du Cinéma* was their temple.[53] The critics of *Les Cahiers du Cinéma* understood, in full, the importance of *Lacombe, Lucien* and devoted a special issue to their dislike for it.[54] The journal was also the first to attempt a detailed comparison of *Lacombe, Lucien* and *The Night Porter*. The Marxist critique of *Les Cahiers du Cinéma* paired these two works as part of a concerted bourgeois effort to rewrite history, using ambiguity in its various forms to blur moral and political boundaries between right and wrong. In the critics' view, alongside the films by Malle and Cavani stood other works of the early 1970s, such as Jean Yanne's occupation parody *Les Chinois à Paris* (*Chinese in Paris*, 1974).

Serge Daney, in particular, saw 1974 as a key year in the bourgeois attack on history and memory. According to *Les Cahiers du Cinéma*, retro-style became the artistic arm of a new cynical ideology, identified with recently-elected President Giscard d'Estaing, aimed at changing traditional representations of Nazi-occupied France, in particular negating the existence of a widespread popular anti-fascist struggle.[55] Bonitzer and Toubiana specifically defined retro-style as 'the snobbish fetishism of period effects (costumes and settings) with little concern for history'.[56] The usefulness of this definition is limited to its applicability to a thematic rather than national trend, which allowed the critics to include *The Night Porter* in their discourse.

Otherwise, Cavani's film fits uneasily in their interpretation of retro-style as a post-Gaullist attempt to replace 'the old lie' with a new one, opposite yet equivalent to it. Interviewed by *Les Cahiers du Cinéma*, the renowned French philosopher and historian Michel Foucault suggested that while after the war de Gaulle played down the idea of a popular struggle by emphasising the heroes of conventional war, in the post-de Gaulle era the middle classes attempted to perpetuate the same lie by suggesting there were no heroes, and consequently no struggle.[57] Whereas before 1968, people were taught to consider action impossible because 'it only happened elsewhere', in post-1968, post-de Gaulle, post-*Sorrow and the Pity* France they were taught that popular action would not happen because it had never happened.

The problem with these critiques of retro-style texts advanced by *Les Cahiers du Cinéma* is that their critics' undoubted ability to read films and identify trends was blunted by the rigidity of their Marxist analysis of both society and art. The twin assumptions that the working class was a homogeneous social group and that this group was progressive, clouded their judgment. These conjectures led most left-wing critics to believe that a film like *Lacombe, Lucien,* shot by a bourgeois film-maker and portraying a young member of the working class as a collaborationist, could not but be a right-wing ploy to discredit the class as a whole.

The arguments advanced by Foucault and his two interviewers, in particular, are more expressly political, referring to both the May elections and the French far left's self-destructing behaviour, and thus apply less to Cavani's film than to Malle's. On the other hand, another critic writing for *Les Cahiers du Cinéma,* Serge Daney, drew a much more effective if still flawed parallel between the content and style of these two films. In a series of articles exploring the role and responsibility of film critics, Daney used them as examples of the resurgence of a right-wing cinema disguised as auteur film.

> In 1974, bourgeois filmmakers (Malle, Cavani etc.) prefer to 'decode' the past, no longer even trying to prove anything at all. Fascinated by the inexplicable, they explain virtually nothing, being content [...] to be 'daring' and show what was still hidden only yesterday (sex and politics and what passes for their privileged meeting point, fascism). [58]

According to Daney, these films employed auteur-film techniques, such as never making their discourse explicit, so that the spectator would not notice 'the poverty and banality (sometimes the sheer stupidity: Cavani) of the lesson'.[59] The critic noticed a cinematic tendency to force the audience to make an implicit choice between two evils: in *Lacombe, Lucien,* this manifested itself in the opposition between naive Lucien and his heinous fellow collaborators; in *The Night Porter,* in that between the increasingly powerless Max and the other former members of the SS, consistently obsessed by power.[60] In Daney's mind, this was a dangerous and misleading trend, ultimately aimed at a reassessment of fascism as an ideology and a historical phenomenon. This is where once again *Les Cahiers du Cinéma*'s analysis failed: while the journal successfully isolated and articulated characteristic themes of retro-style films, its reaction to them –

the bourgeois film critic accusing a bourgeois film-maker of misleading and misrepresenting a class to which neither belonged and which neither understood – became itself a retro-style stereotype.

BETWEEN MORALITY AND MORALISM: *THE NIGHT PORTER* AND THE POPULAR PRESS

If the writers in *Les Cahiers du Cinéma* were successful indiscussing retro-style as a phenomenon, they were unable to distinguish between the individual films. Thus they failed to point out that, while Malle and Cavani share an interest in the relation between victim and persecutor, *Lacombe, Lucien* suggests that the crossing over can be accidental or unconscious, whereas *The Night Porter* implies that each individual is by nature both. Similarly, whereas neither film focuses on the socio-economic interpretation of the rise of Nazism and fascism, Malle, unlike Cavani, does not suggest that Nazism was first and foremost the somatic symptom of a psychoanalytic dysfunction:

> 'We think Nazism is dead. Not at all. It survives still in each of us. That collective sexual phenomenon was nothing but the rise of the sadomasochistic relationship existing within each couple. Hitler was merely a detonator.'[61]

These differences were not considered by French reviewers. Whether they interpreted the films as demystifying or revisionist, they continued to consider them almost as one. The critical association of the two films was facilitated also by the proximity of the two films' dates of release: *Lacombe, Lucien* on 30 January; *The Night Porter* on 3 April 1974. For example, *L'Express* credited Cavani and the film-makers of her generations, including Malle and Drach, with 'having put an end to the John Wayne perspective on the period 1940–1945'.[62] At the opposite end of the spectrum is the opinion of Pascal Bonitzer, who had interviewed Foucault for *Les Cahiers du Cinéma*, who levels the accusation that 'these films that speak of sex and Nazism, do not speak of racism, or deny racism'.[63] His rather unconvincing argument is that, though they refuse racial stereotypes, both films effectively maintain them by reversing them; that is by having Jewesses seduced by Nazis rather than Aryan women led astray by Jews.

Bonitzer's argument rests partly on his assumption that Lucia in *The Night Porter* is a Jewess, whereas her identity in this respect is left deliberately confused. It is interesting, however, that this was the only reference any reviewer made to the issue of the deportations in both films. With regard to *Lacombe, Lucien*, reviewers clearly took the condition of the Jewish family as obvious, completely neglecting the individual characteristics of each of the three Jewish characters. With regard to *The Night Porter*, they did not question the ambiguity of Lucia's personal history. Instead, they took this either for granted or as insignificant, so that, just as Bonitzer assumed that Lucia is Jewish, others arbitrarily decided she was the daughter of a socialist deputy.[64]

Nonetheless, Cavani's film caused considerably less controversy than Malle's. There are several explanations for this. First, the obvious fact that *The Night Porter* was not a French film and did not tackle specifically French issues. Second, because of its very extremism, the film's thesis appeared less applicable and more like a theoretical provocation, a form in which some were prepared to entertain it. Finally, the serious censorial problems the film experienced in Italy caused many French critics to rally around it in the name of freedom of expression. And, at the same time, the fact that France was ready to adopt this persecuted work of art was a reason for national pride.

The Night Porter was censored on two distinct occasions: first, on 4 April 1974 the censorship board remonstrated against the film, finally granting it a visa without cuts on 11 April;[65] then, on 14 April, Rome's district attorney confiscated the film which, after several court hearings, was eventually discharged on 27 May, once again in its integral form, and released nationwide on 30 May. French reviewers took pleasure in highlighting Italian obscurantism by quoting extracts of the, frankly atrocious, court order of the first instance of censorship:

> Forbidden because of obscenity, excessive vulgarity, scenes showing sexual intercourse, which are offensive to good conduct. This film, doubly pernicious because realised by a woman, shows an ignoble scene where one sees the female protagonist take the initiative in the sexual relationship.[66]

Le Journal de Dimanche also dedicated a whole article to the censorship, reporting Italian intellectuals' reactions to it.[67] *Le Monde* had two pieces, one on 30 March and one on 19 April, reporting Cavani's protest at the confiscation.

Nevertheless, censorship was not enough to persuade all reviewers to support the film. Unsurprisingly, given its politics, *Libération* lashed out at 'the phallocratic and reactionary censorship' and Italy's 'Latin Puritanism',[68] without this indignation affecting its entirely negative judgment of the film. Colette Godard questioned 'the theatre of dictatorship, death and disguise', which forgets that 'beauty is not always innocent' and the dangers of suggesting otherwise;[69] Martin Even placed Cavani within the context of a cinema which, he suggested, 'has discovered politics as a romantic theme rather than an ideological practice', forgetting history to seek extreme cases and 'psychological climaxes'.[70] Hélène Cixous, in *Combat*, contested what she saw as the film's 'ideological confusion' and 'disturbing lack of intellectual elaboration'.[71] Cixous's understandable problem, which sums up that of the left as a whole, was in accepting Cavani's separation of Nazism from its ideological, socio-economic and historical context.

The Italian left rejected the film for the same reasons. *L'Unità* accused Cavani of forgetting the economic and social forces behind Nazism, and that history's ambiguity is 'dialectic, not metaphysical'.[72] From a different political perspective, *Il Popolo* shared its communist counterpart's dislike for the film more on technical grounds, it seems, than on ideological or moral ones. The only positive review of *The Night Porter* came from the centrist Roman daily, *Il Messaggero*, which praised the film and specifically its ending, for its morality. According to the reviewer, Lucia and Max redeemed themselves by 'offering themselves in Holocaust'.[73] A year later, speaking of Wertmuller's *Seven Beauties*, another reviewer would criticise the film's main character on the grounds that 'a real man should have offered himself in Holocaust',[74] confirming the introduction of a significant term and, simultaneously, its equally significant misrepresentation. What guilt needs to be atoned for as ever remains unclear.

The persistence of Italy's ignorance of the Shoah, and its considerable distance from France with regard to its treatment in art and history, are manifest also in its reception of *The Night Porter*. In fact, the coverage of Cavani's film was altogether less widespread than in France, and the critical interventions very limited. Whereas in France the film's difficulties with censorship affected some reviewers' judgment, in Italy they simply made them forego judgement altogether. After the confiscation of the film on

14 April, not a single review appeared that engaged with the film's discourse, but only tirades against cultural obscurantism.

Nonetheless, Italian censorship patterns are revealed as extremely interesting. Italy, in this period, was at the height of its incredibly successful erotic film production, which produced hundreds of soft-porn digressions in all traditional genres. *The Night Porter* itself, though obviously not pornographic, was billed as an erotic sensation by its own distributors: they employed advertising lines such as 'A triumphal, delirious success in Paris; watching it is an infernal pleasure', and featured Charlotte Rampling topless in SS uniform on the poster.[75] It is sufficient to glance at the entertainment pages of any contemporary newspaper, including the highbrow and the political dailies, to recognise a trend. Titles such as *Africa Nuda, Africa Violenta* (Mario Gervasi, 1974); *Nuda per Satana* (*Naked for Satan*, Luigi Batzella, 1974), a Gothic horror with some nudity and very little Satan; and *La Profanazione* (Tiziano Longo, 1974) – about a novice – graced the screen at the same time as *The Night Porter*. These, and numerous others, were rated '18' but were not banned.

On the same day, however, that Cavani's film was banned, three others were also banned: *Flavia la Monaca Mussulmana* (*Flavia the Heretic*, Gianfranco Mingozzi, 1974), *Simona* (Patrick Longchamps, 1974), and *Appassionata* (Gianluigi Calderone, 1974). All were concerned not only with sex but also with politics, religion and family. Considering this, it is arguable, first, that Cavani was right when she suggested to *Le Monde* that sexual content was considered acceptable when it did not carry even remote political overtones;[76] and second, that the censors were particularly sensitive in the run-up to the referendum on the divorce law of 11 May 1974.

The latter point is fascinating but less simple to prove. It is clear, in fact, that censorship of certain themes took place before and after April 1974: in May 1974, Bernardo Bertolucci's *Last Tango in Paris* was still awaiting a judicial review after being banned in June 1973, and in June 1974, censorship stopped the release of *La Sensualità è un Attimo di Vita* (Dante Marraccini, 1974), where a naked boy advanced on the audience shouting, 'Family does not exist!'[77] Still, it is not unreasonable to suggest that particular attention may have been paid to themes such as the family in the run-up to the referendum, in a way similar to any other election coverage.

Whatever the intentions of the censorship board, its actions were interpreted as political. On 18 April, *Il Messaggero* carried the news of the film's requisition, claiming that 'Italy is becoming a country in which it is impossible to live, [where] the keyword is to prevent contemporary secular culture from exorcising our thought from atavistic guilt complexes.'[78] The critic concluded by inviting readers to vote against the abrogation of the law on divorce. The same newspaper continued to make a similar point throughout May, while *L'Unità* on 28 May reported the imminent re-release of *The Night Porter,* attacking Christian Democratic censorship albeit without the high moral tones of *Il Messaggero*.[79] No further comment was made on the film itself.

AT A CROSSROAD

The reception of *The Night Porter* and *The Garden* reinforces the feeling that, in the 1970s, Italian critics were unable to analyse Holocaust films in a constructive manner. Sterilised by political opposition and a falsely critical approach to cinema and history, Italian film critics came to mistake rhetoric for insight. Their French counterparts, on the other hand, while equally rhetorical in their language, took a much more analytical approach. Moreover, in the 1970s, this critical ability seems to have moved out of the closed circles of *Les Cahiers du Cinéma* and into mainstream public opinion. A significant quantitative difference emerged: French newspapers dedicated review after review to certain films, often from different perspectives, inviting external contributions, while Italian ones tended to rely on a resident film critic to review offerings.

This is a testament to the development of a different cultural climate and a different place occupied by cinema as an art form within this cultural framework. It also points to the final qualitative decline of the Italian film industry, orphan of neo-realism and hostage to hundreds of commercially successful B-movies. Finally, it signals the immobile nature of Italian popular understanding of history. Italian public opinion remained locked into an ideological struggle between the Christian Democrats and the communists. This conflict, despite gradually losing significance, maintained all its trappings and rhetoric. The Second World War, in all its facets, continued to be interpreted within the context of that struggle. In particular, either ignorance of the

Holocaust as the attempted genocide of European Jewry, or unwillingness to discuss it in those terms persisted.

In contrast, in France a change in perception is evident. Here, the historical circumstances following 1968 and the death of de Gaulle contributed to a radical change in perspective on the war. The release of *The Sorrow and the Pity* launched a reconsideration of the country's past which, by the mid-1970s, had become manifest not just in historiography but also in popular culture. Furthermore, with the re-appraisal of the Vichy regime and collaboration, came also the discovery of the persecution of French Jews and foreign Jews resident in France. Films such as *Lacombe, Lucien* and Michel Drach's *Les Violons du Bal* differed from earlier French fiction film production not just in their representation of the French population, but in the fact that they did not shy away from representing home-grown racial persecution.

In Italy, *The Garden* could have suggested a similar shift, made even more significant by the fact that the film's narrative perspective is a Jewish one. Of all the aspects discussed by the film, however, class relations and romance decidedly outplay that of Jewish identity, if not in the text, then certainly in the interpretation given to it by its contemporaries, including its author. Thus, De Sica's film remained an isolated if remarkable effort. In France, as in Italy, the persecution of the Jews, which had just begun to enter public consciousness after a quarter of a century of neglect, was immediately surpassed by other concerns. Among these, the fascination with suddenly-blurred boundaries between good and evil were particularly fashionable. Applied to the Second World War, these ideas raised questions about the behaviour of victims, persecutors, collaborators and bystanders. Both *Lacombe, Lucien* and *The Night Porter* inscribe themselves within this trend, though with different results. The film-makers' fascination for psychoanalytic explanations of fascism, including sexuality, was not at all new, of course. Rossellini's *Rome, Open City* had explored this as early as 1945. However, what in Rossellini and others had been a fairly straightforward link between sexual deviancy – in particular homosexuality – and personal immorality, in the 1970s evolved into the suggestion that personal issues of identity affect political stance: specifically, the idea that individuals will seek conformity by joining powerful and repressive groups was very popular in the 1970s.

Thus, if on the one hand, French and Italian attitudes

towards the Shoah diverged considerably in the 1970s, on the other hand, the two countries' filmic production, result of much financial as well as cultural cooperation, remained much closer. The French began to manifest a far clearer understanding of the Shoah to that displayed by Italians. Nonetheless, a historically informed discussion of the Shoah did not really materialise. In particular, both countries continued to be unaware of the need to recuperate the voice of the victims: not just of the survivors, but also of the dead. This next step would take ten years and one film – and take one film ten years – and would further aggravate the contrast between France and Italy.

NOTES

1. On all these films see Annette Insdorf, *Indelible Shadows: Film and the Holocaust*, third edition (Cambridge: Cambridge University Press, 2003) and Ilan Avisar, *Screening the Holocaust: Cinema's Images of the Unimaginable* (Bloomington, IN: Indiana University Press, 1988). On Visconti's two films see also Henry Bacon, *Visconti: Explorations of Beauty and Decay* (Cambridge: Cambridge University Press, 1998).
2. For a filmic analysis of *Lacombe, Lucien* see, among others: Charles F. Altman, '*Lacombe, Lucien*: Laughter as Collaboration', *French Review*, 49, 4 (1976), pp.549–58; Naomi Greene, *Landscapes of Loss: The National Past in Post-War French Cinema* (Princeton, NJ: Princeton University Press, 1999), particularly Chapter 3, 'Vichy Revisited'; Harry Roderick Kedward, 'The Anti-Carnival of Collaboration: Louis Malle's *Lacombe, Lucien* (1974)', in Susan Hayward and Ginette Vincendeau (eds), *French Film: Texts and Contexts* (London: Routledge, 2000). For historical contributions on the film see: Richar Golsan, *Vichy's Afterlife: History and Counter-History in Postwar France* (Lincoln, NE: University of Nebraska Press, 2000), pp.57–72; Paul Jankowski, 'In Defence of Fiction', *Journal of Modern History*, 63, 3 (September 1991), pp.457–82; and Henri Rousso, *The Vichy Syndrome: History and Memory in France Since 1944* (Cambridge, MA: Harvard University Press, 1991), pp.230–7. For works on Modiano and the collaboration in literature see Colin W. Nettlebeck and Penelope Hueston, 'D'un Clown Collabo à une France Juive: *Lacombe, Lucien*', in *Patrick Modiano – Pièces d'Identité: Écrire l'Entretemps* (Paris: Lettres Modernes, 1986), pp.53–64.
3. Elie Wiesel, foreword to Insdorf, *Indelible Shadows*, second edition, p.xii.
4. 'Vittorio De Sica: L'Artiste et l'Argent', interview by Véra Volmane, *La Croix*, 10 January 1971.
5. Insdorf, *Indelible Shadows*, second edition, p.120.
6. Volmane, 'L'Artiste et l'Argent'.
7. Giorgio Bassani, *Il Giardino dei Finzi-Contini* (Torino: Einaudi, 1962), p.22. Quoted by Insdorf, *Indelible Shadows*, second edition, p.120.
8. For Levi see Myriam Anissimov, *Primo Levi: Tragedy of an Optimist* (London: Aurum Press, 1998), especially Part I. For Ginzburg, see her own memoirs, Natalia Ginzburg, *Family Sayings* (Manchester: Carcanet, 1984), and Claudia Nocentini, 'Racial Laws and Internment in Natalia Ginzburg's *La Strada Che Va in Città* and *Tutti i Nostri Ieri*', in Thomas DiNapoli (ed.), *The Italian Jewish Experience* (Stony Brook, NY: Forum Italicum Publishing, 2000).
9. Insdorf, *Indelible Shadows*, p.120.
10. Volmane, 'L'Artiste et l'Argent'.
11. The source for the box office figures is Roberto Poppi and Mario Pecoraro (eds), *Dizionario del Cinema Italiano*, vol. 4 (Rome: Gremese, 1996). In addition, many reviewers and newspaper adverts of the time explicitly referred to the film's financial success.

12. Aggeo Savioli (Ag. Sa.), *L'Unità*, 23 December 1970.
13. Paolo Valmarana, *Il Popolo*, 23 December 1970.
14. G.M., *La Stampa*, 5 December 1973.
15. *Il Corriere della Sera*, 5 December 1970.
16. Bir., *Il Messaggero*, 23 December 1970.
17. Giovanni Grazzini, *Il Corriere della Sera*, 5 December 1970.
18. See, among others, Valmarana, *Il Popolo*, 23 December 1970 and Françoise Wagener, *Le Monde*, 9 December 1971.
19. Especially successful were the Hercules and Maciste subgroupings, including increasingly far-fetched titles such as *Ulysses versus Hercules* (1962), *Zorro versus Maciste* (1964), *Maciste in Genghis Khan's Hell* (1965) and many others.
20. On the transition from the original story to the film, through several versions of the screenplay, see Colin Partridge, *Senso: Visconti's Film and Boito's Novella: A Case Study in the Relation between Literature and Film* (Lewiston, ME: E. Mellen Press, 1992) and Clotilde Bertoni, 'Dalla Pagina allo Schermo: Il Senso Sospeso di un Racconto', in Camillo Boito, *Senso* (Lecce: Piero Manni, 2002), pp.5–18 and 63–144.
21. Bir., *Il Messaggero*, 23 December 1970.
22. Ibid.
23. François Maurin, 'Le Retour de De Sica', *L'Humanité*, 11 December 1971.
24. Jean Rochereau, *La Croix*, 23 December 1971.
25. Wagener, *Le Monde*, 9 December 1971.
26. Rochereau, *La Croix*, 23 December 1971.
27. Pierre Viansson-Ponté in *Le Monde*, 18 February 1974.
28.. David Wilson (ed.), *Les Cahiers du Cinéma – Vol. 4: 1973–1978: History, Ideology, Cultural Struggle* (London: Routledge, 2000), p.58.
29. Patrick Modiano, interviewed in *Politique Hebdo*, 7 February 1974.
30. Insdorf, *Indelible Shadows*, p.126.
31. Alan Morris, *Collaboration and Resistance Revisited: Writers and the 'Mode Rétro' in Post-Gaullist France* (New York: Berg, 1992).
32. *Le Point*, 28 January 1974.
33. Delfeil de Ton, *Charlie Hebdo*, cited in *Le Monde*, 14 February 1974.
34. Ibid.
35. Viansson-Ponté, *Le Monde*, 18 February 1974.
36. Ibid.
37. Mona Ouzouf, *Le Nouvel Observateur*, 25 March 1974.
38. Ibid.
39. Ibid.
40. Janvier, 'Les Ficelles de Louis Malle', *Libération*, 28 February 1974.
41. *Quinzaine Littéraire*, 2 February 1974.
42. *Politique Hebdo*, 7 February 1974.
43. Jean-Louis Bory, *Le Nouvel Observateur*, 28 January 1974.
44. Jean de Baroncelli, *Le Monde*, 31 January 1974.
45. Louis Malle interviewed by former Resistance leader René Andrieu, *L'Humanité-Dimanche*, 3 April 1974.
46. Modiano, interviewed in *Politique Hebdo*, 7 February 1974.
47. Philip French (ed.), *Malle on Malle* (London: Faber & Faber, 1993), chapter 3, 'Scenes from Provincial Life', pp.81–116.
48. Delfeil de Ton, *Charlie Hebdo*, cited in *Le Monde*, 14 February 1974.
49. Gerard Lefort, *Libération*, 28 February 1974.
50. Ibid.
51. Jacques Bertin, *Tribune Socialiste*, 20 February 1974.
52. Michel Flacon, *Le Point*, 11 March 1974.
53. Nick Browne (ed.), *Les Cahiers du Cinéma 1969–1972: The Politics of Representation* (Cambridge, MA: Harvard University Press, 1990).
54. *Les Cahiers du Cinéma*, special issue on *Lacombe, Lucien*, 251 (July–August 1974).
55. Pascal Bonitzer and Serge Toubiana, 'Anti-Rétro: Entretien avec Michel Foucault', *Les Cahiers du Cinéma*, 251, (July–August 1974), cited in Wilson (ed.), *Les Cahiers du Cinéma – Vol. 4*, p.159.
56. Ibid.

57. Ibid.
58. Serge Daney, 'La Fonction Critique', *Les Cahiers du Cinéma*, 250 (May 1974), cited in Wilson (ed.), *Les Cahiers du Cinéma – Vol. 4*, p.59.
59. Ibid.
60. Daney, 'La Fonction Critique', cited in Wilson (ed.), *Les Cahiers du Cinéma – Vol. 4*, pp.63–4.
61. Liliana Cavani, cited in *L'Express*, 1 March 1974.
62. *L'Express*, 1 March 1974.
63. Pascal Bonitzer, *Libération*, 18 April 1974.
64. Claude-Marie Tremois, *Télérama*, 6 April 1974; Aggeo Savioli, *L'Unità*, 11 April 1974.
65. *The Night Porter*, censorship visa number 64254 of 4 April 1974; source: online archive of ANICA (National Association of Audiovisual and Cinematographic Industries), www.anica.it.
66. *Le Nouvel Observateur*, 8 April 1974
67. *Le Journal de Dimanche*, 31 March 1974.
68. Bonitzer, *Libération*, 18 April 1974.
69. Colette Godard, 'Le theatre de la dictature, de la mort et du travesty', *Le Monde*, 18 April 1974.
70. Martin Even, 'Les créateurs font marche arrière', *Le Monde*, 18 April 1974.
71. Hélène Cixous, 'Est-ce que le Nazisme c'était ça?', *Combat*, 11 April 1974.
72. Aggeo Savioli, 'Il nazismo intimista', *L'Unitá*, 11 April 1974.
73. Bir., *Il Messaggero*, 14 April 1974.
74. Giovanni Grazzini, *Il Corriere della Sera*, 20 December 1975.
75. *Il Messaggero*, 11 April 1974.
76. J.N., '*Portier de Nuit* saisi à Rome', *Le Monde*, 19 April 1974.
77. The film was eventually released on 18 March 1975, censorship visa number 64326. Source: online archive of ANICA (National Association of Audiovisual and Cinematographic Industries), www.anica.it.
78. Bir., *Il Messaggero*, 18 April 1974.
79. *L'Unità*, 28 May 1974.

6

From Recognition to Representation: Claude Lanzmann's *Shoah*

Ten years of work, 350 hours of interviews resulting in 563 minutes of the most demanding, shocking and rewarding analysis. These are the numbers of *Shoah* but this is not *Shoah*. The documentary Claude Lanzmann began making in 1974, which was finally released in French cinemas in 1985, has attracted much attention and praise, yet it has also defied critical scrutiny. Not because of its size, certainly intimidating, but because of its subject matter and the uncompromising and relentless way in which it tackles it. Much has been written about *Shoah* that has been both thoughtful and thorough, yet arguably its essence still eludes explanation. We can apply the techniques of the historian or the film scholar to it, explain each scene or interpret the contributions of interviewer and interviewee, but somehow the work as a whole seems to result in more than the sum of its parts. Evidently, it is necessary to look at *Shoah* in the same way as it looks at the Shoah: distinguishing the film from its author, but also putting aside rhetoric, metaphor and powerful but inaccurate images as it (almost always) refuses symbolism, archival footage and reconstruction. In taking this approach, this chapter will seek to go back to the film itself – to its structure, images, words and silences – to analyse it from a historical perspective while also discussing at length its reception in France and Italy, which has hitherto been overlooked by academic scholarship.

After *Night and Fog* and *The Sorrow and the Pity*, *Shoah* is the third French Holocaust documentary to be analysed in this book. Placed strategically across the period of this study, they form its backbone and illustrate both the change in the understanding of

Figure 6.1. *Shoah*: 'Resnais's tracking shot of the Auschwitz ramp, his intuition in seeking the signs of the past in the present, is clearly echoed by Lanzmann.' Lanzmann's shot, however, assumes a new, first-person perspective. (© Claude Lanzmann.)

the Shoah over three decades and the gradual development of a dichotomy between Italy and France. And while they are quite different from each other, they share a distinct interest in the idea of memory. Resnais's tracking shot of the Auschwitz ramp, his intuition in seeking the signs of the past in the present, is clearly echoed in Lanzmann's endless shots of the eerie fields and forests of modern-day Chelmno, Sobibor and Treblinka (Figure 6.1). And Lanzmann's attention to testimony and use of editing as corroboration or rebuttal are reminiscent of Ophuls's revolutionary interviewing style.

For its own merits, and for the influence it has had on other texts, *Shoah* has become the paradigm of modern documentary representation of the genocide. A film such as Louis Malle's *Au Revoir, les Enfants* (*Goodbye, Children,* 1987), which represented more effectively the arrival of the Shoah in public consciousness through cinema, could not have existed or obtained the same success without Lanzmann's film. Its scope, subject matter, methodology and style are unique. While mostly highbrow, the enthusiastic reception of *Shoah* provides an interesting window on French cultural values and readiness to address the past at the time of its release, particularly if compared to the less kind treatment of *Night and Fog* or *The Sorrow and Pity*. The fact that it was distributed at all, being not only a documentary but a remarkably lengthy one, is in itself significant. Its box office figures, in turn, may have been low in absolute terms but nonetheless were unexpectedly high for a film of its kind.

Shoah was the first film to adopt the Hebrew word for the Nazi genocide of Europe's Jewry, which carries a notably different meaning from the term 'Holocaust'. The word 'Shoah' loses all connotations of ritual sacrifice and simply signifies 'destruction'. And the destruction of European, and particularly Eastern European Judaism, is exactly what the film addresses, with meticulous attention to detail. Identifying it as a specifically Jewish tragedy, Lanzmann's perspective is diametrically opposed to that of Alain Resnais, who identified the genocide as a conflict of opposing ideologies and moralities belonging to and affecting all humanity. In the mid-1980s, *Shoah* marked the arrival point of the journey towards the recognition of the Shoah as the unprecedented, orchestrated Nazi attempt to annihilate all Europe's Jews by modern industrial means. At the same time, it signalled the definitive Jewish reappropriation of their own memory and history, the right to tell it and demand acknowledgment and, where possible, reparation.

With a detailed analysis of the film, this chapter will show exactly why, thematically and aesthetically, *Shoah* was revolutionary. This analysis will argue that, by avoiding all references to France, Lanzmann wrenched the anti-Jewish persecution from the context of wartime collaboration, in which it had been considered ever since *The Sorrow and the Pity*. Thus, while *Shoah* did not match the revelatory effect of Ophuls's film, it greatly influenced French perceptions of the Shoah by shifting the debate around the destruction, detailing the reality behind by then familiar names and concepts. Furthermore, the chapter will assess the film's reception, comparing it with the Italian reception of *Shoah*'s television showing. The French response to the film was superficial and overawed, and reveals an uneasiness in dealing with the Jewish genocide; critics preferred to focus on issues such as Polish anti-Semitism or the Barbie trial.

SHOAH

The nine-and-a-half hours of *Shoah* are divided into two eras, each in turn composed of two parts. Rather than restricting himself, however, to a chronological discussion, Lanzmann chose a structure of concentric circles, which Rachel Ertel has described as 'a vertiginous downward spiral [in which] the camera becomes a drilling instrument'.[1] Instead of attempting to discuss the process of persecution, deportation and execution of the Jews, as for example Resnais had done in *Night and Fog*, Lanzmann isolated the latter, making it the hub around which the film is built and to which it cyclically returns. Even more specifically, the director identified not just murder, but the industrial, systematic nature of the Nazi genocide as the mainstay of his work.

His film only very occasionally concerns itself with the 'conditions of living' of the persecuted Jews; instead it concentrates on the 'conditions of dying'. The life of the Jews, alongside their Christian neighbours before the war, for example, or in the ghettos and camps during it, is never the central topic of any interview but always discussed in passing, en route to the focal point of the film: their annihilation. Thus while Poland and Polish anti-Semitism may at times seem to be the central theme of the film, they are not. The film is concerned with Poland because Poland is where the killing took place. Similarly, almost all of the survivors interviewed are East European Jews because they were more often involved in the killing mechanism than West European ones.

The film opens in modern-day Chelmno, where gas vans were first employed, and the first part of the first era deals mostly with the lagers of 'Operation Reinhardt': Belzec, Sobibor and Treblinka.[2] Here, Lanzmann traces the initial Nazi experiments with murder by carbon dioxide poisoning, either in vans or in the first gas chambers. This initial part introduces the concept and method of extermination. It also establishes one of the recurring themes of the film: the difficulty of reading the signs left by the camps, where the Nazis and time have conspired to erase them. It was necessary for Lanzmann to establish that Jews had been present in the Polish countryside, that they had been taken from there, and that they had been gassed in the now peaceful-looking fields and forests of Chelmno, Sobibor and Treblinka. To do this, Lanzmann makes widespread use of witnesses: the few remaining Jewish survivors, and also German guards and Polish residents of the nearby villages.

Their testimonies are superimposed so as to corroborate each other, establishing not only that the massacres had taken place,

Figure 6.2. *Shoah*: 'Henrik Gawkowski can still drive the engine of a steam train, as he did when he took their human cargo to Treblinka.' (© Claude Lanzmann.)

but also that the Polish population had been fully aware of the fact, and that anti-Semitism among the locals had been rife. Poles remember the Jewish communities in their towns, such as Oswieçim, sadly more famous under its Germanised name, which before the war had been 80 per cent Jewish. Chelmno peasants remember Simon Srebnik who, as a teenager, had walked around the town in chains as part of the Jewish work detail of the camp. Treblinka peasants remember working their fields alongside the perimeter of the lager, smelling the stench of burnt flesh, or warning the incoming Jews with signs of slitting their throats. So, too, did Henrik Gawkowski, who can still drive a steam engine, as he did when he took the trains with their human cargo to Treblinka (Figure 6.2).

By the end of 1943, both Treblinka and Sobibor had been razed to the ground after revolts.[3] In 1942, the Nazis had decided to use the specifically-developed Zyklon B poison gas instead of carbon monoxide, which nonetheless continued to be used in Chelmno until 1945.[4] To maximise its deadly potential, they built new, larger and 'more efficient' gas chambers in the Auschwitz Birkenau lager.

The first part of the film is closed by Franz Suchomel, the first SS witness interviewed by Claude Lanzmann. Filmed secretly, he is the missing link, with Jewish and Polish witnesses forming the third element of the film's concentric structure. With deserved delight and a touch of arrogance, Lanzmann flaunts the fact that he filmed this interview without the German's permission: it is his revenge. Formerly a guard at Treblinka, Suchomel is able to explain as no one else can the functioning and capabilities of the gas chamber there. For example, he can point out the shocking fact that, in Treblinka, the gas chambers were the only permanent structure. Suchomel allows Lanzmann to move his investigation further along the production line of death, and although there are a few German witnesses in the film, his naturalness renders him free from inhibition.

The second part of the first era perseveres in oscillating between the outside and inside of the camps, now edging a little further into them, now stepping back outside to focus on the Polish population's memory of a past with Jews and life in a present without them. It is not until the second era that Lanzmann crosses the boundary of the gas chambers themselves, attempting to recover the perspective of those who died there through the testimonies of those few people who saw them and survived: Abraham Bomba, who was a barber in the antechamber of the Treblinka gas chamber, and Filip Müller, who belonged to five different Sonderkommandos. The former saw the victims enter the chamber; the latter witnessed its effects. All that is left unsaid, as decency and necessity demand, is the suffering within it.

The final section takes a step back. It focuses on the attempts to alert the world to the catastrophe, though it stops short of directly indicting the Allies for their passivity. Lanzmann encounters Rudolf Vrba, who escaped successfully from Auschwitz on 7 April 1944, and Jan Karski, an emissary of the Polish government-in-exile who secretly visited the Warsaw Ghetto. The ghetto uprising, the details of which are left out of the film, leads Lanzmann to end his film in Israel, at the Ghetto Fighters Kibbutz, with two of the leaders of the uprising, Yitzhak Zuckerman and Simha Rottem. Here, survival, the renewal of life, armed resistance and the Jewish state could combine to achieve a miraculously uplifting, stirring finale. Yet Lanzmann refuses it: there is no happiness in Rottem and Zuckerman, no triumph in a survival haunted by death.

'AND I WILL GIVE THEM AN EVERLASTING NAME'[5]

Around the same time as Shoah was first distributed, Primo Levi wrote in *The Drowned and the Saved* about survivors such as himself: 'We are those who by prevarication or ability or good fortune, did not reach the bottom. Those who did [...] have not returned or have returned voiceless.'[6] Lanzmann is interested in those who did not return; those who are often commemorated, but seldom understood; those of whose very existence we have no record; those who are left with no grave, no history and no name.

If, as Lanzmann contested, the Nazis' greatest crime was not simply to have killed the Jews, but to have erased the evidence of their passing, then to avenge them he would recapture their memory. The biblical epigraph of *Shoah* immediately establishes Lanzmann's mission. The author himself explained this often in interviews, declaring his intention to be 'to resuscitate these people, the Jews, and then kill them once more, with me; accompanying them'.[7] This task presented challenges on two levels: the historiographical one and also, perhaps especially, the representational one. The two are indeed inextricably linked, for the obstinacy demanded by the pursuit of accuracy did not allow Lanzmann much leeway in terms of what he would choose to do with the images.

There exists only one two-minute, mute film of Nazi Einsatzgruppen murdering Jews by shooting in Latvia, made by Germany naval officer Reinhard Wiener in 1941.[8] There are also four still images, taken secretly by unknown members of the Sonderkommando in August 1944, of dead bodies being burned in open pits and naked women being herded towards the gas chamber of Crematorium V in Auschwitz.[9] The shortage of visual evidence posed two problems: first, it raised the question of how to convey, while filming on site, what those places had witnessed; second, it immediately precluded the conventional mixture of archival footage and interviews.

The crucial part of Lanzmann's solution rested on the selection of the contributors: it was not enough for them to have experienced the concentration camps; they had to have witnessed first-hand the process of industrial annihilation, to be able to testify also on behalf of those who were gassed immediately after arrival and of whom we have no record. Yet very few such witnesses existed.

Of the Chelmno Sonderkommando, there are but two survivors, both left for dead when the camp was finally abandoned in January 1945. Simon Srebnik was a teenager when he was shot in the head by the retreating Germans. Lanzmann found him in Israel and brought him back to Poland:

> It's hard to recognise, but it was here. They burned people here. A lot of people were burned here. Yes, this is the place. […] It was always this peaceful here. Always. When they burned two thousand people – Jews – everyday, it was just as peaceful. No one shouted. Everyone went about his work. It was silent. Peaceful. Just as it is now.[10]

With these words, the first witness opens *Shoah* by standing on the very fields where he had unloaded the gas vans' deadly cargo: eighty people in each van, all day long, between 7 December 1941 and Spring 1944, and then again between June 1944 and January 1945: 400,000 people overall.[11] There he dreamt that, should he survive, he would find himself alone, the last man on earth. Srebnik's testimony is of special significance because of how candidly he remembers death as routine. Locked in the Łodz Ghetto as little more than a boy, he recalls thinking death was normality. His words, spoken in Yiddish, almost symbolise the challenges faced by the film-maker and the historian. Just as we need a translator to understand Srebnik's language, we need the survivor to translate the secrets of the deceptively peaceful landscape. The relationship between survivor, language, land and film-maker is absolutely central to *Shoah*.[12]

Whenever possible, as in Simon Srebnik's case, Lanzmann persuaded the survivors to visit the sites with him. When he could not convince them to do so, he attempted to stage his interview in as suggestive a setting as possible, to stimulate not just recollections but emotions. For example Yitzhak Dugin and Motke Zaïdl, survivors of the Vilna Ghetto, are interviewed in an Israeli forest that resembles the Latvian Ponari forest, where Vilna Jews were massacred. Significantly, Lanzmann does not pretend the two are the same; he admits his artifice and thus simultaneously manages to avoid misleading the audience and to make the witnesses engage with the place. Dugin and Zaïdl, who recognised their families when forced to unearth and burn the Jews buried in Ponari, are rare living witnesses not just of the

Nazis' murderous crimes, but also crucially of their attempt to erase any trace of them.

Lanzmann had to overcome the reluctance of some survivors to recount their experiences. Zaïdl's daughter relates how Lanzmann's visit had been the first time she heard her father tell his story. Podchlebnik, the other survivor of Chelmno, also resisted talking. Understandably, they both wished to live and forget. Podchlebnik says it quite candidly, though it is immediately obvious he has forgotten nothing. There is more than a small element of violence in Lanzmann's insistent, forceful, provocative prodding. His approach is violent not just towards the witness but the audience as well, which would surely like to rebel against his intransigence.

This is most evident when he interviews Abraham Bomba. Bomba is not unwilling to talk. On the contrary, he is eager to do so and seems understandably aware of the need for objectivity. At times, he seems almost too objective: the monotone, impersonal recollections are effectively equivalent to Podchlebnik's silence. A retired barber, Bomba had been selected to work shaving the condemned. One day, Lanzmann decided to film him in a Tel Aviv barber's shop, where the director asked him to re-enact the procedure followed in Auschwitz. Whereas Bomba had until then been almost mechanical in his recollections, the evocative setting of his interview caused him to break down, bringing back memories which he had otherwise kept for himself.

> Claude Lanzmann: Go on, Abe. You must go on. You have to.
>
> Abraham Bomba: I can't. It's too horrible. Please.
>
> C.L. We have to do it. You know it.
>
> A.B. I won't be able to do it.
>
> C.L. You have to do it. I know it's very hard. I know and I apologize.
>
> A.B. Don't make me go on please.
>
> C.L. Please. We must go on.[13]

The scene of Abraham Bomba's barber's shop interview poses very serious questions about Lanzmann's mission and methods. It is obvious that Lanzmann believes it is not merely his duty to explain the death of millions, but also the duty of the witnesses.

Shoshana Felman has analysed the issue of testimony as central to *Shoah*, even suggesting that this is a film as much about testimony as about the Shoah. She draws on Elie Wiesel's statement that 'if someone else could have written my scripts, I would not have written them', to explain why, however unpleasant and unsettling bearing witness may be, it is essential, in jurisprudence as in historiography as in *Shoah*, that it is her or himself and no one else who relates her or his experience.[14]

Shoah's revolution, then, is in its approach to Holocaust testimony: it questions survivors about their experiences in order to capture, or at least grasp for a moment, the experiences of those who did not survive. Lanzmann does not ask them about their emotions but about their actions and, by doing so, he brings the issue back to a field where semantic conventions still hold. He does not ask Abraham Bomba how it felt to shave the hair of countless doomed innocents. To do so would have been asking something that is impossible for Bomba to convey and for us to understand. Instead, he asks him to show his technique. Thus, *Shoah* overcomes the problem of expression and perception to which Wiesel referred, and makes it possible for the survivors, collectively, to recover and communicate 'the essential', which Levi thought unspeakable and Wiesel feared 'buried in the ash'.[15]

Survivors of the Sonderkommandos are pivotal to Lanzmann's achievement. This is the reason why only one historian appears in the film. Raul Hilberg provides a link between testimonies and expertise whenever it becomes necessary to interpret original historical documents. Still further, it is essential to Lanzmann that witnesses should talk in their own language, and that no short cuts should be used in their interpretation. Lanzmann speaks Hebrew, English, German and Italian, as well as French. Whenever he can, he communicates directly with the witness. When he cannot do so, he allows himself a translator, yet significantly he subtitles only the translator's words, not those of the witness, so that the audience has to follow the same process of comprehension as the interviewer.

Bernard Cuau has explored the issue of language in *Shoah*, drawing a parallel between the film itself as a new cinematic language, and the idioms within it. He noted among other things how language seems to be on the side of the Germans, who are the only ones still able to speak their own language in their own country. 'The [Jewish] Czechs and Poles who have survived the Camps, today speak English in New York, Hebrew in Israel, German in Basle.'[16] They are, Cuau suggests, '*malade avec la langue*': each Jew struggles to find the right word to describe what they have seen and felt. Yet the old Nazis, too, are uncomfortable with language. Apart from Franz Suchomel, who obviously enjoys the memory of those days, every German interviewed is vague, amnesiac, or mute. Having functioned in a system that hid behind a combination of orderliness and ambiguity, they have lost the protection of both, yet they are still enslaved to them.

Franz Schalling, a German policeman at Chelmno, is the only person able to report willingly and precisely. Joseph Oberhauser, a Belzec SS whom Lanzmann found pouring beer in a Bavarian beer-house, nervously ignores cameras and questions; Frau Michelsohn remembers the cries of terror of Jews waiting to be gassed at Chelmno, but is unsure of whether there were 40,000 or 400,000; Walter Stier, former head of Reich Railways Department Thirty-Three, in charge of special trains to the death camps, insists unconvincingly that he was unaware of the fate of those who travelled on them; Franz Grassler, the deputy to Dr Auerswald, Nazi commissioner of the Warsaw Ghetto, claims to have forgotten everything of the war years and maintains that the German administration worked for the survival of the ghetto, not its destruction. Despite working in Krakow, Stier denies any knowledge of the scope of the massacre until the end of 1944, all the while slyly questioning the slaughter itself. Grassler, on the other hand, seems unsettled by memory and knowledge: he does not question the facts, yet even at the end of his interview he refers to deportations from Warsaw as 'evacuations'.

Whereas among Jewish witnesses silence, ambiguity, hesitation and reticence denote pain, among the Germans they suggests only embarrassment, cowardliness or indifference. The empathy Lanzmann feels for the Jewish survivors, even in his persistence, becomes obvious when compared to his merciless questioning of German witnesses. There is a brilliant perversity in Lanzmann, when he asks Suchomel to sing again the Treblinka song: 'Once more, but louder!' It is part of his attempt to obtain recollections unmediated by reason, by calculation, by self-consciousness: it is what he termed 'reliving' as opposed to mere 'remembering'. Getting Suchomel to sing the Treblinka anthem is equivalent to asking Bomba to imitate cutting women's hair in Auschwitz, or Srebnik to revisit the killing fields of Chelmno. The result is the same: with the exception of Oberhauser they all eventually talk.

In fact, as Cuau suggests, the only witnesses truly at ease with language are the Poles, rather than the Germans. At the time of the film's release, Lanzmann was attacked by the Polish government, who felt he had misrepresented its people as ignorant, anti-Semitic peasants whose indifference is revealed as expectant cowardliness rather than imposed impotence. It was suggested that Lanzmann had carefully selected peasants who would unwittingly accuse themselves; that he had disregarded urban and educated Poles despite the fact that cities like Krakow, Łodz and Warsaw had been major Jewish centres until the war; that he ignored numerous incidents in which Poles helped Jews despite the most severe penalties.[17]

It is certainly true that, for the most part, Poles in *Shoah* appear greedy, spiteful and endemically anti-Semitic. There is no doubt that Lanzmann could have given more emphasis to episodes of empathy and bravery among the Poles, but his position hardly amounts to a deliberate anti-Polish resolve. On the contrary, Lanzmann's interest in the Poles seems to be perfectly coherent with *Shoah*'s mandate. It made perfect sense that Lanzmann should interview those who lived nearest the death camps, who smelt death even when they did not see it. The meeting between Simon Srebnik and the populace of Chelmno, during a Catholic festival outside the church where Jews were locked up while awaiting their slaughter, is one of the most inspired moments in *Shoah*. Surrounded by well-wishers, Srebnik seems quite alone, as in his wartime dream. What is most astonishing is not the Poles' anti-Semitism, but their almost complete lack of empathy, as if unaware of the crimes committed there.

When it is present, Polish anti-Semitism can hardly be blamed on mistranslation or malicious editing on the part of Lanzmann. The Grabow men claiming the Jews smelt bad, or Chelmno's Mr Kantarowski's story of how the Jews themselves accepted their death as just punishment for the death of Jesus, cannot be attributed to misinterpretation. Neither can the general feeling that these rural communities were, at the time of filming, not displeased with being rid of their Jewish neighbours, not least because they drew considerable economic benefit from reduced competition and the seizure of property.

But not all the Poles in *Shoah* lack empathy. Jan Karski is an educated Pole whose sadness in recalling the Warsaw Ghetto betrays not just empathy but unjustified guilt at having been impotent against the atrocities committed there. The tears of the Treblinka rail worker recalling the obscenities he saw on the ramp are not those of an anti-Semite. The train driver, Gawkowski, seems genuinely shaken by the memory of his work for the Nazis, which had been made neither less clear nor more justifiable by the alcoholic haze in which he had performed it. When he spontaneously turns back from the engine towards the camera and makes the sign of slitting his throat, Lanzmann could make him look like a monster, but he does not. It becomes clear that Lanzmann's aim is the same as it has been with Jewish or German witnesses: not moulding their testimonies to his own ideas, but facilitating, even forcing, a deeper descent into memory.

Poles, Germans, Jews and, around them all, the land and the crime there perpetrated, become characters in Lanzmann's play. Because although *Shoah* is at no point fake, it does contain an element of fiction throughout. The prologue reads: 'The story begins in the present day at Chelmno.' As Cuau has pointed out, in the original French 'the story' is '*l'action*', which makes the cinematic reference even more explicit.[18] The fictional element of *Shoah* is interesting to consider in the context of Lanzmann's refusal to make use of traditional documentary features such as archival footage, and more recent ones such as recreation and re-enactment.

Recreation is the fictional reproduction of a historical event, a common device in historical documentaries seeking a synthesis between authenticity and engagement of the audience. Re-enactment is a form of historical recreation which implies engaging actors in reproducing known or alleged historical situations. While re-enactment is a technique used in recreation, the latter can assume forms that do not require the former. At its worst, re-enacted historical recreation was used recently by immensely successful television documentaries such as David Starkey's *The Six Wives of Henry VIII*,[19] or Simon Schama's *A History of Britain*.[20] To show a ginger-bearded Henry VIII strolling around Hampton Court with a flirtatious Anne Boleyn, or a slow-motion shot of clashing spears accompanying the narration of the battle of Hastings, smacks of a false authenticity whose only purpose is to tantalise the audiences with the possibility of action, either romantic or violent.

Because the extermination process was central to *Shoah*, this kind of recreation or re-enactment was not an available option. Death never appears in *Shoah*, neither real nor fake. The filming, or more accurately the re-enactment, of death immediately raised philosophical and moral concerns in which Lanzmann's own ideas about the uniqueness of the Shoah married the theories of Bazin and Bèla Balász on the subject of death as taboo for the camera.[21] This concept fitted Lanzmann's certainty that the Shoah was impossible both to represent and to understand. Lanzmann's rejection not only of recreation but also of all archival footage is ultimately dependent on this premise. As has been argued in the case of *Night and Fog*, to employ footage of Mauthausen while discussing Auschwitz would result in illustration by proxy or, worse, in outright deception.

The question of perspective is also essential. By using footage shot by the Nazis, and especially by using it out of context, Lanzmann would effectively perpetuate an image of Jews created by their murderers for their own propagandistic aims. But by using post-Liberation Soviet or Anglo-American film, he would convey an image of compassion, of tragedy mitigated by renewed freedom, infinitely different from the reality of captivity. In either case, the spectator would witness a foreign perspective of the Jews, one that robbed them of agency and did not grasp the nature and meaning of the Shoah for its victims.

Lanzmann has always argued that he did not use footage of the Shoah simply because none existed.[22] Yet also well known is the director's statement that, if he found footage of the gas chamber, he would not only not use it but destroy it. The key to understanding *Shoah* is the realisation that we cannot cross the threshold of the gas chambers. Even in the present-day filming, Lanzmann does not go into what remains of the Auschwitz gas chambers and crematoria, even though the narration takes him there. It is as though he were suspicious of relics, uneasy with their potential to mislead the audience in believing that those remains are the gas chambers, while the contrast with their original essence goes well beyond their appearance. Lanzmann is altogether more comfortable around the clarity of what is entirely absent: Chelmno, Sobibor and Treblinka.

There are occasions on which Lanzmann seems to contradict its own rigid code, and indulge to some extent in artifice. What else is borrowing a barber's shop for Bomba's interview, if not a recreation? Of similar nature are many other scenes: mounting the camera on a car, driving it into the Chelmno forest and superimposing its images onto Srebnik's narration; renting an original steam engine for Gawkoski to drive on the same Treblinka tracks; even panning over a miniature of the Birkenau crematoria. Perhaps with the exception of the subjective shot of the Chelmno gas van's route – whose purpose is clearly to reinforce the witness's words – the crucial difference is that the aim of Lanzmann's pretence is never to deceive the spectator. Similarly, though Lanzmann occasionally asks his interviewees to 're-live' their past actions, notably he never employs somebody else to re-enact them. Artifice in *Shoah* is always either obvious or acknowledged, and symbolism is not used as the replacement of one thing with another but as an aide to stimulate the interviewee. Hence, Lanzmann's resolution is to seek not authenticity through accurate but essentially false representation, but reality by engaging the witnesses in meaningful recollections.

OUTSIDE HISTORY

The radicalism of Lanzmann's attitude to the representation of the Shoah is matched by his interpretation of its history. 'One cannot drown the Holocaust in the universal problem of evil. Nor assimilate it to the horrors of war or other genocides', he has said in one of many statements to the same effect. [23] To Lanzmann, the Shoah is the absolute crime, unique – it cannot be relativised or compared to other historical events – and 'outside history'.[24] This definition is perplexing, especially given the meticulousness with which the film locates the events discussed. No detail is too insignificant: many are the times when Lanzmann insists on getting witnesses to perform the precise enactment of a gesture, clarify the exact functioning of machinery, or the accuracy of the geographical and temporal situation of specific events. In fact, one of the strengths of *Shoah* is that it places the Shoah firmly in time.

Yet, on closer inspection, a distinction becomes evident in Lanzmann's conceptualisation, between the plethora of events, communities, deportations, camps and murders, that were part of the Shoah, and the Shoah as a whole. He seems to suggest that the attempted genocide consists of more than the simple sum of its parts. It is not a finite historical event that was concluded with the liberation of the camps, it continues to exist not just through its memory but through the places of extermination, however unrecognisable. It continues to exist because of the very fact that it once took place. Hence also *Shoah*'s insistence on present-day images is explained, as an indication that the destruction continues to exist, even if it has ceased to renew itself.

This should be read as a provocation, the aim of which is to release the Shoah from the bonds of historical analysis, chronology and concatenation between cause and effect. All relativity and contextualisation are deliberately excluded from the film. The result is that it focuses uniquely on Jews. While most other films – and most books and commemorations – tend to acknowledge the heterogeneous composition of Nazi victims, *Shoah* considers only Jews. The knowledge that Jews were treated uniquely by the Nazis is such that Lanzmann does not even feel it necessary to make his reasoning explicit. The fact that the Jews were singled out at all stages of the persecution is not in question, yet one would be quite wrong to see in Lanzmann's efforts the establishment of a sort of hierarchy of suffering. On the contrary, this distinction resides in the theme of the film which, at every stage and with remarkable obstinacy, remains the gas chamber as the preferred instrument of the Nazi solution to the Jewish Question.

Shoah can be perceived as intransigent, but the film is more about coherence than about exclusiveness. By refusing comparisons between the Shoah and other historical events, Lanzmann does not claim any special status for the Nazi attempted genocide of the Jews. Despite the impression some of Lanzmann's statements in the press may give, the French director does not place the Shoah 'above' other genocides exactly because it rejects any relativism. What is most important is that *Shoah* succeeded in what it set out to do: the film identified, in the systematic and unprecedented killing by industrial means, the defining features of the attempted annihilation of Europe's Jewry by the Nazis between 1941 and 1945; it reclaimed the perspective of the victims while acknowledging the impossibility of grasping, or representing their experience. Indeed, even more significantly, such an acknowledgment is crucial to Lanzmann's success in reclaiming the victims' perspective. In 1985 the film was the first to achieve this task, and it did so with discretion, honesty and rigour, in which it still remains unsurpassed. It is arguable that it needed these qualities to allow viewers to withstand *Shoah*'s nine-and-a-half hours, in which our natural tendency to seek in a film comfort and reassurance is relentlessly rejected.

THE RECEPTION OF *SHOAH*

It cannot be said of many films that their making spanned two presidential terms: *Shoah* was conceived in Valéry Giscard d'Estaing's France but released in François Mitterrand's. Despite the apparent shift from centre-right to centre-left, the France of these two presidents was not so very different. Under both presidents, France was still seeking to grapple with its past. The need to commemorate the First World War, honour sacrifice and revamp past national grandeur did not always coexist smoothly with the need to remember the Second World War, acknowledge racism and accommodate new supranational institutions. On Armistice Day in 1978, Giscard d'Estaing ordered a wreath to be laid at Marshal Pétain's grave on the Île d'Yeu, as de Gaulle had done ten years earlier. If the Gaullist idea of a thirty-years war had initially made it easier to play down Vichy's importance, it now made it impossible to pay tribute to the hero of Verdun without also remembering the dictator.

Three years later the presidential elections pitted Giscard d'Estaing against the Socialist Party's Mitterrand, ten years his senior, who was presented as the candidate of the Resistance, of which he had been part. During the campaign, however, Mitterrand's record was questioned, as his position in Vichy's organisation for prisoners of war until 1943 came under scrutiny.[25] This was used by the right to allege that, far from being a Republican idealist, he had been nothing more than an opportunist. Not until a decade later would it be revealed that not only had Mitterrand worked for the Vichy government, but that from the 1930s he had been involved in the Croix de Feu and that, after the war, he had been a friend of René Bousquet, chief of the Parisian police during the Rafle du Vél d'Hiv, who had been murdered in June 1993 before he could be tried for crimes against humanity. The fact that these issues were raised at all and the passion with which they were approached show the enduring sensitivity of the subject. It also demonstrates that, perhaps surprisingly, it was believed that this issue could still decide an election.

Whether or not this was an overestimation is difficult to say, yet Mitterrand won in 1981 as the candidate who embodied the values and legacy of the Popular Front. This was partly in response to scandals that had blighted the right's years in government: Georges Pompidou had had to deal with the Touvier affair; Giscard d'Estaing with the Darquier de Pellepoix-Bousquet affair, the emergence of Faurisson and, in election year, the first revelations about Papon. Yet, while Mitterrand's presidency attributed great importance to historical consciousness, it also continued earlier attempts to establish national unity through a sanitised version of national history. Hand in hand with strengthening ties with West Germany and France's commitment to the European Union, Mitterrand pursued national reconciliation. He shook hands with Chancellor Kohl at Verdun in 1984, and had yet another wreath laid at Pétain's tomb, a gesture he repeated in 1986, and each year between 1988 and 1991.[26]

Yet the context had changed. The generation of the war had begun to dwindle – Mitterrand would be the last president born before 1939. New challenges had surfaced in the form of revisionism and the emergence of the Front National, whose leader, Jean-Marie Le Pen, declared in 1987 that the gas chambers were 'a point of detail in the Second World War'.[27] But with these developments a new awareness also began to materialise. Certainly, by the mid-1980s, the Shoah had been placed high on the historical and political agenda: it was taught in schools, and its hard-won status was now carefully protected by academic historiography as well as by determined Jewish organisations. These developments contributed, in 1992, to Mitterrand transferring the yearly laying of Pétain's wreath from the Île d'Yeu to Verdun. Henceforth the warrior was to be honoured independently of the man.

Within this context, *Shoah* opened in three Parisian cinemas on 30 April 1985: the Logos-Reflets and the Monte-Carlo, which screened it in two parts on alternate days, and the Olimpic, which bravely projected it each day in its entirety. It was not a film destined for popular success. Overall, during the period of its general release in France, it was watched by between 60,000 and 70,000 people, about half of whom lived in Paris.[28] The length of the film, not to mention its extensive subtitling, were certainly not conducive to mass audiences, though *The Sorrow and the Pity*, itself over four hours long, was seen by ten times as many people, and many French cinemas regularly screened subtitled foreign films, which attracted large audiences. Yet it is a little unfair to compare Lanzmann's *Shoah* with Ophuls's film, the theme of which had an altogether different relevance to France. The fact that a film with *Shoah*'s characteristics was released at all, let alone that it achieved a respectable box office result, is remarkable. It further attests to France's passion for history at this time. It is interesting that, as Lanzmann himself suggests, the film was not well received by France's Jewish community.[29]

There is no doubt, however, that the film's importance was felt by its contemporaries. Whether convinced by its argument, touched by its humanity, or simply overawed by its scale, few commentators were left unaffected, and even fewer negatively so. In fact, apart from Robert Faurisson's rabid distortion of Lanzmann's work,[30] it is hard to find a single negatively critical review of *Shoah* in the French press. The only adverse criticism, first moved by Jean-Francis Held in *L'Événement du Jeudi*, was of the film's excessive length, which, Held suggested, saturated the viewers, exhausting their ability 'to live in the abyss'.[31] Identifying arbitrarily the audience's attention span as six hours, he concluded that it was 'a pity to have amalgamated the dimensions of the film with those of the Holocaust'.[32]

Otherwise, from *Libération* to *Figaro*, critics were enthusiastic. The recurrent features of this uniform praise were Lanzmann's painstaking detective work, his refusal to use footage, his ability to 'make places speak', the concept of the Shoah as outside history, the essentiality of the testimonies, at once terrible and awe-inspiring. Yet the critics' words often seem hollow: undoubtedly sincere, yet as if the writers were perhaps overwhelmed by a film which requires more than one viewing and is ill-suited to being reviewed in a few hundred words. In any case, contemporary critiques read like varyingly competent variations on Lanzmann's own opinions about his film. These were expressed, both vociferously and intransigently, in a number of interviews. Held defensively noted Lanzmann's impatience with criticism, but justified his own comments as 'not disrespectful' because motivated by 'concern for the film's effectiveness'.[33]

Yet French reaction also reflects a new attitude towards the genocide. This was due, in part, to an increased awareness of history, which was facilitated partly by historiography and partly by an institutional acceptance. In this regard, it was significant that Mitterrand attended the premiere of *Shoah*. In particular, comparing the reception of Lanzmann's film to that of earlier works, such as *Night and Fog* and *The Sorrow and the Pity*, suggests a much stronger understanding of the Shoah as a specifically Jewish experience. *L'Humanité* wrote:

> Partisans were deported, massacred. They were combatants. Communists were tortured, executed. They were the indomitable enemies of the Nazis. Soviet officers, soldiers were exterminated in the camps. Their revolution had made empires vacillate. They all were killed without pity. They knew, we knew, why. Six million Jews, almost the totality of that people in Europe, were scattered in smoke. Whole families gassed. Why?[34]

These words show the distance travelled since the days of *Night and Fog* and *Enclosure*. The vision of the *univers concentrationnaire* as a battlefield between fascism and anti-fascism no longer dominates. *L'Humanité*'s Marxist orientation meant it saw partisans, communists and Soviet troops as, essentially, embodiments of a shared ideology engaged in a life and death struggle against Nazism. Many other victims of the Nazis – Poles or homosexuals, for example – are still ignored by this organ of the French left. But the massacre of the Jews now assumes an absolute centrality for *L'Humanité*, that marks a complete change in French understanding of the Final Solution.

This revelation of Jewish suffering, shared by all the press, is a remarkable one. Remarkable, yet made much easier by the fact that the film was deliberately not about France and the French, Jewish or otherwise. Lanzmann suggested various reasons for neglecting his homeland. Among these was the subject matter: the film was not about Vichy or collaboration but about the Shoah. In addition, the absence in France of survivors of the Sonderkommandos militated against a French focus. Finally, Lanzmann felt he was too close to France to guarantee the necessary objectivity. The result of the self-conscious exclusion of France from the material treated by Lanzmann is that *Shoah* was greeted with praise as unanimous as had been the controversy engendered by *The Sorrow and the Pity*. It is tempting to speculate that the reason for the uniformly positive response to Lanzmann's film had less to do with his objectivity than with his readiness to steer clear of opening old wounds.

Only in one article did a critic detect any relevance to France in *Shoah*. Journalist and novelist Claire Devarrieux, writing in *Le Monde*, drew a lesson from the film, which she believed valuable for her country, acknowledging that in France there still existed an everyday racism that, while possibly more sophisticated in essence, differed little from the Polish anti-Semitism represented in Lanzmann's work: a racism which 'wishes certain people would leave of their own will'.[35] *Shoah*, Devarrieux felt, quietly established the possibility of a connection between this 'ordinary intolerance' and 'the Final Solution'.[36] Lanzmann did this 'not to nurture our sense of guilt but to prevent it',[37] she concluded, presumably referring to Ophuls.

Perhaps, then, the best way to confront such delicate domestic issues was to rely on the audience's ability to recognise these similarities. Or perhaps not, since Devarrieux's thesis remained isolated. Much more interest was raised by Poland's anti-Semitism, occasionally in tones suggesting that, despite all the introspection and debate over the past, France's memory was short. The fact that the Polish government had taken offence at what it perceived to be an incomplete and biased representation of its people appeared to the French as outrageous. It was conveniently forgotten that consecutive French governments had reacted in much the same way to *The Sorrow and the Pity* and, more decisively and recently, to films about Algeria.[38]

The Polish government had initially protested strongly against the planned screening on French television of *Shoah*, which 'contains insulting insinuations about the Polish people's alleged collaboration in the Holocaust'.[39] 'Surprised and outraged' by President Mitterrand's presence at the premiere, the Polish government was reportedly supported by the public – albeit controlled by an oppressive communist state – in denouncing the film and France. Indeed, French anti-Semitism was vilified: according to Szymon Szurmiej, the president of the Polish governmental socio-cultural Jewish association, in France 'Jews are very often killed in the streets.'[40] This was, of course, a gross exaggeration but it may nonetheless have resonated among those individuals, apparently unrepresented within the press, who remembered the attacks on Jewish sites in Paris's Rue Copernic in 1980, and the Marais in 1982.[41]

The French press concentrated on Poland to the point of presenting Polish anti-Semitism as the key issue in Lanzmann's film. The left-wing press, in particular, sought, both simplistically and arbitrarily, to see in the Polish censorship of *Shoah* another symptom of the struggle between Wałesa's Solidarity – hailed as tolerant, democratic and anti-fascist – and Jaruzelski's totalitarian regime. *Libération*'s first article on *Shoah*, five days before its release, was entitled 'Poland in the dock' and read: 'the black legend of the Holocaust, interwoven with the monstrous reality resuscitated by Lanzmann, telescoped the golden legend of Solidarity, interwoven with heroic truth. Myth against myth, forgotten reality against modern reality.'[42]

Among the things that *Shoah* is not about, 1980s Poland is high on the list, especially since the film was started years before the birth of Solidarity. Moreover, General Jaruzelski's totalitarian regime not only allowed national television to screen a radically abridged version of the film on 30 October 1985, but also permitted the integral version to be released in one Warsaw theatre. It is among the most striking aspects of this affair that nobody remarked upon the apparent inexplicability of this decision.

EITHER SIDE OF THE ALPS, EITHER SIDE OF MEMORY: TWO TELEVISION SCREENINGS

Shoah did not have to wait ten years for its first screening on French television: only two. Still, it was broadcast in West Germany, Holland, Sweden, Denmark, Switzerland and Italy, before France. In West Germany, *Shoah* was shown in March 1986, by the Westdeutscher Rundfunk (West Germany Broadcasting, WDR), an ensemble of regional channels each of which arranged its schedule independently. The film was televised everywhere over several evenings, except in Catholic Bavaria where, after an initial refusal to buy the rights on the grounds that 'we know it all by heart',[43] Bayerische Rundfunk broadcast it in two parts on Sunday mornings, in competition with Mass.[44]

In Italy, Lanzmann's documentary was aired in four parts,

between 3 and 6 December 1986. Comparing the Italian and French television broadcasts of *Shoah* is extremely interesting. The difference could not be more striking, and is only partly explained by the French origin of the film, whose theme was equally relevant to both countries. In Italy, the rights of the film were acquired by the state television, RAI, which allocated it to its least popular and most highbrow channel, RAI Tre, historically controlled by the Communist Party.[45] Here, it was initially scheduled just before midnight, until a strong protest by the Associazione Nazionale Ex-Deportati Politici nei Campi Nazisti (National Association of Political Deportees to Nazi Camps, ANED), the national association of former political deportees, managed at the last moment to have it moved to an earlier time. The result was complete chaos. The last-minute change meant that, on 3 December, many television listings carried the original time of 23.55, rather than the new one of 23.05. The hasty reshuffle also caused the film to be shown over four days at four different times: 22.05 on 4 December, 22.40 on 5 December and finally 23.15 on 6 December. Newspapers, especially those of the left, seem to have made much of the initial controversy, but very little of the film.[46] Among these, *L'Unitá* was alone in announcing the film, and the controversy, the day before its broadcast, and in a front page article.[47]

The fight, largely perceived as a victory for historical memory, and, therefore, a political victory, assumed more importance than the content of the film on whose behalf the battle had been fought. After 3 December only one article appeared in the Italian press: in *La Repubblica* of 5 December, in the 'Comments' section, a thoughtful piece by Jewish journalist and author Rosellina Balbi engaged with the film and drew a contemporary lesson from it. A film 'about testimony and indifference', Balbi writes, it demonstrates that 'although our testimony cannot be the same as theirs, our indifference today, may well be as guilty as that of the Poles then'.[48]

Two matters appear noteworthy in this affair. First, the fact that in Italy an association of former deportees could still, in the late 1980s, force a television channel to alter its schedule. Although admittedly RAI Tre's political line meant it was more likely to listen to such an organisation, the fact still points at the very least to the left's continued reverence for the Resistance. Second, it is telling that Jewish deportees were still represented by an organisation of political deportees. This, in particular, appears to suggest that Italian Jewish organisations had not yet gained the same role as their French counterparts.

Italy's failure fully to understand the Jewish perspective of the Shoah appears to be twofold: on the one hand, there lurked an historical refusal to consider the Shoah as a phenomenon with a domestic dimension; on the other, there was a fairly generalised lack of interest in the Shoah as an essentially foreign matter. Consequently, an Italian equivalent to *Shoah* does not exist. Yet, at the same time, when Lanzmann's film was shown it hardly made news, since its content was perceived as foreign. Proof of this is in the fact that the only real interest *Shoah* created was with regard to RAI's perceived passive censorship. Yet, while a section of the public complained about this, the public's own indifference towards the film itself amounted to much the same.

At the end of 1986, Italy obtained two unflattering records: it was the only country to show *Shoah* at four different times, and the only one to show it dubbed. When Lanzmann protested against RAI's decision to dub his film, he was allegedly told: 'Consider yourself lucky that the film is broadcast at all; you should know that racism is not dead.'[49] And although RAI Tre replayed the first episode on 10 March 1987 at 20.30, preceded by an interview with the 1986 Nobel Peace Prize winner Elie Wiesel, popular indifference was confirmed by a total audience of only 640,000, equal to a share of 2.74 per cent of the viewing public. This time the poor showing was not explicable by the late-night showing. Furthermore, well into the 1990s, Italy remained the only European country where *Shoah* was not available on video, and where the screenplay, first published by Rizzoli in 1987, was not reprinted until Bompiani acquired the rights in 2000. In the face of these facts it is hard not to agree with Frediano Sessi who, in 1998, identified this silence as yet another symptom of Italy's 'active forgetfulness' of fascism's responsibility in the Shoah.[50]

In comparison, *Shoah*'s French television debut was triumphant. Even so, the delay in its taking place did not go unnoticed: *Libération* published an article, '*Shoah* storms the small screen.'[51] State television TF1 had first bought the rights in 1979, before the film's completion, yet a tentative scheduling in August 1986 had angered Lanzmann, who considered that broadcasting it at the height of holiday season was tantamount to not showing it at all. It was not until TF1 was privatised by Mitterrand's government that *Shoah* appeared in French film-houses during four nights between 30 June and 2 July 1987. This should not be misconstrued as a gesture to memory, for it made perfect commercial sense, despite the appropriate absence of any adverts.[52] On consecutive nights, it attracted an average of four million viewers, with peaks of six-and-a-half million.[53] The new TF1 broke records and established for itself a new cultural image, while Lanzmann saw his film's audience multiplied by a factor of almost sixty.

Both the broadcast and the critical and popular attention it achieved are easily explained: the trial of Klaus Barbie had once again thrust the Shoah into the limelight. Though Lanzmann categorically denied there was any connection between the screening of his film and the trial,[54] it is clear that TF1 strategically placed it shortly before the court case's climatic conclusion. Similarly, it can be argued that the atmosphere created by Barbie's trial contributed to the film's large audience. It is apparent that connections can be created even when they are absent, and cannot then be easily dismissed, even if they do not become legitimate.

The connection between the two events was not primarily between the events narrated in the film and the crimes being judged by the Lyon assize court. Rather, the two events were linked because the Barbie trial, turned by Vergès into a public re-examination of the country's history, facilitated the television screening of *Shoah* and loaded the French perception of it with political meaning. Despite being a German Nazi rather than a French collaborator such as Touvier, Papon and Bousquet, Barbie caused a wave of introspection. This led *Shoah* to be perceived, in 1987, as a film more relevant to France than it was just two years earlier. *Libération* declared that the 'interest triggered by the Barbie trial has shown the existence of a need for history which rekindles some hope for the future'.[55]

In 1985, the same paper had praised *Shoah* but had seen it principally as an anti-Polish exposé. Now *Libération* changed its tune: *Shoah* had become simultaneously both a 'monument to the world's memory' and, crucially, 'another challenge to France's memory'.[56] It was also perceived as the answer to France's hunger for history. In an article entitled 'Why one must watch *Shoah*', *L'Événement du Jeudi* exhorted families to watch it together, because 'in a time when Decaux sings Brasillach's praises on state television [...], in the time of the Barbie trial [...], a real history lesson cannot but improve our intelligence'.[57] *La Vie Ouvrière* also saw in *Shoah* a direct, relevant and valuable response to recurrent French anti-Semitism, sympathy for Barbie, 'Le Pen's troops' and Holocaust denial.[58] The record audiences were widely reported and *Libération* followed up its earlier pieces by sending six reporters to watch the film with members of the public in three Parisian locations, as well as in Nancy, Lille and Avignon. *Libération*'s piece, which perhaps attempted too much in the short space available, was an uninteresting collection of superlatives and reiterations of the importance of historical memory.[59] Its short article on the reactions of the Jewish community is little better. The article revealed mixed feelings: not simply the praise for a beautiful and valuable film, but also the angst of those who could not bring themselves to watch it, and the disenchantment of those who believed it to be a fundamental film that was nonetheless powerless to prevent future and inevitable anti-Semitism.[60] Perhaps these responses, rather than shedding light on France's perception of the Shoah, reflected the disillusioned zeal of the days when *Shoah* was on television, Barbie in the dock, and Kurt Waldheim in the plush salons of the Vatican.

FROM RECOGNITION TO REPRESENTATION

There is something of this disillusionment in the reception of *Shoah*. This was not caused by the film failing to fulfil expectations. On the contrary, artistically and historically, the film was treated with respect bordering on reverence. Press reaction simply lacked the sense of immediate importance, of much-awaited revelation that had pervaded the response to *The Sorrow and the Pity* and, to a lesser extent, to *Lacombe, Lucien*. Although the reception of the 1987 television broadcast revealed the intuition of a momentous occasion, France did not react to *Shoah* as viscerally as it had done to those earlier films. Except for the Poles, nobody really found *Shoah* controversial. They found it shattering in the way it moves the viewer without relying on over-exploited emotional techniques, but it was an expected and in many respects alien shock. In this sense, the press's surprise at *Shoah*'s poor box-office showing was naive: the public's desertion did not amount to a want of interest in history any more than the press's praise amounted to serious analysis.

That public opinion in 1980s France was still interested in Vichy is evidenced by the importance accorded to it in politics and the media, as well as in the academic milieu. It is equally clear that, by this point, the extent and consequences of Vichy's anti-Semitism were well-known. Varyingly caricatured, porcine-faced, greasy-haired French anti-Semites were now commonplace in French films about the Second World War.[61] Nonetheless, the public still found it very hard to accept the degree to which Vichy colluded in the Jewish genocide. *Shoah* undoubtedly helped hammer home further the chilling consequences of such collusion.

The vast majority of the public avoided watching *Shoah* not because it was uninterested in those historical events but because it is not an easy film to watch: the integral projection of the film especially would require the daunting prospect of a whole day. Moreover, the film's format – its refusal to use archival footage in favour of interviews, rightly hailed as highly original in the press – made it appear nonetheless as an endless sequence of talking heads which would have scared even the most *engagé* of cinephiles. More than twice as long as *The Sorrow and the Pity*, *Shoah* lacks the irony of Ophuls's film, and also its provocative and uplifting ending. Unlike *The Sorrow and the Pity*, moreover, Lanzmann's is not a film about France and as such commanded less popular interest.

The trial of Klaus Barbie re-established as related events the Final Solution and the repression of the French Resistance. This bond, formed immediately after the war, had been severed in the effort to claim visibility for the Shoah's Jewish dimension. The seven counts on which the former SS captain was charged included the deportation of Jews and also the murder of Jean Moulin and other Resistance leaders, some of whom were themselves Jews.[62] The argument over the definition of crimes against humanity that accompanied the trial spilled into it almost to the point of derailing it, when Vergès's line of defence was revealed to rest entirely on establishing an equation between colonialist and Nazi crimes. Consequently, the Lyon proceedings struck at the heart of French memory, connecting the history of France with that of the Shoah. By association, thanks mostly to TF1's intelligent scheduling, *Shoah* came to be perceived, and therefore to an extent became, a film about France.

This is evident in the reviews of June–July 1987, and especially in the interviews with the director. Lanzmann strongly refused to accept any connection between his work and the trial, the importance of which he considered greatly overestimated by public opinion.[63] In an interview included in *Archives d'un Procès: Klaus Barbie*, he repeatedly scorned the case as a show, and the pedagogical value attributed to it as shallow.[64] 'France has treated itself to a mini-Eichmann trial', in which, he resentfully suggested, his film was not mentioned once.[65] Even so, the prosecution of Barbie played an important role in improving the visibility and fame of a film which otherwise could have remained the lonely territory of specialists and film buffs.

Shoah's fame has been central to its impact on popular memory, yet one feels its long-term effect will reside in maintaining its cult status, rather than in achieving mass distribution. Despite release on video and,[66] in 2003, on DVD,[67] still more people have heard of *Shoah* than have watched it. It remains a difficult text to use as a teaching aid in schools, or to be shown on television. *Night and Fog* is still by far the easier option. This has haunted every step of Lanzmann's film. The discovery in 1987 that a Parisian cinema was screening *Night and Fog* immediately followed by *Shoah* infuriated Lanzmann, who forced the theatre to pull Resnais's film.[68]

His was an overreaction, which revealed little faith in his own audience; his lack of trust was perhaps justified but nonetheless unpleasant. Yet his interpretation of *Night and Fog*'s failings was not completely off the mark. *Shoah* to this day is still the only film to have tackled the Shoah head-on, to have moved it from background to centre of the narrative. Lanzmann's great achievement is to have understood the essence of the catastrophe, while remaining at an appropriate distance from it. Correcting Resnais's interpretation, his film demonstrates that it is possible to capture simultaneously the Shoah's universality and its Jewish specificity. Its importance is and will continue to be located in this, rather than in how many people have watched the film.

Night and Fog and *Shoah* related to the periods in which they were made and answered their different needs: in the collective silence of 1955, *Night and Fog* needed to place the Shoah on the map, albeit rather approximately; in 1974, when it was begun, *Shoah* was necessary to establish the facts clearly and restore the proper name to the event. That is exactly what it did. In contributing to the recognition of the Shoah as a Jewish tragedy, however, it also played a fundamental part in its representation. In the 1990s, this would be attempted in a greater variety of ways than ever before: exploring genres previously deemed inappropriate for the subject; seeking new stories to tell; crossing hitherto uncrossed boundaries; suggesting different meanings; and above all offering countless images, from the abstract to the most explicit ones, to depict the Shoah. Thus Lanzmann, the self-proclaimed guarantor of the impossibility of representing the Shoah, paradoxically also signalled its entrance into the realm of the representable.

NOTES

1. Rachel Ertel, 'Le Noir Miracle', in Claude Lanzmann (ed.), *Au Sujet de Shoah: Le Film de Claude Lanzmann* (Paris: Belin, 1990), p.50. An Italian version of her article is available in Francesco Monicelli and Carlo Saletti (eds), *Il Racconto della Catastrofe: Il Cinema di Fronte ad Auschwitz* (Verona: Cierre Edizioni, 1998), pp.44–9).
2. Yitzhak Arad, *Belzec, Sobibor, Treblinka: The Operation Reinhard Death Camps* (Bloomington, IN: Indiana University Press, 1987), is a meticulous study on all aspects of the camps' history.
3. On the revolt at Treblinka and Sobibor see the following memoirs: Samuel Willenberg, *Surviving Treblinka* (Oxford: Basil Blackwell, 1989) and Thomas Toivi Blatt, *From the Ashes of Sobibor: A Story of Survival* (Evanston, IL: Northwestern University Press, 1997). Richard Rashke, *Escape from Sobibor* (London: Sphere, 1982), is a valuable text which collates the recollections of several survivors of Sobibor. Two films have been made on the Sobibor revolt: Jack Gold's *Escape from Sobibor* (USA, 1987) and Lanzmann's own *Sobibor 14 Octobre, 16 Heures* (France, 2001).
4. See Arad, *Belzec, Sobibor, Treblinka*; Raul Hilberg, *The Destruction of European Jews* (Chicago, IL: Quadrangle, 1961); and Mathias Beer, 'Die Entwicklung der Gaswagen beim Mord an den Juden', in *Vierteljahreshefte fuer Zeitgeschichte*, 37, 3, pp.403–17, translated into English by the author and available at http://dss.ucsd.edu/~lzamos c/chelm10.htm.
5. Isaiah, 56:5.
6. Primo Levi, *I Sommersi e i Salvati* (Torino: Einaudi, 1986), p.64. The book has been published in English under the tile *The Drowned and the Saved* (New York: Summit Books, 1988).
7. Claude Lanzmann, interviewed by François Gantheret, 'Les Non-Lieux de la Mémoire', in Lanzmann (ed.), *Au Sujet de Shoah*, pp.280–92. The interview was originally published as 'L'Amour de la Haine', *Nouvelle Revue de Psychanalyse*, 33 (Spring 1986).
8. A copy is held by the Washington Holocaust Memorial Museum. See Joshua Hirsch, *Afterimage: Film, Trauma and the Holocaust* (Philadelphia, PA: Temple University Press, 2004), pp.1–3.
9. Negatives 278–82, State Museum of Auschwitz-Birkenau. See Georges Didi-Hubermann, *Images Malgré Tout* (Paris: Les Éditions de Minuit, 2003).
10. Simon Srebnik, survivor of Chelmno, in Claude Lanzmann, *Shoah: The Complete Text of the Acclaimed Holocaust Film* (New York: Da Capo Press, 1995), p.3.
11. Ibid., p.1.
12. On the issue of language in *Shoah*, see Cuau, in Lanzmann (ed.), *Au Sujet de Shoah*, pp.13–19.
13. Lanzmann, *Shoah*, pp.107–8.
14. Shoshana Felman, 'A l'Âge du Temoignage', in Lanzmann (ed.), *Au Sujet de Shoah*.
15. Elie Wiesel, in the foreword to A. Insdorf, *Indelible Shadows: Film and the Holocaust*, second edition (Cambridge: Cambridge University Press, 1989), p.xi.

16. Cuau, 'Dans le Cinéma une Langue Étrangère', in Lanzmann (ed.), *Au Sujet de Shoah*, p.13.
17. Jean-Charles Szurek, 'De la Question Juive à la Question Polonaise', in Lanzmann (ed.), *Au Sujet de Shoah*, pp.258–78. See also Neal Ascherson, 'La Controversie Autour de *Shoah*' (pp.226–35) and Jacek Kuron, 'On a Condamné à Mort les Juifs parce qu'ils étaient Juifs' (pp.256–7), in Lanzmann (ed.), *Au Sujet de Shoah*.
18. Ibid., p.14.
19. Davis Starkey, *David Starkey's The Six Wives of Henry VIII* (Channel Four Productions, 2002).
20. Simon Schama, *A History of Britain* (BBC Productions, 2000).
21. André Bazin, *Qu'est-ce que le Cinéma?*, vol. 1: 'Ontologie et Langage' (Paris: Éditions Cerf, 1958), pp.65–70; Bèla Balász, 'Filming Death', in Barry Keith Grant and Jeannette Sloniowski (eds), *Documenting the Documentary: Close Readings of Documentary Film and Video* (Detroit, MI: Wayne State University Press, 1998), pp.29–32. Balázs's essay was originally published in Bèla Balász, *Theory of the Film* (London: Dennis Dobson, 1952).
22. Interview by Sophie Lannes, *L'Express*, 10 August 1985.
23. Ibid.
24. Ibid.
25. Pierre Péan, *Une Jeunesse Française: François Mitterrand, 1934–1947* (Paris: Fayard, 1994) and Jean Lacouture, *Mitterrand: Une Histoire de Français*, two vols (Paris: Éditions du Seuil, 1998).
26. Robert Gildea, *France Since 1945* (Oxford: Oxford University Press, 1996), p.66; Nicholas Atkin, *The Fifth French Republic* (Basingstoke: Palgrave-Macmillan, 2005), pp.156–63.
27. Jean-Marie Le Pen used to serve in the parachute corps and was a Poujadist before forming the Front National (FN) in 1972. Since the 1980s, Le Pen has exploited fears raised by the growth of immigration to make the FN a major political player in France. The election of the socialist Mitterrand, in 1981, may also have played a part in the rise of right-wing extremism, but Le Pen's appeal has not shown any signs of decreasing since the right returned to power with Chirac in 1995. While anti-Semitism is not central to the FN's doctrine, Le Pen's comments in 1987 on the gas chambers carry echoes of the negationist thesis, confirming that Holocaust denial has been allowed to gain a small but solid foothold in France. On Le Pen and his party see Harvey G. Simmons, *The French National Front: The Extremist Challenge to Democracy* (Oxford: Westview, 1996); Julian Wolfreys, 'Neither Right nor Left? Towards an Integrated Analysis of the Front National', in Nicholas Atkin and Frank Tallett (eds), *The Right in France from Revolution to Le Pen*, second edition (London: I.B. Tauris, 2003), pp.261–76.
28. The rough estimate is Lanzmann's own, in an interview by Bernard Le Saux in *Le Matin*, 29 June 1987. The precise figure of the Parisian box office is 35,319 over fifty-seven weeks in just three screens (source: Bibliothèque du Film, Paris, www.bifi.fr).
29. Annette Levy-Willard and Laurent Joffrin, 'La marche entravée d'un film géant', *Libération*, 29 June 1987.
30. Robert Faurisson, '*Shoah*' (review of the film), *Journal of Historical Review* (Spring 1988), pp.85–92
31. Jean-Francis Held, 'Shoah ou l'épopée de la solution finale', *L'Événement du Jeudi*, 2 May 1985.
32. Ibid.
33. Ibid.
34. Bernard Frederick, *L'Humanité*, 30 April 1985.
35. Claire Devarrieux, 'Les champs de la conscience', *Le Monde*, 28 April 1985.
36. Ibid.
37. Ibid.
38. On censorship against fiction about the Algerian War see Philip Dine, *Images of the Algerian War* (Oxford: Clarendon Press, 1994).
39. 'La Pologne veut interdire *Shoah*', *Le Matin*, 2 May 1985.
40. Ibid.
41. Rousso, *Vichy Syndrome: Hisory and Memory in France since 1944* (Cambridge, MA: Harvard University Press, 1991), pp.161–7. Rousso argues that the attacks were not related to the 'Vichy syndrome', but rather the result of new anti-Zionism and anti-Semitism. On the resurgence of these see Pierre-André Taguieff, *Rising from the Muck: The New Anti-Semitism in Europe* (Chicago, IL: Ivan R. Dee, 2004).
42. Laurent Joffrin, 'La Pologne au banc des accusés', *Libération*, 25 April 1985.

43. Levy-Willard and Joffrin, 'La marche entravée'.
44. Antoine Spire and Marc Schlikin, '*Shoah* déchire l'Allemagne', *Le Matin*, 10 March 1986.
45. P. Ginsborg, *A History of Contemporary Italy, 1943–1988* (Harmondsworth: Penguin, 1990), especially pp.177–81 and 286–90, is an excellent introduction to clientelism in Italian politics and the *lottizzazione*, the practice of sharing the control of public institutions. P. Ginsborg, *Italy and its Discontents* (London: Allen Lane, 2002), takes this analysis beyond the corruption scandals, and shatters the idea that clientelism ended with the so-called *prima repubblica*. Specifically on the political sharing of state media see Franco Rositi, *Mercati di Cultura: Politica e Lottizzazione dei Mass Media in Italia* (Bari: De Donato, 1982).
46. Articles dedicated to ANED's successful complaint appeared on 2 and 3 December 1986 in *La Stampa*, p.19, signed respectively by Si. Ro. and Ugo Buzzolan; on 3 December anonymously in *Il Manifesto*, p.8, and *La Repubblica*, p.27.
47. Michele Anselmi, *L'Unitá*, 2 December 1986, pp.1 and 24.
48. Rosellina Balbi, *La Repubblica*, 5 December 1986, p.8. Balbi is also the author of a 1988 volume aimed at warning Italian society against the rise of racism.
49. Levy-Willard and Joffrin, 'La marche entravée'.
50. Frediano Sessi, 'Attorno a un capolavoro: annotazione su *Shoah* di Claude Lanzmann', in Monicelli and Saletti (eds), *Il Racconto della Catastrofe*, pp.51–8.
51. Annette Levy-Willard and Laurent Joffrin, '*Shoah* force le petit écran', *Libération*, 29 June 1987.
52. Patrice Lestrohan, '*Shoah*: jamais tant d'écoute à une telle heure', *L'Événement du Jeudi*, 9 July 1987. In the archive of the Bibliothèque du Film, in Paris, this article appears under the incorrect date of 9 May 1987.
53. Ibid.
54. Interviewed by Bernard Le Saux, *Le Matin*, 29 June 1987.
55. Levy-Willard and Joffrin, '*Shoah* force le petit écran.'
56. Ibid.
57. Florence Assouline, 'Pourquoi il faut voir *Shoah*', *L'Événement du Jeudi*, 25 June 1987. Historian Alain Decaux presented historical programmes on state-owned Antènne 2 between 1969 and 1988. He spearheaded a re-evaluation of Robert Brasillach, who had been a productive, much-admired novelist in the 1930s but also a freelance journalist close to the fascist Action Française and on the editorial team of the party's paper, *Je suis Partout*, until late 1942. He was a collaborator and a vicious anti-Semite. Tried and executed in February 1945, he was the most prominent intellectual to be condemned for treason. For a thorough account of his spectacular fall from grace see Alice Kaplan, *The Collaborator: The Trial and Execution of Robert Brasillach* (Chicago, IL: University of Chicago Press, 2000).
58. Serge Zeyons, 'Sur les lieux du crime', *La Vie Ouvrière*, 29 June 1987.
59. Alain Léauthier et al., 'Les shoah des téléspetateurs', *Libération*, 3 July 1987.
60. Philippe Lançon, 'Du coté de la communauté juive', *Libération*, 3 July 1987.
61. See, for example, the character of Daxiat in Truffaut's *Le Dernier Métro* (1980).
62. Rousso, *Vichy Syndrome*, p.210. On Jean Moulin and the fuss that ensued over his betrayal see Daniel Cordier, *Jean Moulin: L'Inconnu du Panthéon*, three vols (Paris: Lattés, 1989–1993) and Alan Clinton, *Jean Moulin, 1899–1943: The French Resistance and the Republic* (Basingstoke: Palgrave, 2002).
63. Lanzmann: 'Personally, I have always expressed the deepest reservations on this trial. I do not think a trial is the most appropriate setting to evoke the Holocaust. I do not think either that this is the trial of the century, as has been suggested here and there.' In an interview by Bernard Le Saux, *Le Matin*, 29 June 1987.
64. Sylvie Lévy, '*Shoah* et la Shoah: Entretien avec Claude Lanzmann', in Bernard-Henri Lévy, *Archives d'un Procès: Klaus Barbie* (Paris: Globe, 1986), pp.51–8.
65. Ibid., p.54. Years later, when France attempted to prosecute Bousquet, Touvier and Papon, Lanzmann elaborated his distrust of trials by accusing France of using them to provide a resolution, and effectively archive the Shoah. Interview with Serge Grünberg, *Globe Hebdo*, 30 June 1993.
66. *Shoah*, on VHS, is distributed by René Chateau Video, Paris.
67. *Shoah*, on DVD, is distributed by New Yorker Films Artwork.
68. 'People could say to themselves: I have the Holocaust in 20 minutes for ten francs, why bear nine hours for forty-eight francs.' In Vincent Löwy, *L'Histoire Infilmable: Les Camps d'Extermination Nazis à l'Écran* (Paris: L'Harmattan, 2001), p.86.

7

La Vita è Bella and *Train de Vie*: 'Preventing the eyes from seeing' versus 'Cleaning the eyes that have seen too much'

The 1990s oversaw the relentless entry of the Shoah into popular discourse. Cinema contributed integrally and significantly to this process, arguably launching it through Steven Spielberg's *Schindler's List* (1993). 1980s American television films, such as *Holocaust* (1978), *Playing for Time* (1980) and *Escape from Sobibor* (1987), had already signalled the acceptance of the Shoah as a subject of mainstream popular culture, but Spielberg's film represented its definitive, global adoption by the big screen. As the previous chapters have shown, however, the popularisation of the Shoah was not simply a trend imported from the USA. France and Italy had each undergone its own evolution in the way the Shoah was remembered and represented, and now they offered their own characteristic, home-made versions of the Holocaust blockbusters.

In France, the widespread popular and critical acclaim of Louis Malle's *Au Revoir, les Enfants* (*Goodbye, Children*, 1987) signalled that the Shoah had been accepted into popular culture. Malle, who after *Lacombe, Lucien* had spent thirteen years in self-imposed exile in the United States, returned to French cinema with a long-planned work based on his own experiences as a young boy during the *années noires*. The triumphant reception of *Goodbye, Children* certainly points to the greater degree of acceptability of the topic in 1987 France. This not only confirms the impression given by the reaction to *Shoah*, but also considerably strengthens it because Malle's film, unlike Lanzmann's, made France central to its discourse and attacked the cowardliness of the French bourgeoisie.

Notwithstanding this, the film's success should be ascribed also, perhaps primarily, to the fact that *Goodbye, Children* subtly relegated the discussion of French collaboration to the periphery of the narrative. *Goodbye, Children* is utterly different from *Lacombe, Lucien*. In his 1987 work, Malle significantly shifted French responsibility in the persecution of Jews away from the centre stage, which it firmly occupied in his 1974 film. Gloomy greys and blues and oppressive winter weather replaced the scorching sunshine and shining colours of the *Midi*. The boundary between good and evil, which had been not just blurred but deliberately ignored in *Lacombe, Lucien*, was firmly reinstated.

Most crucially of all, the character of Lucien, once the protagonist, was transformed into that of Joseph, the kitchen hand who betrays the two Jewish boys out of class jealousy and spite for the school that had unfairly sacked him. Lucien and Joseph are clearly the same character: young, poor and somewhat raw. Nevertheless, where Lucien had been handsome and healthy, Joseph was now repulsive and crippled; where Lucien had been popular with his comrades and romantically successful, Joseph was now bullied and frustrated. Moreover, the disturbing lack of motivations that accompanied Lucien's collaboration – and that had so enraged French critics in 1974 – was replaced by unoriginal psychological and sociological explanations: namely jealousy and the social injustice of the education system. Therefore, while honestly and emotionally representing the tragedy of the deportations, Malle offered the French public a more acceptable view of collaboration.

In Italy, films such as Roberto Faenza's *Jona che Visse nella Balena* (*Jonah who Lived in the Whale*, 1994) and especially Francesco Rosi's *La Tregua* (*The Truce*, 1997), arguably highlighted the same, belated, shift. Here too, however, the transformation of the Shoah as a subject of mainstream cinema was not painless. *Jonah*, which in keeping with Italian Holocaust filmography set its action abroad, was a box-office flop, grossing a mere 1,127,517,000 Italian lire.[1] An ambitious, expensive, international production, starring John Turturro as Levi, Rosi's work establishes Levi's identity as an Italian, an anti-fascist and an intellectual, all but ignoring his Judaism. With a careful blend of selective and inaccurate adaptation of the book, Rosi completely revolutionised Levi's identity. Levi always credited luck with his survival; Rosi ignored this to turn him into an all-seeing being who stood out from the crowd. Rosi cheaply used romance to symbolise Levi's return to life, making it utterly devoid of the necessary complexity. Worst of all, and against all of Levi's writings, Rosi converted Levi's pursuit of justice into a pursuit of forgiveness. The disappointing result is the portrait of a man at peace, not one of a man living through an atrocious truce.

Despite some controversy, *The Truce*'s seductive and deceptive offer of closure received some critical acclaim and was financially more successful than *Jonah*.[2] Nevertheless, Rosi's reinterpretation of Levi as an all-seeing, all-forgiving, left-wing Italian intellectual proved that popularisation runs the very real risk of banalisation.[3] Even Rosi's success, however, was slight when compared to Roberto Benigni's *La Vita è Bella* (*Life is Beautiful*, 1998), which won numerous prizes and awards including the film 'Grand Prix de la Jury' at the Cannes Film Festival in 1998, and Academy Awards for Best Actor to Benigni, Best Original Dramatic Score for Nicola Piovani's music, and Best Foreign Language Film, in 1999.[4]

The recent appearance of concentration camp comedies is a reminder that, while commentators were still discussing the implications of a popularised Shoah, cinema had already moved on, beginning to look for new ways of describing the tragedy. Having argued in previous chapters for the validity of the historical use of cinema as reflection and agent of society's attitudes to history, this final chapter will concentrate on two examples of Holocaust comedy: one Italian, *Life is Beautiful* and one French, Radu Mihaileanu's *Train de Vie* (*Train of Life*, 1998).[5] Although contrasting starkly in many aspects, these films are also remarkably similar: they share the year of production, both are comedies, and both are constructed as fables. The purpose of this direct comparison is to trace the most recent developments in the representation and memory of the Shoah in France and Italy, thus concluding this comparative investigation of the two countries' attitudes towards the Shoah.

The second aim of this concluding case study is to expose an essential flaw in the debate over Shoah mass representation. As Hilene Flanzbaum has pointed out, too often critics and viewers forget that a work of art, even the most historically accurate one, cannot be in any way a substitute for either witnessing the events it depicts, or their study through academic history.[6] Instead, increasingly often, critics seek to judge Holocaust films merely on the grounds of realism. To name one example, which shall be analysed in this chapter, *Life is Beautiful* was both hailed as an appropriate educational surrogate, and condemned for its lack of realism. It is our contention that this kind of debate is often futile for two reasons: first, because it seeks in cinema something that cinema cannot offer; second, because it prevents the discussion of more relevant points concerning the films.

In the first part, this chapter will address the two films, while trying to place them in the tradition of Holocaust representation, and Holocaust comedy in particular. In the second part, it will examine public and critical response to *Life is Beautiful* and *Train of Life* in France and Italy, before drawing a few conclusions about how such a response affects the analysis of French and Italian perceptions of the Shoah. Commercial decisions and individual taste undoubtedly affected the different reception accorded to each film. This chapter will argue, however, that these differing reactions also show a pattern in how, and how much, French and Italians are prepared to think and talk about the Shoah.

TWO MODELS OF HOLOCAUST REPRESENTATION

Despite the similarities I have pointed out, *Life is Beautiful* and *Train of Life* are entirely different in style, humour and even content. One is very much the product of a certain Italian comic tradition with very little influence from Jewish culture;[7] the other is a thoroughly Yiddish comedy, drenched in Ashkenazi Jewish humour, a stylised reflection of that Eastern European Jewish society which was all but brought to extinction by the Nazi persecution.[8] Both films are fairy tales about the Shoah, yet their attitudes towards both the genocide and their own fairy-tale nature are in opposition. Benigni's film uses the Shoah as the background for an uplifting survival narrative, while Mihaileanu makes the Shoah the centre of his commemoration of the victims. Similarly, the two films' relationships with their fairy-tale narrative structure are in stark contrast: the former upholds the fable until the end; the latter rejects it utterly. It is the combination of these differences and similarities that make a comparison worthwhile, indeed essential. Given this, it is also surprising that despite the wealth of literature about *Life is Beautiful*, this comparison has not hitherto been attempted.[9] This

Figure 7.1. *Train of Life*: 'Mihaileanu works by reversal.' Here, the shtetl's Jews queue to contribute to preparations for their journey. (© Radu Mihaileanu.)

absence is explained in part by *Train of Life*'s lack of popularity and a less than enthusiastic media response, and in part by insufficient distribution.[10] This chapter will argue, however, that the considerable discrepancy in the reception of these two films, in both France and Italy, points to a general inability, perhaps even unwillingness, to consider the Shoah in the terms suggested by the French–Romanian director.

Train of Life is a powerful Yiddish homage to pre-war Eastern European Jewry, its life and culture. It tells the story of a shtetl, which, informed by its 'village idiot', Shlomo, of the imminent arrival of the Germans, decides to assemble a false deportation train and deport itself to Palestine. The villagers assume the roles of both the Nazis and their prisoners in a desperate bid to escape their fate. But this attempt is only a superficial one, which must be understood metaphorically. By the film's end, it is clear that their only aim, in Shlomo's words, is 'to clean the eyes that have seen too much'. It is through Shlomo's eyes, the only ones unbound by rationality, thanks to his supposed madness, that the viewer understands fully the tragedy behind this comedy. At one point in the film, the train's gentle puffing becomes Shlomo's heavy breathing as the carriages slow down, approaching an all too familiar scene of night and fog. Through Shlomo's eyes one sees the Germans arriving; the shtetl's synagogue being burnt down; one of the Jews being arrested – until, in a shocking finale, he reveals the falsity of his own story.

In order to achieve this, Mihaileanu works by reversal. In other words, he shows the audience what it knows is the truth, by showing us its opposite. This is a technique which serves simultaneously a historical and a comic purpose. The work the shtetl undertakes to build the train and prepare for departure is voluntary work with a clear and productive aim, the opposite of the slave labour enforced by the Nazis. Similarly, the traditional imagery of the deportations is reversed by Mihaileanu's representation of the Jews eagerly waiting to board the train, accompanied by the rabbi's blessing. The initial collection of money mocks, perhaps unwittingly, Nazi confiscation of Jewish property and goods (Figure 7.1). Even the puppies some of the characters use to track down fellow Jews on the run are the opposite of the Germans' ferocious hounds. Following this rationale, the fact that the entire shtetl survives suggests in fact that they are all dead. The train itself, far from assuming the deadly symbolism it is usually given in Holocaust films, becomes a symbol of life. *Train of Life*'s greatness is that through the comic life of the village fool – who would have been a rabbi had the place not been taken already – and all the other characters of traditional Yiddish theatre, the spectator witnesses every step of the terrible path leading to their extermination.

This is something, which *Life is Beautiful* fails to do. The plot of Benigni's film is well known: it is the story of a father, Guido Orefice, who attempts to protect his child, Giosuè, in an unnamed death camp by shielding him both physically and psychologically from the horrors of such place. The first half of the film establishes its fairy-tale nature, setting the love-story between Jewish Guido and his gentile princess against the background of rising Italian anti-Semitism; the second half opens with the family's deportation and separation, including the murder of Guido's uncle in the gas chambers, and traces the father's attempts to invent an intricate game to help Giosuè withstand the situation. Until, with the ultimate sacrifice, Guido saves Giosuè who will find his mother again in an emotional, happy ending.[11]

Although *Life is Beautiful* deals with several aspects of the

Shoah, it does not do so in ways as subtle or as effective as those used in *Train of Life*. Where Mihaileanu uses widespread symbolism and a clever if perhaps uninventive montage, Benigni employs a visibly realistic, yet infinitely diluted, version of the events. Hence *Life is Beautiful*'s passing references to the smoke from the chimney; medical selections; tattoos; and the final German attempt to destroy evidence, give the impression of being rushed concessions to its historical consultant, Marcello Pezzetti, rather than genuine attempts to inform the public. In comparison, *Train of Life* perhaps presumes a certain historical knowledge from its viewers but risks less in terms of misleading them.

A separate point should be made about the sequence in *Life is Beautiful*, where Guido carries his sleeping son back to their hut at night, immersed in an eerie fog, and Guido fantasises about the whole camp being a dream in what is truly a rather dream-like night. Rather than a nice cup of milky coffee, however, an enormous pile of corpses appears out of the mist. By this point the viewer, especially the second-time viewer, has realised that that mist is the same as in the initial sequence of the film, where a voice-over warned audiences that 'this is a simple story, but it is not an easy one to tell. Like a fable, there is sorrow, and, like a fable, it is full of wonder and happiness.'[12] This is a statement backed up by the entire first half, which masterfully sets the fairy-tale tone through its stress on riddles and magic. Even the cinematography in the first half is aimed at establishing this fairy-tale setting: the large, lightly coloured halls of the Grand Hotel and the theatrical streets of the little Tuscan town point to this. Even the three headlights of the Auschwitz-bound train, which are turned on one by one before the night-time entrance into the camp, are a statement of fictitiousness.

While masterfully establishing the film's tone, the first half also succeeds in making many important points on Italian fascism and on Italian society in general. As we have seen, before *Life is Beautiful*, only De Sica's *The Garden of the Finzi-Contini* had made references to the Italian racial laws, issued independently by Mussolini and willingly signed by the King. Benigni's mock lesson on the alleged superiority of the Italian race is a small masterpiece of extremely serious comedy. Some elements and characters of the fascist bureaucracy, too, amount to more than mere ridiculing of its idiosyncrasies: they make significant points through satire. The way Sig. Rodolfo, the fascist official, abuses his power over the weaker Guido, but bows servile to the town's prefect, is a bitter but gracious critique of the mixture of arrogance, clientelism and pusillanimity on which the regime was built.

The inconsistency, however, between these parts of the film and large sections of the second half are perplexing. The representation of the camp was always going to be the most problematic task Benigni was likely to face, and it is from that point onwards that the film's ambiguity becomes evident. Some of the elements of Benigni's camp are not simple inaccuracies aimed at sketching out a fairy-tale environment, but seriously misleading errors of judgment. The linguistic opposition between guards and inmates, for example, fails to point out the role played in the process of de-humanisation by the impossibility of communication. An assimilated Italian Jew like Guido would arrive at a camp exhausted and disorientated after several days of travel, separation from his family, and physical humiliation, and would understand nothing either the guards or his 'fellow' Jews told him. If, like Guido, he was not religious, he would not even enjoy the comfort of a common religion. Instead, this opposition suggests solidarity, an us-versus-them mentality rather than the each-one-for-himself logic of the camps.

This is not to attack the film's lack of realism, since the film at no point claims to be realistic; that is why this book will not criticise the physical representation of the camp. The physical details of the camp, Guido's ability to defy and deride the guards, these are legitimate narrative tools in a comic, fairy tale narrative. Instead, the target here is the film's lack of accuracy and the authors' inability to grasp the concentration camp experience. Language, solidarity, physical humiliation, these are key issues in explaining the concentration camp as a separate universe and the displacement of the individual thrown into this universe. Benigni's failure, then, is not that he represents this displacement in an unrealistic style, but that he does not represent it.

Furthermore, by employing well-known symbols of the Shoah, such as the smoke from the chimney, in a context not intended to be realistic, Benigni's attempt to represent the camp is ambiguous. These forays into realism contradict the film's own claim, expressed in the opening voice-over, that it is a fairy

Figure 7.2. The end? Benigni seeks closure in relief while Mihaileanu finds it in honesty. *Life is Beautiful* (© 1997 Melampo Cinematografica) and *Train de Vie* (© Radu Mihaileanu).

tale. The ending of the film reinforces its ambiguity: even overlooking the desperately bad taste of the American tank; the perfect tan of the soldier who emerges from it; the green grass; the once again sunny sky; one cannot but be stunned at the final revelation that the initial voice-over was in fact the voice of Giosuè's older self. This establishes him as a survivor, who can confidently state: 'We've won!' On top of this, the words used in the final voice-over, clearly spoken in the indicative mode and in the perfect tense, place what the viewer has just witnessed in a definite moment in the past and, thus, suggest that the fact has indeed taken place. As Ruth Ben-Ghiat has argued, 'this desire for closure [...] takes on special meaning in a country that has been slow to acknowledge the consequence of its history as a Nazi ally and participant in state anti-Semitism'.'[13]

The ending of *Life is Beautiful* has exactly the opposite effect to the ending of *Train of Life*. Whereas the latter erases the feel-good effect created by the film's comic tone, to reveal the only possible ending for the population of a shtetl, the former contrasts the heaps of corpses and the death of our hero by reassuring us that the 'good guys' have won. By telling the story of a community that is now effectively extinct, through its traditional humour and wit, *Train of Life* sketches out a way of living that is no more, giving a stunning sense of collective pain. The sorrow that one does feel in *Life is Beautiful*, on the contrary, is very much an individual one: the audience is emotionally touched by the beauty of the father–child relationship, and by the extreme sacrifice of a father who dies to save his offspring, rather than by the planned systematic annihilation of an entire people.

Thus, though both films effectively employ multiple endings to give the audience an option between a tragic truthful ending and an uplifting but false finale, the results are quite different (Figure 7.2). An interesting alternative way is shown by another recent Holocaust comedy, *Jacob the Liar* (USA, 1999),[14] starring Robin Williams. In this film, *Train of Life*'s ending is reversed: the audience is first told that all the Jews are gassed, but then witnesses an alternative ending where the Jews are all saved. The three films enjoy different degrees of sensitivity and success. However, by offering the audience a solution that is both historically accurate and uplifting, *Life is Beautiful, Train of Life* and *Jacob the Liar* reveal a deliberate effort to make the Shoah acceptable to mass mainstream audiences.

Benigni and co-scriptwriter Vincenzo Cerami, having set up, in the first half of the film, the 'beautiful life' of Trotsky's quotation[15] which inspired the title, go about destroying it, showing that life is all too often not beautiful, especially when people are persecuted, humiliated and systematically exterminated.[16] Thus the film gradually reveals that there is no solution to its own riddle, denying itself the way out granted to most fairy tales. It is in the second half of the film that Guido understands the gravity and scale of what is happening. After the night on which he sees the corpses, there will be no more jokes. Had the film ended with Guido's murder it would have been a great deal more convincing. Barry Langford, speaking in 2001, suggested polemically that perhaps today one can only make a truthful film about the Shoah by lying about it and then admitting the film's fictitiousness.[17] It is arguable that the fairy tale of *Life is Beautiful* would have been much more acceptable had it followed *Train of Life*'s cue in eventually revealing its own fictitiousness. In the final analysis, here lies the film's contradiction, and its failure, in not having the courage to finish what it starts. It makes little difference whether this was brought about by the producers' pressure or by the demands of mainstream American audiences, or the public's expectations of a film released at Christmas.

The reason behind the contradiction inherent in *Life is Beautiful* is probably that it is not a film about the Shoah. It is mainly a film about a father's attempt to save his child. It is around this theme that Benigni builds his fairy tale. It is a story about saving childhood and saving imagination, and that is perfectly adaptable to the struggle against the rationality, discipline and industrial, systematic nature of the Nazis' attempt to annihilate the Jews. The Holocaust setting was ideal, yet not essential, for the sort of extreme conditions in which Benigni wanted to place his story. Similarly, the setting in provincial Italy during the Second World War is only fundamental insofar as it suited perfectly Benigni's personal history and his brand of political satire. Guido's Judaism seems to be even less indispensable for the film, indeed almost accidental. His detachment is different from that of the unreligious, assimilated Jew of the 1930s, who nonetheless looked worriedly at the world's developments. The memory of the Holocaust does not seem among Benigni's top priorities.

Train of Life also makes one of its central themes the role of

Figure 7.3. *Train of Life*: one soul of European Judaism – the assimilated, sophisticated Swiss Jew – trains the Yiddish-speaking rural Jews of the shtetl to behave like Germans. 'L'humour juif c'est comme l'humour allemand, l'humour en plus.' (© Radu Mihaileanu.)

imagination and humour as the ultimate defence of humanity and dignity: in Shlomo's initial speech to the council of the wise and then throughout, it seems to suggest that innocence and irrationality walk side by side. 'Shtetl, shtetl, little shtetl, do not erase from people's eyes what still keeps me alive: their small follies', sings Shlomo's voice-over at the very end. It seems no coincidence, therefore, that the children are the keenest supporters of Shlomo's idea of the train, or that the communists and the fake-Nazis, two disciplinarian groups, are those who endanger the unity of the community itself. The whole film is dependent on Shlomo's attempt to use imagination to begin to heal the wounds inflicted by reality.

This is the fundamental difference in approach between the two film-makers: while Shlomo attempts to clean the eyes that have seen too much, *Life is Beautiful* places emphasis on preventing Giosuè's eyes from seeing in the first place. One film attempts to recapture innocence; the other to prevent its loss. This explains the fact that while *Train of Life* contains a strong element of mourning for the dead, *Life is Beautiful* is completely devoid of mourning, even after Guido's death and Giosuè's liberation.

Mihaileanu shows he is aware that even narratives of survival exist within a context of absolute loss; Benigni does not. As a result, while Benigni's Giosuè proclaims his triumph, Mihaileanu's Jews cannot win. They laugh, they dream, they fear; they live and they die, perhaps they survive. Most of all they beg not to be forgotten.[18] If *Life is Beautiful* has very loudly posed the question, 'Can we make a comedy about the Shoah?', *Train of Life* is a whispered but irrefutable answer.

THE RECEPTION OF *LIFE IS BEAUTIFUL* AND *TRAIN OF LIFE*

The differences between *Life is Beautiful* and *Train of Life* are not only of content and style. They also enjoyed very dissimilar commercial fortunes. Benigni's film was distributed worldwide; it won three Academy Awards; it broke box-office records.[19] In Italy alone, *Life is Beautiful* grossed 93,933,265,000 Italian lire (45.9 million dollars), the most successful Italian film ever made. In France, it was shown in more than 455 screens, seen by 4,315,283 people, with the best spectator–copy ratio of 1998.[20] Its success and fame ensured that it had a great impact on Italian and international awareness of the Shoah. In addition, it made an important point about Holocaust representation, stressing comedy's role as a cinematic language equal in value to any other. *Train of Life*, instead, went almost unnoticed by the public and, as we will see, by critics. It was rather successful at various festivals, yet in France, its country of origin, it was released in only 79 screens for a total of twenty weeks, exactly half the duration of *Life is Beautiful*'s distribution.[21] It was seen by only 216,348 people, coming 122nd in the annual table of most-watched films, as opposed to *Life is Beautiful*'s third place.[22] In Italy it was appreciated, but still did not break out from the circle of art cinemas; it was eventually distributed in the USA, in the wake of Benigni's success, without gaining widespread acclaim. Despite having been subtitled in English for the US audience, it has never been distributed commercially in the United Kingdom.

Most film scholars have approached *Train of Life* only in an attempt to defend Benigni's film from the perhaps undeserved accusation of trivialising the Holocaust. The comic language spoken by the French film was seen as a legitimisation of its Italian counterpart. Various comedies have been made about the Holocaust, however, and countless ones have centred on the ridiculing of Nazi-fascism. Famous pre-1945 films such as Lubitsch's *To Be Or Not To Be*, set in Warsaw in the 1940s,[23] or Chaplin's *The Great Dictator*,[24] were also repeatedly called to the rescue of *Life is Beautiful*.

Yet whereas these films make it seem all but obvious that there cannot be a prejudice against comedy in the treatment of the Nazi persecution of the Jews, the critics have been less concerned with how they treat this subject. Most articles on *Life is Beautiful* emphasised the comic tone of the aforementioned classics; none, however, considered that these remarkable films were made before the Allies had discovered the death camps and the gas chambers, or the scale and systematic nature of the genocide. It would not be too far-fetched to suggest that Chaplin and Lubitsch would not have made their films in the same way, and maybe not made the films at all, in 1945. Years after the Second World War, Chaplin himself said that 'had I known of the actual horrors of the German concentration camps, I could not have made *The Great Dictator*: I could not have made fun of the homicidal insanity of the Nazis.'[25]

Train of Life suffered a similar fate in this respect, as reviewers showed more interest in its comic style than in an analysis of its content. Sander Gilman, in an article tracing the history of the relation between 'laughter and the Holocaust', reserved just a few lines for *Train of Life*, sketching out a very basic account of what the film is about.[26] In an inaccurate and potentially misleading way, Gilman refers to Shlomo's dream of survival as 'masquerading' as a German and leading his fellow Jews to Palestine. Indeed, it is not by chance that Shlomo does not lead the shtetl's train, or that at no point does he impersonate a German. Whereas Benigni's film, especially in its second half, is entirely a vehicle for Guido's antics, *Train of Life*'s strength resides in its collectiveness.

La Repubblica was among very few Italian newspapers to dedicate an article of its own to *Train of Life*. On 27 March 1999, almost the entire first page of the entertainment section was given over to an interview with Mihaileanu, although half the page was occupied by a photograph of the film's beautiful female lead. Entitled 'Comedy and the Shoah', the piece did not analyse the film in any depth. After asking Mihaileanu about his view on comic representation of history and the dangers of attempting to represent the Shoah, the interviewer gives in: 'A reference to Benigni is inevitable ... ', and then: 'Did you like *Life is Beautiful*?'[27] Mihaileanu's thoughts on Benigni's film are not of particular interest here. Instead, the interviewer's question clearly shows how *Train of Life* effectively came to be seen as a corollary of *Life is Beautiful*. Yet this is hardly surprising, coming from an Italian newspaper in the year that an Italian film won three Oscars and earned more money than any before it.

As Gilman suggests – perhaps harshly but understandably, given the near unanimity of ecstatic Italian reviewers – 'for Italian commentators there is no question of the substance of the film, only its Italian provenance'.[28] The reason *Life is Beautiful* did so well in Italy is not only a matter of national pride but also of national taste: Benigni's film is intrinsically Italian, especially but by no means exclusively in its first half: Guido's political satire, matched not by political commitment but by an innate optimism for an ever-uncertain future, is an Italian characteristic; the use of a child's perspective is also a favourite narrative artifice which has won Italian cinema international awards from De Sica's *Ladri di Biciclette* (*Bicycle Thieves*, 1948) to Giuseppe Tornatore's *Nuovo Cinema Paradiso* (*Cinema Paradiso*, 1989). Also appealing to Italian audiences is Guido's ability to make the most of difficult situations, the art of *arrangiarsi*, a formidable Italian passion. Whereas in Lina Wertmuller's *Seven Beauties* these peculiarities had come across as a cynical and selfish survival technique, in Benigni's film they personify joviality and harmlessness, courage and wit.

It would be unfair to say that French commentators have hated *Train of Life*. In fact, it would seem that the film had the rather more unfortunate fate of leaving reviewers indifferent, which to a certain extent explains why it did not exactly draw crowds. Although the 'Public's Award' it won at the 1998 Miami Film Festival seems to suggest a degree of popular success, it appears that French critics did not share this positive opinion. 'Banal' and 'heavy' were recurring criticisms. Articles in *Les Echos* and *Télérama* both compared it – not with the intention of praising it – to Asterix, the former branding it 'Asterix and the rabbis'.[29] In the same article, Annie Copperman concluded in a rather patronising tone that it was 'Slightly heavy, clumsy, but endearing' [*sympathique*].[30]

An examination of the terms used by French daily newspapers reveal a degree of snobbery towards a film produced by an almost unknown director and acted largely by unknown actors, filled with a kind of humour which the French adore in its sophisticated Manhattan variety but evidently not in the more rustic form of its roots. *Le Monde* dismissed it as 'une pantalonnade', literally slapstick, and claimed that only Rufus – one of few better-known actors in the cast – 'pulls his weight'.[31] Other criticisms, such as those of 'impersonal filming', 'standard colour photography' and melodramatic moments of 'guilty conscience',[32] entirely ignore the substance and sensitivity of the film. Instead they condemn, even seek patronisingly to correct, what seems like an unforgivable lack of sophistication on the part of Mihaileanu.

French newspapers dedicated nine articles to *Train of Life*, as opposed to the thirty-eight that were written about *Life is Beautiful*. Specialised journals dedicated extensive coverage to the latter, reviewing it seven times, whereas only four short columns, little more than mentions, were reserved for the former. Although these are merely quantitative considerations, the impression is that Mihaileanu's film both suffered and benefited from the fame of *Life is Beautiful*. On the one hand, *Train of Life* was undoubtedly favoured by the publicity which surrounded the whole topic of Holocaust representation in the months between the French release of *Life is Beautiful* in October 1998 and the Academy Awards early the following year; on the other hand, it could not compete with Miramax's enormous distribution and marketing power. Undoubtedly, *Train of Life* was less glamorous and, because of its peculiarly Jewish culture and humour, less inclusive than Benigni's film.

Only the Catholic *La Croix* praised *Train of Life* without reservation.[33] Similarly, in specialised film journals there was general indifference to the film, only one reviewer enjoying Mihaileanu's effort. Jean-Pierre Lavoignat, writing in *Studio*,[34] awarded it two stars, one more than *Godzilla*, though two fewer than *Saving Private Ryan*. He called it 'clumsy' and 'often too naive', although he was not overwhelmingly critical. In *Positif*,[35] the film critic Yannick Dahan was equally unimpressed although not entirely negative. He did not see in *Train of Life* the ability to use laughter 'to penetrate history, question it', a quality which he found, instead, in *Life is Beautiful*. Y. D. Katelan, a reviewer for the monthly magazine *Première*, was even less generous: 'Excellent idea but a guilty conscience, [...] the screenplay's structure is but a series of clumsy sketches, [...] the female character is ridiculous, [...]

and even its set pieces are too artificial to be moving.'[36] In fact, *Première*'s eight reviewers awarded *Train of Life* an average of one-and-a-half stars, less than half what they gave *Life is Beautiful*.[37] This kind of indifferent criticism reveals an inability, even a downright reluctance, to engage with Jewish humour.

Against the trend, as ever, was *Les Cahiers du Cinéma*. From its highbrow approach it paid tribute to *Train of Life*. The critic pointed out the film's musical score, before moving on to an analysis of its final shot, which he called 'unforgettable'. To sum up, he wrote: '*Train of Life* is a perfectly coherent and morally indisputable work.'[38] By means of this finale, Mihaileanu concluded his film's theory by denying its hypothesis: he showed that it is impossible 'to clean the eyes that have seen too much'. This is something Benigni failed to do, insisting until the final curtain that innocent eyes can be prevented from seeing the truth. *Les Cahiers du Cinéma* was alone in recognising this. Like *Train of Life*'s reviewer, another critic writing in the same issue about *Life is Beautiful* noticed the intrinsic ambiguity of that film's second part. After the scene of the translation, he suggested, in a piece conspicuous for its brevity, that the film 'seems to be an obstinate attempt to not see by laughter, to lose all tragic memory thanks to comedy'.[39] With regard to Benigni's film too, *Les Cahiers du Cinéma* seems to go against the trend, not least by reserving it such little visibility. This chapter will return later on to the implications of this stance. First, however, it will be useful to examine other reactions to this controversial film.

It is difficult to assess the outcome of a debate like the one that surrounded *Life is Beautiful* between its Italian release at Christmas 1997, its festival triumphs in Cannes and Jerusalem, and the 1999 Academy Awards. The film had the undoubted merit of unleashing in people an emotional reaction, but this in turn exasperated the debate and at times prevented a more profitable and balanced exchange of opinions. The result was the formation of two opposing camps: one was almost censorious, including David Denby's accusation that the film was 'a benign form of Holocaust denial', playing on the director's name;[40] the other idolising. For French critics, writing on the eve of the film's release in France, in October 1998, when the controversy was rife, it was especially difficult to escape from this dualism.

Les Inrockuptibles's Serge Kaganski is a telling example. The same man who had mildly disapproved of *Train of Life* suddenly assumed a moral high ground: 'From beginning to end, *Life is Beautiful* is false',[41] he wrote. And, astonishingly, he continued: 'filming fairy tales on the Shoah should be forbidden'.[42] Kaganski acknowledged Lanzmann's stance and made it his own, but surprisingly the writer had none of these reservations about *Train of Life* which, after all, was an equally fictional film about the Shoah. He concluded: 'when the cultural elites swim in semantic confusion [...] the falsifiers of history have won one battle in their doubtful fight'.[43]

A similar ethical fervour was displayed by *L'Humanité,* in whose pages Benigni was accused of transforming 'a death camp into a factory with a slightly tough discipline, [...] and the programmed, systematic extermination of six million children, women, and men into a glossy soap-opera'.[44] Moreover, this reviewer called the film 'obscene' and scorned Benigni for comparing himself to Chaplin who, he explained, 'filmed *The great dictator* and not *Charlot in the gas chambers*'.[45] More restrained but perhaps more incisive was *Le Monde,* which said: 'Of course, Benigni does not tell us to forget, quite the contrary, but his cult of remembrance already displays the signs of amnesia.'[46]

An altogether more balanced approach was taken by Pascal Merigeau of *Le Nouvel Observateur*. He realised that 'commercial needs justify happy endings' and, although worried that laughter might assuage the trauma and anaesthetise the pain, Merigeau did not seem to have moral reservations about the film itself. Nonetheless, he turned to Bazin and the theorists of the French New Wave, to assert that Benigni should consider himself morally responsible for any misunderstanding in his audiences. He quoted the warning one of Bazin's collaborators, the film-maker Rivette, issued about the over-familiarity of horrific images:

> If (the director) dares to represent a fact as if it were *reality* [italics in original], and in a manner which is physically bearable for the spectator [...] and each person becomes accustomed to the horror [...] then who, next time, will be outraged by what, in effect, will have become less shocking?[47]

Merigeau and others formed a sort of 'third way' of interpreting *Life is Beautiful.* Although they did not doubt Benigni's good faith, they were concerned that the combination of the film's success, its comic power, its uplifting ending, and the many prime-time television showings it was destined to receive, might influence negatively the viewer's perception of the Shoah. Merigeau was also worried that this film might obscure other, more worthy, works on the Shoah: on this point he wrote: 'in twenty, in thirty years time, what will be the importance of Resnais' *Night and Fog*, of the nine-and-a-half hours of *Shoah*, of the pages of Primo Levi? What importance will History have?'[48]

Didier Peron, of the left-wing paper *Libération*, argued along the same lines. 'The public is always willing to let itself be exorcised by laughter and tears for faults it is not guilty of, and of which, most importantly, it does not want to bear the weight.'[49] Peron regretted most of all what seemed to him like an imposed choice between considering *Life is Beautiful* as a masterpiece or as a work of historical revisionism. Annie Copperman, in *Les Echos*, concluded a positive review of the film by voicing her concern: 'the question is not over Benigni's talent, or even his good intentions, it is over how the film will be interpreted'.[50] Jorge Semprun, a survivor of Buchenwald, writing in the same paper, praised the film's emphasis on the absurdity on which the Nazi regime was built, but remained sceptical about what the public would think after watching it.

The majority of articles in French newspapers were overwhelmingly positive about the film. Rather than proposing a specific reading of it, however, these often amounted to nothing more than passionate reactions against perceived threats of censorship. In defence of *Life is Beautiful*, the critics cited now freedom of speech, now the healing powers of imagination, now the opinion of individual survivors of the camps as well as, of course, the precedents of Charlie Chaplin and Ernst Lubitsch. Along these lines moved, for example, Jean-François Bouthors in *La Croix*, who at least remained consistent with his earlier praise of *Train of Life*.[51] Or *L'Evénement du Jeudi*, which again brought forward the views of writer and survivor Jorge Semprun.[52] More perceptive was Jean-Claude Loiseau in *Télérama*, who suggested that having to choose 'between the unfilmable and the overfilmed [Benigni] rid his film of all realism in order not to betray history'.[53]

Italian reviewers were remarkably united in exalting Benigni's film before, and especially after, the Academy Awards ceremony. He became a sort of national hero. In February 1999, halfway through the life of the first left-wing government in

Italian post-war history, the Italian state-television RAI broadcast the ceremony live from Benigni's native Tuscan village of Veiano. The programme was staged in Veiano's Casa del Popolo, the former communist-sponsored cultural and recreation centre. In May 2000, the film's Oscar-winning theme music, 'Life is Beautiful', now turned into a song with new lyrics in English, was performed for Pope John Paul II, in St. Peter's square in Rome, by the composer Nicola Piovani and the Israeli singer Noah.[54]

This is not irrelevant because politics, more than any other single factor, has influenced the Italian debate on *Life is Beautiful*. Benigni had been an outspoken anti-clerical and left-wing militant for many years, and his *vis comica* had always been drenched in political fervour. In the 1980s, his jokes about the Church and his satire of the then ruling Socialists earned him an unofficial ban from appearing on RAI.[55] In the light of these considerations, the papal audience assumes a fundamental importance. It essentially sanctioned Benigni's evolution from icon of the Italian left to national hero.

Evidence for this is that two years after the 1999 Academy Awards, *Life is Beautiful* could still draw much attention to itself. At 20.50 on 22 October 2001, RAI Uno screened the terrestrial premiere of the film. It recorded the highest audience rating ever for a film, with sixteen million and eighty thousand viewers, a share of 53.6 per cent.[56] Apart from the obvious popularity of the film, this data points to a number of other interesting factors. First, RAI Uno had planned to broadcast the film on 3 October 2001, before its director Agostino Saccà decided to postpone it in order to arrange more extensive advertising for the film's launch. The final instalment of this advertising campaign was, on 20 October, a half-hour documentary retracing the fortunes of *Life is Beautiful* through various interviews granted by Benigni to the channel's film critic, Vincenzo Mollica. As a further demonstration of the attention and affection Italians still had for the film, it is worth pointing out that Italian public opinion helped RAI advertise both the film's broadcast and its record audience. Turin's *La Stampa*, for example, dedicated to the film an article on 22 October, and as many as three on Wednesday 24 October, when the ratings results were made public.[57]

Second, only the Sanremo Festival of Italian Popular Song – broadcast on radio and then on television in February every year since 1939 – and Italian football internationals, the two defining events of Italian national–popular culture, have ever achieved higher ratings.[58] This spells out how remarkable Benigni's achievement has been. Third, the viewing share peaked at 22.55, reaching a stunning 63.2 per cent of all viewers. Whereas this could no doubt have been caused by viewers turning over to RAI Uno at the end of other programmes on different channels, it seems no coincidence that spectators tuned in just in time for the film's emotional ending. This at the same time proves the paramount importance of the ending within the structure of the film, and suggests that the reunion of young Giosuè with his mother holds the key to understanding the full extent of the film's success.

Finally, the programming choice of the other Italian channels is telling. RAI Due, the second of three state-owned television channels, staged a last-minute change of schedule by showing Sylvester Stallone's *Cliffhanger*, which had already been aired, and RAI Tre broadcast a weekly quiz, *Novecento*, which retraced the history of the twentieth century through Italian popular culture. Similarly, two of Silvio Berlusconi's three private television channels, Rete Quattro and Italia Uno, did not try to compete with RAI Uno's blockbuster. His third and main channel, Canale Cinque, however, decided to match *Life is Beautiful* with a special extended evening episode of *Il Grande Fratello* (*Big Brother*), the immensely popular reality-TV show. On top of that, Canale Cinque announced that the episode would contain the week's nominations for eviction from the contestants' communal house.

The show's producers were quick to point out that the special episode had been planned to make up for the one postponed on the evening of September 11 2001, in the wake of the terrorist attacks on New York. The producer, Marco Bassetti, as well as the channel's director, Giovanni Modica, also said how pleased they were by *Life is Beautiful*'s result.[59] Vincenzo Cerami, the film's co-scriptwriter, seemed less persuaded by Canale Cinque's choice of programme, suggesting that it was 'an unfortunate choice, […] which made the programme's vulgarity even more evident'.[60] Considering the amount of forethought television channels put into their schedule, it seems indeed very unlikely that the clash was accidental. Moreover, this possibility starts to look remote in the light of the long-term tension between Berlusconi and Benigni.

The first evidence of this confrontation goes back to 1996, during a heated election campaign, when Benigni toured the country with a show, *Tuttobenigni '96*, in which he openly attacked Berlusconi and his cronies as corrupt and false.[61] Accordingly, two years later, when the film came out in time for Christmas 1997 and enjoyed a remarkable success with both public and press, one newspaper alone attacked it with vehemence. *Il Foglio*, a daily paper directed by Giuliano Ferrara,[62] published an article entitled 'Those who love it and those who loathe it', signed by an unknown Buttafuoco (Mr Spitfire). Not much was said of 'those who love it', but in return 'those who loathe it' found adequate space to express themselves. Buttafuoco was clearly no other than Ferrara, himself brutally ridiculed for his obesity by Benigni in his 1996 show. He later confessed that he had not seen the film, adding that his criticisms were of a 'Dadaist' nature.

The result was enormous outrage, led by Aldo Tassone of *La Repubblica*, a moderate left-wing paper. Italian intellectuals rallied around the film, which was shortly afterwards selected for the Cannes Film Festival.[63] Two years later, Ferrara, having seen the film, signed a more elaborate if no less polemical critique of the film. Here, he acutely accused it of 'denying the right to the elaboration of pain and mourning of many who cannot laugh about Auschwitz', and of being 'spiritually lazy, uninterested in understanding [the Shoah] and helping everyone else pretend that they have not understood'.[64]

In his very thorough article on *Life is Beautiful*, film scholar Maurizio Viano has reviewed American reaction to the film, pointing to much the same conclusion: that the film was often talked about but seldom understood.[65] Whereas in Italy this has much to do with politics, elsewhere it might be because of Benigni's wildly comic and anti-conformist personality, which everyone witnessed at the Cannes Festival and Academy Awards ceremonies. This might explain why so many newspapers and film magazines have dedicated pages and articles to interviews with the Italian actor–director, rather than to the analysis of his film. It is astonishing that *Première, Positif* and *Studio*[66] all decided to interview Benigni at length, but contained no critique whatsoever of the film. Conversely, it is striking that in Britain, where Benigni is considerably less well-known than in France, *Sight and Sound* analysed in depth the film and its role in the context of Holocaust representation.[67]

Viano asked scholars to take Benigni's film seriously, 'as a text whose value exceeds the contingent polemics it has stirred'.[68] He pointed out a pattern in the American response to the film, according to which enthusiastic daily newspaper reviews were followed by less impressed critiques on the part of weekly 'cultural' magazines and even less warm ones by specialised journals. Indeed, Viano suggested that film scholars chose to ignore the film. In support of his argument he used the failure of *Les Cahiers du Cinéma* 'to give the film even the recognition of an attack'.[69] There is some truth in Viano's theory, although it applies more to the United States than to continental Europe.

More importantly for the comparative purpose of the present analysis, the reception of *Train of Life* seems to have followed the opposite pattern. Viano acknowledged Mihaileanu's film but did not feel the need to call for the same recognition that he craved for Benigni's. This is surprising, considering that *Train of Life* has not enjoyed the media attention, the marketing effort, the width of distribution, the public success or the critical fervour reserved for *Life is Beautiful*. In a final analysis, it will be these all-important economic factors, more than academic attention, that will allow Benigni's work to make some lasting contribution to a collective memory of the Shoah, certainly in Italy, and quite possibly elsewhere. What remains to be assessed is the quality of this contribution, which will be important if the film is shown and talked about in the context of other Holocaust films and documentaries, and supported by a thorough knowledge of history, but could be misleading if it was to be considered as a surrogate for historical study.

As audiences continue to rely on film to construct their histories, both the wisdom of embracing cinema as a legitimate historical source and the need thoroughly to contextualise it become more evident. This is extremely clear in the analysis of Holocaust survival narratives, whose success highlights both the offer and the demand for closure. In popular culture as in politics and history, closure may be legitimately demanded though never justifiably imposed. Furthermore, if these two films show anything, they show that this craving for the resolution of past traumas can be satisfied in different ways; that the demand for closure itself is not a threat to the accurate and sensitive commemoration of the past, but the crowd-pleasing offer of an uplifting resolution almost inevitably is; that it is impossible to clean eyes that have seen too much but it is disconcertingly easy to prevent eyes from seeing in the first place.

NOTES

1. Enrico Lancia (ed.), *Dizionario del Cinema Italiano*, vol. 6 (Roma: Gremese, 2002).
2. 6,148,256,000 Italian lire. Lancia (ed.), *Dizionario*, vol. 6.
3. On Rosi's film see Bryan Cheyette, 'Levi's *The Truce*: From Text to Film', in Nancy Horrowitz, *Primo Levi: Witnessing, Memory and Writing* (New Haven, CT: University Press of New England, 1999).
4. Roberto Benigni, *La Vita è Bella*, Italy, 1997.
5. Radu Mihaileanu, *Train de Vie*, France, 1998, produced by Noé Productions and Raphael Films *et al.*, distributed by TF1 and AB Video. The film won the Critics' Prize and the 'Premio Anica Flash' at the 1998 Venice Film Festival, as well as at the Mostra de Sao Paulo in the same year, and the Miami Film Festival and the Sundance Film Festival in 1999.
6. Hilene Flanzbaum, '"But wasn't it terrific?" A Defense of Liking *Life is Beautiful*', *Yale Journal of Criticism*, 14, 1 (2001), pp.273–86.
7. Benigni claims to have inspired himself with Primo Levi's writings, among other things, but this is not necessarily apparent in his film. 'Benigni: Régard d'un Clown', interview with Michel Rebichon, *Studio* (November 1998), pp.97–100.
8. Before leaving Romania for Paris in 1980, Mihaileanu was an actor at Bucharest Yiddish Theatre. For an exploration of the Yiddish theatrical tradition see Nahma Sandrow, *Vagabond Stars: A World History of Yiddish Theatre*, Limelight Editions (New York: Seth Press, 1985).
9. As we will see in due course, very few articles have acknowledged *Train of Life*'s existence. Among these are Maurizio Viano, '*Life is Beautiful*: Reception, Allegory and Holocaust Laughter', *Annali d'Italianistica*, 17 (1999) and Sander Gilman, 'Is Life Beautiful? Can the Shoah be Funny? Some Thoughts on Recent and Older Films', *Critical Inquiry* (Winter 2000).
10. This was Mihaileanu's second feature-length film; his first was the little-known *Trahir* (*Betrayal*, 1993), which evoked the communist dictatorship, which he had fled in 1980, going briefly to Israel and then France.
11. Anita Kertzer, 'Like a Fable, not a Pretty Picture: Holocaust Representation in Roberto Benigni and Anita Lobel', *Michigan Quarterly Review*, 39, 2 (Spring 2000), pp.279–300.
12. The initial voice-over was not there when the film was first released in 1997. Benigni added it to the film and cut six minutes off the first part between the release in Italy and Cannes. The director tells us that Harvey Weinstein, whose distribution giant Miramax was buying the film for the US market, asked him to do so. Allegedly, he was worried that the American public's inadequate knowledge of Second World War history would lead to misunderstandings. Interview with Benigni, *Studio* (November 1998), p.99.
13. Ruth Ben-Ghiat, 'The Secret Histories of Roberto Benigni's *Life is Beautiful*', *Yale Journal of Criticism*, 14, 1 (2001), pp.253–66.
14. Peter Kassovitz, *Jacob the Liar*, USA–France–Hungary, 1999. The film was shot in 1996, before *Life is Beautiful*, but released only in the wake of Benigni's film.
15. 'Natasha has just come up to the window from the courtyard and opened it wider so that the air may enter more freely into my room. I can see the bright green strip of grass beneath the wall, and the clear blue sky above the wall, and sunlight everywhere. Life is Beautiful. Let the future generations cleanse it of all evil, oppression and violence, and enjoy it to the full.' Of course, Trotsky died; he did not walk out of the bunker shouting: 'I've won!' For one view on the title's relevance see Viano, '*Life is Beautiful*'.
16. In this respect, legendary French film-maker Jean-Luc Godard replied to journalists

asking about Benigni's film by saying he had not seen it, because the film should have been entitled *Life is Beautiful at Auschwitz*. Rebichon, 'Régard d'un Clown', p.99.

17. Dr Barry Langford speaking at a seminar on Italian Holocaust Film, held at University College London, 22 March 2001.
18. 'Shtetl, shtetl, shtetl, ne m'oublie pas shtetl/Je suis parti un jour en train pour aller très loin', are the first two lines of the final voice-over.
19. The highest-grossing foreign film in Italian history is *Titanic*, which grossed $70.9 million. Lancia (ed.), *Dizionario*, vol. 6.
20. This ratio was of 8,495 spectators per distributed copy; see Simon Simsi, *Ciné Référence: Les Films et les Chiffres* (Paris: Dixit, 2000).
21. Ibid.
22. Ibid.
23. Ernst Lubitsch, *To Be Or Not To Be*, USA, 1942.
24. Charles Chaplin, *The Great Dictator*, USA, 1940.
25. David Robinson, *Chaplin: His Life and Art* (London: Collins, 1985), p.485.
26. Gilman, 'Is Life Beautiful?'
27. 'La Commedia e la Shoah', *La Repubblica*, 27 March 1999.
28. Gilman, 'Is Life Beautiful?'
29. Annie Copperman, *Les Echos*, 17 September 1998.
30. Ibid.
31. *Le Monde*, 16 September 1998.
32. Serge Kaganski, *Les Inrockuptibles*, 16 September 1998.
33. Jean-François Bouthors, *La Croix*, 17 September 1998.
34. Jean-Pierre Lavoignat, *Studio*, 137 (September 1998).
35. Yannick Dahan, *Positif*, 452 (October 1998).
36. Y. D. Katelan, *Première*, 259 (October 1998).
37. *Première*, 260 (November 1998).
38. E.H., *Les Cahiers du Cinéma*, 528 (October 1998).
39. A. d. B., *Les Cahiers du Cinéma*, 528 (October 1998).
40. David Denby, '*Life is Beautiful*', *The New Yorker*, 15 March 1999, pp.96–9. See also Denby, 'Darkness out of light', *The New Yorker*, 16 November 1998, p.116.
41. Kaganski, *Les Inrockuptibles*, 21 October 2001, p.48.
42. Ibid.
43. Ibid.
44. M. G., *L'Humanité*, 18 May 1998.
45. Ibid.
46. Samuel Blumenfeld, *Le Monde*, 22 October 1998.
47. Pascal Merigeau , *Le Nouvel Observateur*, 15 October 1998.
48. Ibid.
49. Didier Peron, *Libération*, 21 October 1998.
50. Annie Copperman, *Les Echos*, 21 October 1998.
51. Jean-François Bouthors, *La Croix*, 21 October 1998.
52. Jorge Semprun, *L'Evénement du Jeudi*, 22 October 1998.
53. Jean-Claude Loiseau, *Télérama*, 21 October 1998.
54. 'Un primo maggio tra Papa e rock', *La Nazione*, 30 April, 2000.
55. It is worth pointing out that under Bettino Craxi's leadership, the Socialist Party (PSI) – which had already taken centrist positions since the mid-1960s – had abandoned any pretence of being a left-wing party.
56. The Auditel (Italian television ratings agency) data are available from www.auditel.it.
57. Fulvia Caprara, 'Benigni sfida il Grande Fratello', *La Stampa*, 22 October 2001; Lietta Tornabuoni, 'Benigni: "Grazie Italiani" ', 24 October 2001; Fulvia Caprara 'Per *La Vita è Bella* 16 milioni di telespettatori' and 'Roberto felice', 24 October 2001.
58. On the role of the San Remo Festival of Italian Music in Italian popular culture see Stephen Gundle, 'Memory and Identity: Popular Culture in Post-War Italy', in Patrick McCarthy (ed.), *Italy Since 1945* (Oxford: Oxford University Press), pp.183–96.
59. *La Stampa*, 24 October 2001.
60. Ibid.
61. Roberto Benigni, *Tuttobenigni '96*, Italy, 1996.
62. Giuliano Ferrara is a well-known television and press journalist. Son of a renowned

trade unionist, Ferrara was a communist activist and student leader in 1968, before shifting towards Bettino Craxi's Socialist Party (PSI), and eventually migrating in the 1990s into Berlusconi's Forza Italia, where he served in government as a Minister for Relations with Parliament.

63. The Italian row over *Life is Beautiful* was reported in France by Sophie Grassim, *L'Express*, 22 October 1998.
64. Giuliano Ferrara, 'Non basta un Oscar a far bella la vita', *Panorama*, 18 February 1999, p.29.
65. Maurizio Viano, '*Life is Beautiful*'.
66. *Positif*, 452 (October 1998); *Studio*, 139 (November 1998); *Première*, 260 (November 1998).
67. J. Hoberman 'Dreaming the Unthinkable', *Sight and Sound*, 9, 2, (February 1999), pp.20–4.
68. Viano, '*Life is Beautiful*''.
69. Ibid.

Conclusion: Beyond Benigni

For a period of about two decades, the memory of the Shoah developed along broadly parallel lines in Italy and France. After the Second World War, both countries failed to acknowledge the extent and systematic nature of the specific anti-Jewish persecution. Furthermore, as the commemorative ceremonies at Père Lachaise demonstrate,[1] the Jewish identity of the victims was incorporated into the wider process of commemoration of victimised nationals, especially the targets of political persecution. Film mirrored and contributed to this process. For a decade after the war, no film was made to deal primarily with the persecution of the Jews.

Moreover, the Holocaust films eventually made between the mid-1950s and early 1960s clearly show both countries' inability and unwillingness to consider the Shoah as anything other than another battlefield in the wider war between fascism and anti-fascism. In 1956, *Night and Fog*'s failure to refer directly to Jewish victims epitomised this attitude. The reception of *Night and Fog* further proves this point. In reviewing the film, no French critic mentioned Jews, or that Auschwitz – footage of which occupies much of the film – was primarily a place dedicated to their slaughter. In accordance with this view, if Jews were considered victims of the war they were innocent civilian casualties, not specific targets of a genocidal policy. Furthermore, films such as *Enclosure* and, to a certain extent, *Kapo* and *The Gold of Rome* seem to consider Jews guilty of not having actively joined the anti-fascist camp, either out of lack of ideological awareness or cowardliness. Thus, although these films are not devoid of compassion, the deaths of David in *Enclosure*, Edith in *Kapo* and Giulia in *The Gold of Rome* suggest a degree of guilt, to be expiated only through martyrdom.

Nonetheless, the fact itself that a documentary such as *Night and Fog* was commissioned by the government, made and shown – in spite of considerable difficulties – in France rather than in Italy, suggests a different level of interest in the subject from an early stage. Resnais's neglect of the Jews detracts little from the fact that his film seeks to understand the concentration camp system and the concept and scale of annihilation by gas. As a result of his thematic choices, *Night and Fog* is no mere commemoration of fallen comrades, but a worthwhile investigation into an enormous crime. Nothing of the sort exists in Italy to this day. Similarly, the responses to *Kapo* and *The Gold of Rome* in Italy, and to the former and *The Enclosure* in France, prove that, already by 1960, French commentators had a better grasp of the history of the Shoah. Also, the many references to Resnais's documentary in the French reception of these two fiction films prove that *Night and Fog* had become the paradigmatic work on the death camps.

With the release of Marcel Ophuls's *The Sorrow and the Pity*, in 1971, these differences became more marked. Ophuls's film seized the generational challenge of 1968 to force a rethink of the Gaullist and communist resistancialist myths. *The Sorrow and the Pity* was, in part, the result of a specifically French Jewish effort to obtain recognition of the crimes committed against Jews, and French involvement in them. But France's 1970s reassessment of its wartime experiences was not driven only by the efforts of the Jewish community. The pervasiveness and susceptibility of the debate sparked by *The Sorrow and the Pity* reveals a wider French desire to deal with the truth about French collaboration. French introspection is evident in the deluge of films, novels and historiography that followed Ophuls's example.

By the 1970s, Italy, like France, had achieved a clearer understanding of the Shoah. De Sica's *The Garden of the Finzi-Contini* shows this by dealing, more specifically than any Italian film before it, with the plight of Italian Jews well before the German occupation. As discussed earlier in this book, however, the film's reception – including comments by the director himself – challenged what the film plainly shows: that Italian anti-Semitism was not a German import and that Italians were actively involved in theorising and carrying out the persecution. This is the most striking difference between French and Italian attitudes towards the Shoah: on the one hand, France rapidly began to develop an obsession with uncovering its own collusion with the Shoah; on the other hand, Italy continued to portray the genocide as an alien event. This is proven further by the fact that, while film-makers from both countries became fascinated with the murky underworld of collaboration, Italian film-makers set their narratives abroad while French ones almost inevitably placed them at home. Cavani's *The Night Porter* situated its action in Austria, but Malle's *Lacombe, Lucien*, Drach's *Les Violons du Bal* and Losey's *Mr Klein* all used French characters in a French context.

What Italy and France shared, in the 1970s, was a distinct inability to tell Holocaust narratives from a Jewish perspective. Films such as *The Night Porter*, *Lacombe, Lucien*, *Mr Klein* and, to a lesser extent, *The Garden* either follow non-Jewish characters or use different concepts – such as class, gender or provenance – to construct their identity. This inability to adopt a Jewish perspective in narrating Holocaust experiences is also reflected in the reception of these films. Commentators failed to turn the increase in films set during the Shoah into a historically-informed discussion of the Shoah. In particular, film-makers and critics alike failed to see that, in order fully to grasp and represent the Shoah, it was paramount to recuperate the voice of the victims: not just those who escaped or survived deportation, but also those who perished.

In France this complex task was accomplished by the gargantuan effort of Claude Lanzmann. His 1985 documentary *Shoah* sought to assume the perspective of those who had been murdered and, therefore, had no voice of their own with which to testify. Lanzmann's film also served the purpose of offering, through cinema, a comprehensive analysis of the detailed functioning of the Nazi extermination procedure. *Shoah* left no doubt as to what this procedure was or against whom it was applied. The reception of *Shoah* reveals a certain degree of difficulty in coming to terms with the sheer scope both of the persecution and of the film, but also an immense respect for Lanzmann's undertaking, and the desire to use it, particularly against the threat of revisionism and Holocaust denial.

Whereas many film-makers before Lanzmann had chosen

the Shoah as a setting for their narratives, *Shoah* was perhaps the first film truly about the genocide of the Jews. Furthermore, by rejecting the sacrificial overtones of the term 'Holocaust', Lanzmann restored to the event its proper name. There is no overestimating the uniqueness and significance of *Shoah*. Nonetheless, the film also performed an unforeseen role: in making the gas chambers its central theme, *Shoah* also contributed to making more acceptable the fictional representation of the extermination process. In the 1990s, this would be attempted in more ways than ever before, producing a vast corpus of images, from the abstract to the most explicit ones.

Since the 1990s, French and Italian film-makers have been fascinated with the Shoah. Constantly seeking untold stories, the concentration camp experience has become the most extreme setting for uplifting stories of resistance and survival. Benigni's *Life is Beautiful* simultaneously symbolised this trend and a recent Italian effort to accept Italy's role in the persecution. On the one hand, it shows how film-makers have sought new genres and styles to approach the subject; on the other hand, the first half of *Life is Beautiful*, and particularly Benigni's savage critique of the racial laws, mirrors the institutional effort to condemn the 1938 discriminatory legislation on its sixtieth anniversary. The second half of the film, however, confirms that the Italian investigation of the persecution of Italian Jews was in its infancy in 1997. Furthermore, the comparative analysis of *Life is Beautiful* and *Train of Life* suggests that France still enjoys more familiarity with Judaism and Jewishness. This is reinforced further by Francesco Rosi's 1997 *The Truce*, which completely disregards the Jewish side of Primo Levi's identity. While *Train of Life* shows that French film-makers, too, are trying to tackle the Shoah with alternative modes of representation, Mihaileanu's ability to tell a fictional Holocaust story from a Jewish perspective, and forego survival as an uplifting finale, epitomises how deeply the different paths chosen by Italy and France have affected their shared memory of the Shoah.

With reference to the Italian and French memory of the Shoah, 'shared memory' is a more accurate term than 'national memory' or 'collective memory'. The evidence analysed in this study suggests that a collective memory of the Shoah did not exist independently of that of other aspects of the war. A Jewish memory of the Shoah, however, was there in each country throughout the post-war period. This was expressed privately in the home or publicly through memoirs, lobbying for recognition. But the difficulty most film-makers and reviewers have shown, in understanding the Shoah as a Jewish tragedy, suggests that the Shoah was not a trauma of the majority of French or Italian citizens. Hence – while cinema is undoubtedly only one of a number of aspects that should be analysed to offer a more complete answer – this study suggests that looking for a national memory of the Shoah will prove less fruitful than analysing the interaction between different memories of a shared history.

If the attempted genocide of the Jews has not been, in either country, a trauma of the majority, then the Freudian trauma–repression–expression cycle – which may yet be applicable to other traumatic experiences of the Second World War, such as the occupation – does not successfully explain the unease with which the Shoah has been approached. Instead, there are other reasons for this unease: on the one hand the ignorance of the extent of the genocide and its systematic nature; on the other hand the unwillingness to accept the collusion of part of the local population with the genocide. In fact, when these conditions have been partly overcome – in 1970s France and 1990s Italy – public understanding of the Shoah has also improved.

THE FUTURE OF HOLOCAUST REPRESENTATION

With historiography studying every aspect of the Shoah from ever-different perspectives and remembrance becoming increasingly a public and institutional issue, the mode of representation is the main challenge facing contemporary Holocaust film narratives. How far into a concentration camp should we take the camera? How realistic should our representation of suffering be? Should there be any taboo subjects in Holocaust representation – such as the gas chambers, for instance? At times, the absolutist tones of the controversy that surrounded *Life is Beautiful* seemed to suggest the film had pushed representational boundaries so far that they could not be strained any further. Already, only a few years after *Life is Beautiful*, it seems clear that those representational boundaries will be stretched further still.

As a result of this dominant approach, which sells realism as accuracy, even the gas chamber is no longer a taboo of Holocaust representation. In 1999, Donna Deitch's US television movie, *The Devil's Arithmetic*, showed a gas chamber in action, yet this remains an isolated example. In Costa-Gavras's *Amen* (France, 2000), SS officers observed through a spyhole the effects of Zyklon B. The camera remained a third party throughout, refraining from showing the audience what the officers' gaze beheld. Three years later, in 2003, Tim Blake-Nelson's *The Grey Zone* changed perspective and went further, mounting a shoulder-held camera on an imaginary child being led by his naked mother into the Auschwitz gas chamber. The subjective angle ended as the pair entered, stopping short of showing us the functioning and consequences of the chambers.

This approach is not all-encompassing, and fiction and documentary film-makers alike have rejected the misguided notion that the understanding of history is directly proportional to the graphicness of its representation. In the adaptation of Martin Sherman's play *Bent* (Great Britain, 1997), Sean Mathias represented the camp as a white, oppressive, empty space, shunning traditional imagery of the lager such as crowded barracks and muddy compounds. In 2005 and 2006, two documentary films, Rex Bloomstein's *KZ* and Alan Marcus's *Beautiful Dachau*, have filmed present-day Matthausen and Dachau, rejecting archival footage by breaking down the boundaries between past and present in a way that resonates with Lanzmann. Nevertheless, in spite of these challenges, the constant quest for more extreme narrative settings – such as the Sonderkommandos in *The Grey Zone*, or Hitler's bunker in *Der Untergang* (*Downfall*, Oliver Hirschbiegel, Germany, 2005) – it seems likely that, eventually, other film-makers will follow and surpass Deitch.

Since 1998, in France and Italy as in the rest of Europe and in the United States, the Shoah has become an immensely popular subject with film-makers and audiences, and therefore also with producers. In the 2001 film *Concorrenza Sleale* (*Unfair Competition*), Ettore Scola decided to change the setting of his story of discrimination and solidarity from the experiences of an immigrant in modern-day Italy, imagined in the original script, to those of a Roman Jewish family in 1938. While the film-maker rejected the idea that the change of setting altered the crux of the film, it was a telling choice that further proved the entrance of the Italian discrimination of Jews into the realm of admissible memory.[2] In that sense, Scola's film is very much the direct result of the Italian government's acknowledgement, since 1998, of Italian responsibility in the persecution.

Like *Unfair Competition*, Andrea and Antonio Frazzi's *Il Cielo Cade* (*The Sky is Falling*, Italy, 2000) and Gerard Jugnot's *Monsieur Batignole* (France, 2002) are Holocaust stories told from the perspective of a child. *The Sky is Falling* is an adaptation of the true story of the family of Albert Einstein's cousin, murdered in Tuscany shortly before the liberation. It is a film of uncommon sensitivity, discretion, and emotion. Unlike *Unfair Competition* and *Monsieur Batignole*, *The Sky is Falling* does not seek to offset tragedy by using comic elements. Instead, Jugnot's film exalts the simple courage of the average Frenchman, on this occasion embodied by a porcine-looking butcher who ditches his self-centred indifference to save a Jewish boy, in whose parents' capture the butcher had been instrumental. *Monsieur Batignole* points to a recent French trend – confirmed also by *Laissez Passer* (*Safe Conduct*, Bernard Tavernier, France, 2000), and *Bon Voyage* (Paul Rappeneau, France, 2003) – which aims to celebrate an apolitical bravery, triggered by a loosely-defined personal malaise.

In the choice of a child as narrator and in the reliance on comedy, these films confirm the impact of *Life is Beautiful* on current Holocaust fiction. They perhaps point to a partial settlement of Italian and French understanding of the Shoah, but also of their preferred kind of Holocaust narratives: one that shuns political and collective interpretations of the tragedy and focuses on individual choice and suffering, preferably eased by a suggestion of the continuation of life. They also signal the continuing evolution of the popular understanding of the Shoah. And perhaps they warn that in the age of Holocaust Memorial Day – as facts become more easily available and their interpretation safeguarded – society's ability to accept the trauma of one of its minorities may yet be hampered by being engulfed into a different memory of the majority, staged punctually and pompously on 27 January each year.

NOTES

1. Annette Wieviorka, *Déportation et Génocide: Entre la Mémoire et l'Oubli* (Paris: Hachette Littératures, 1992), pp. 136–42.
2. Leonardo Jattarelli, 'Scola: il razzismo è dietro l'angolo', *Il Messaggero*, 22 February 2001, p. 23.

Filmography and Bibliography

The filmography that follows is by no means a complete list of all French and Italian films on the Shoah, but simply acknowledges the cinematic works cited in the book. Similarly, the bibliography does not claim to be a comprehensive catalogue of the vast literature on the Second World War and its memory in France and Italy, but is designed to offer a sample of the intellectual sources which influenced the making of this book.

FILMS

Benigni, R., *La Vita é Bella* (*Life is Beautiful*, Italy, 1997).

Beyer, F., *Jakob der Lugner* (*Jacob the Liar*, East Germany, 1975).

Bloomstein, R., *KZ* (Great Britain, 2005).

Cavani, L., *Il Portiere di Notte* (*The Night Porter*, Italy, 1974).

Chabrol, C., *L'Oeuil de Vichy* (*The Eye of Vichy*, France, 1993).

Chomsky, M., *Holocaust* (USA, 1978).

Costa-Gavras K., *Amen* (France, 2002).

De Sica, V., *I Condannati di Altona* (*The Condemned of Altona*, Italy, 1962).

——— *Il Giardino dei Finzi-Contini* (*The Garden of the Finzi-Contini*, Italy, 1970).

Drach, M., *Les Violons du Bal* (*Violins at the Ball*, France, 1974).

Faenza, R., *Jona che Visse nella Balena* (*Jonah who Lived in the Whale*, Italy, 1993).

Finkelstein, E., *Voyages* (France, 1999).

Frazzi, A. and Frazzi, A., *Il Cielo Cade* (*The Sky is Falling*, Italy, 2000).

Gatti, A., *L'Enclos* (*The Enclosure*, France, 1961).
Jugnot, G., *Monsieur Batignole* (France, 2002).
Kassovitz, P., *Jakob the Liar* (USA, 1999).
Lanzmann, C., *Shoah* (France, 1985).
——— *Un Vivant qui Passe* (*A Visitor from the Living*, France, 1997).
——— *Sobibor 14 Octobre 1943, 16 heures* (*Sobibor, 14 October 1943, 4 p.m.*, France, 2001).
Lizzani, C., *L'Oro di Roma* (*The Gold of Rome*, Italy, 1961).
Losey, J., *Mr Klein* (France, 1976).
Malle, L., *Lacombe, Lucien* (France, 1974).
——— *Au Revoir, les Enfants* (*Goodbye, Children*, France, 1987).
Marcus, A., *Beautiful Dachau* (Great Britain, 2006).
Ophuls, M., *Le Chagrin et la Pitié* (*The Sorrow and the Pity*, France, 1971)
——— *Hotel Terminus* (France, 1987).
Pontecorvo, G., *Kapò* (*Kapo*, Italy, 1960).
Rappeneau, P., *Bon Voyage* (France, 2003).
Resnais A., *Nuit et Brouillard* (*Night and Fog*, France, 1956).
Rosi, F., *La Tregua* (*The Truce*, Italy, 1997).
Rossellini, R., *Roma, Città Aperta* (*Rome, Open City*, Italy, 1945).
——— *Il Generale della Rovere* (*General della Rovere*, Italy, 1959).
Scola, E., *Concorrenza Sleale* (*Unfair Competition*, Italy, 2001).
Spielberg, S., *Schindler's List* (USA, 1993).
Tavernier, B., *Laissez Passer* (*Safe Passage*, France, 2000).
Truffaut, F., *Le Dernier Metro* (*The Last Metro*, 1980).
Visconti, L., *Vaghe Stelle dell'Orsa* (*Sandra*, Italy, 1965).
——— *La Caduta degli Dei* (*The Damned*, Italy, 1969).
Wertmuller, L., *Pasqualino Settebellezze* (*Seven Beauties*, Italy, 1974).

BOOKS

Abadie, F. and Corcelette, J.-P., *Georges Pompidou, 1911–1974* (Paris: Balland, 1994).
——— *Valéry Giscard d'Estaing* (Paris: Balland, 1997).
Amouroux, H., *La Grande Histoire des Francais sous l'Occupation* (Paris: Robert Laffont, 1998).
Anissimov, M., *Primo Levi: Tragedy of an Optimist* (London: Aurum Press, 1998).
Antonini, S., *Delasem: Storia della Piú? Grande Organizzazione Ebraica Italiana di Soccorso durante la Seconda Guerra Mondiale* (Geneva: De Ferrari, 2000).

Arad, Y., *Belzec, Sobibor, Treblinka: The Operation Reinhard Death Camps* (Bloomington, IN: Indiana University Press, 1987).

Arian Levi, G., *Fuori dal Ghetto:Il 1848 degli Ebrei* (Roma: Editori Riuniti, 1998).

Armes, R., *The Cinema of Alain Resnais* (London: Zwemmer, 1968).

Aron, R. and Elgey, G., *Histoire de Vichy: 1940–1944*, 2 vols (Paris: Fayard, 1954).

Atack, M., *May '68 in French Fiction and Film* (Oxford: Oxford University Press, 1999).

Atkin N. and Tallett F. (eds), *The Right in France from Revolution to Le Pen* (London: I.B. Tauris, 2003).

Atkin, N., *Pétain* (London: Addison Wesley Longman, 1997).

——— *The French at War, 1934–44* (London: Pearson Education, 2001).

——— *The Fifth French Republic* (Basingstoke: Palgrave-Macmillan, 2005).

Avisar, I., *Screening the Holocaust: Cinema's Images of the Unimaginable* (Bloomington, IN: Indiana University Press, 1988).

Bacon, H., *Visconti: Explorations of Beauty and Decay* (Cambridge: Cambridge University Press, 1998).

Balász, B., *Theory of the Film* (London: Dennis Dobson, 1952).

Baranski, Z. and Lumley, R. (eds), *Culture and Conflict in Postwar Italy* (London: Macmillan, 1990).

Bar-On, D., *Fear and Hope: Three Generations of the Holocaust* (Cambridge, MA: Harvard University Press, 1995).

——— *The Indescribable and the Undiscussable: Reconstructing Human Discourse after Trauma* (Plymouth: Central European University Press, 1999).

Bassani, G., *Il Giardino dei Finzi-Contini* (Torino: Einaudi, 1962).

Bauer, Y., *Rethinking the Holocaust* (New Haven, CT: Yale University Press, 2001).

Bazin, A., *Qu'est-ce que le Cinéma?* (Paris: Éditions Cerf, 1958).

Bea, Cardinal A., *The Church and the Jewish People: A Commentary on the Second Vatican Council's Declaration on the Relation of the Church to Non-Christian Religions* (London: G. Chapman, 1966).

Becker, A., *Maurice Halbwachs: Un Intellectuel en Guerres Mondiales 1914–1945* (Paris: A. Viénot, 2003).

Becker, J. and Wieviorka, A. (eds), *Les Juifs de France de la Révolution à Nos Jours* (Paris: Liana Levi, 1998).

Behr, E., *Thank Heaven for Little Girls: The True Story of Maurice Chevalier's Life and Times* (London: Hutchinson, 1993).
Ben-Amos, A., *Funerals, Politics, and Memory in Modern France, 1789–1996* (Oxford: Oxford University Press, 2000).
Bergan, R., *Jean Renoir: Projections of Paradise* (New York: Overlook Press 1994).
Bernstein, S and Rioux, J.-P., *The Pompidou Years, 1970–1974* (Cambridge: Cambridge University Press, 2002).
Bertelli, P., *La Dittatura dello Schermo: Telefoni Bianchi e Camice Nere* (Catania: Anarchismo, 1984).
Bessy, M. and Beylie, C., *Jean Renoir* (Paris: Pygmalion, 1989).
Betz, A. and Martens, S. (eds), *Les Intellectuels et l'Occupation, 1940–1944: Collaborer, Partir, Résister* (Paris: Autrement, 2004).
Billig, J., *Le Commissariat Général aux Questions Juives*, 3 vols (Paris: CDJC, 1955–1960).
Boito, C., *Senso* (Lecce: Piero Manni, 2002).
Bon, S., *Gli Ebrei a Trieste 1930–1945: Identità, Persecuzione, Risposte* (Gorizia: Libreria Editrice Goriziana, 2000).
Bondanella, P., *Italian Cinema from Neo-Realism to the Present* (New York: F. Ungar, 1983).
——— *Italian Cinema from Neo-Realism to the Present* (New York: Continuum, 1990).
——— *The Films of Roberto Rossellini* (Cambridge: Cambridge University Press, 1993).
Bonfil, R., *Gli Ebrei in Italia nell'Epoca del Rinascimento* (Firenze: Sansoni, 1991).
Bosworth, R.J.S. and Dogliani, P., *Italian Fascism: History, Memory and Representation* (London: Macmillan, 1999).
Bottum J. and Dalin D. G. (eds), *The Pius War: Responses to the Critics of Pius XII* (Lanham, MD: Lexington Books, 2004).
Bourg, J. (ed.), *After the Deluge: New Perspectives on the Intellectual and Cultural History of Postwar France* (Lanham, MD: Lexington Books, 2004).
Bravo A., Pelaja, M., Pescarolo, A. and Scaraffia, L., *Storia Sociale delle Donne nell'Italia Contemporanea* (Roma: Laterza, 2001).
Brenner, M., Caron, V. and Kauffman, U. (eds), *Jewish Emancipation Reconsidered: The French and German Models* (Tübingen: Mohr Siebeck, 2003).
Broggini, R., *La Frontiera della Speranza : Gli Ebrei dall'Italia verso la Svizzera, 1943–1945* (Milano: Mondadori, 1998).

Brossat, A., *Les Tondues: Un Carnaval Moche* (Paris: Hachètte, 1994).
Browne, N. (ed.), *Cahiers du Cinéma 1969–1972: The Politics of Representation* (Cambridge, MA: Harvard University Press, 1990).
Brunetta, G.-P., *Storia del Cinema Italiano* (Roma: Editori Riuniti, 2001).
——— *Gli Intellettuali Italiani e il Cinema* (Milano: Mondadori, 2004).
Brunette, P., *Roberto Rossellini* (Oxford: Oxford University Press, 1987).
Bruno, J. and de Monicault, F., *L'Affaire Papon: Bordeaux, 1942–1944* (Paris: Tilandier, 1997).
Campani, E., *L'Anticonformista* (Firenze: Edizioni Cadmo, 1998).
Capedevielle, J. and Mouriaux R., *L'Entre-Deux de la Modernité. Histoire de Trente Ans* (Paris: FNSP, 1988).
Carrier, P., *Holocaust Monuments and National Memory Cultures in France and Germany since 1989: The Origins and Political Function of the Vél d'Hiv in Paris and the Holocaust Monument in Berlin* (New York: Berghahn, 2004).
Caruth, C. (ed.), *Trauma: Explorations in Memory* (Baltimore, MD: Johns Hopkins University Press, 1995).
Cayrol, J., *Poèmes de la Nuit et du Brouillard* (Paris: Seghers, 1946).
Cento Bull, A. and Gilbert, M., *The Lega Nord and the Northern Question in Italian Politics* (Basingstoke: Palgrave, 2001).
Chiavola Birnbaum, L., *Liberazione della Donna: Feminism in Italy* (Middletown, CT: Wesleyan University Press, 1986).
Chiti, R. and Pecorari, M. (eds), *Dizionario del Cinema Italiano*, vol. 2 (Roma: Gremese, 1991).
Clinton, A., *Jean Moulin, 1899–1943: The French Resistance and the Republic* (Basingstoke: Palgrave, 2002).
Cointet, J-P., *Sigmaringen: Une France en Allemagne (Septembre 1944–Avril 1945)* (Paris: Perrin, 2003).
Cole, A., *François Mitterrand: A Study in Political Leadership* (New York: Routledge, 1994).
Collins Weitz, M., *Sisters in the Resistance: How Women Fought to Free France, 1940 to 1945* (New York: John Wiley, 1995).
Colombat, A.-P., *The Holocaust in French Film* (London: Scarecrow Press, 1993).
Comité d'Histoire de la Télévision, Fondation Nationale des Sciences Politique, *Mai '68 à l'ORTF* (Paris: DF/Radio-

France/INA, 1987).

Conan, E. and Henry, R., *Vichy, Un Passé Qui Ne Passe Pas* (Paris: Librarie Arthème Fayard, 1994).

Cordier, D., *Jean Moulin: L'Inconnu du Panthéon*, 3 vols (Paris: Lattés, 1989–93).

Cornwell, J., *Hitler's Pope: The Secret History of Pius XII* (London: Viking, 1999).

Coser, L. (ed.), *Maurice Halbwachs on Collective Memory* (Chicago: Chicago University Press, 1992).

Courtois, S., *Le PCF dans la Guerre* (Paris: Ramsay, 1980).

Crainz, G., Farassino, A., Forcella, E. and Gallerano, N., *La Resistenza Italiana Nei Programme RAI* (Roma: RAI-ERI, 1996).

Curiel, R., *The Ghetto of Venezia* (London: Tauris Parke Brooks, 1990).

Davis, R. and Ravid, B. (eds), *The Jews of Early Modern Venezia* (Baltimore, MD: Johns Hopkins University Press, 2001).

De Chambrun, R., *Les 2,600,000 Otages Français de Hitler: La France Puissance Protectrice de ses Prisonniers* (Paris: France-Empire, 1988).

——— *Mes Combats pour Pierre Laval* (Paris: Perrin, 1993).

De Felice, R., *Intellettuali di Fronte al Fascismo: Saggi e Note Documentarie* (Roma: Bonacci, 1985).

——— *Storia degli Ebrei Italiani Sotto il Fascismo*, fourth edition (Torino: Einaudi, 1993).

De Gaulle, C., *War Memoirs*, 6 vols (London: Collins, 1955).

De Santi, G., *Carlo Lizzani* (Roma: Gremese, 2001).

De Vincenti, G., *Jean Renoir: La Vita, I Film* (Venezia: Marsilio, 1996).

Debenedetti, G., *16 Ottobre 1943* (Palermo: Sellerio, 1993).

Deguy, M. (ed.), *Au Sujet de Shoah* (Paris: Belin, 1990).

Diamond, H., *Women and the Second World War in France, 1939–1948: Choices and Constraints* (London: Longman, 1999).

Didi-Hubermann, G., *Images Malgré Tout* (Paris: Les Éditions de Minuit, 2003).

DiNapoli, Thomas (ed.), *The Italian Jewish Experience* (Sony Brook: Forum Italicum, 2000).

Douzou, L., *La Désobéissance: Histoire d'un Mouvement et d'un Journal Clandestins: Libération-Sud (1940–1944)* (Paris: Odile Jacob, 1995).

Drake, D., *Intellectuals and Politics in Post-War France* (Basingstoke: Palgrave, 2002).

Duchen, C., *Feminism in France from May '68 to Mitterrand*

(London: Routledge, 1986).
Duggan, C. and Wagstaff, C. (eds), *Italy in the Cold War: Politics, Culture, Society 1948–1958* (Oxford: Berg, 1995).
Eden, Lord A., *The Memoirs of the Rt Hon Sir Anthony Eden, KG, PC*, 3 vols (London: Cassell, 2002).
Engler, B. and Muller, K. (eds), *Historiographic Metafiction in Modern American and Canadian Literature* (Paderborn: Schöning, 1994).
Felman, S. and Laub, D., *Testimony: Crisis of Witnessing in Literature, Psychoanalysis and History* (New York: Routledge, 1992).
Ferro, M., *Pétain* (Paris: Fayard, 1987).
Feuilloley, P., *La IVe République à Travers la France* (Paris: L'Harmattan, 1996).
Finkielkraut, A., *L'Avenir d'une Négation* (Paris: Le Seuil, 1982).
Fishman, S. *et al.* (eds), *France at War: Vichy and the Historians* (Oxford: Berg, 2000).
Fishman, S., *We Will Wait! The Wives of French Prisoners of War, 1940–1945* (New Haven, CT: Yale University Press, 1991).
Forgacs, D., Lutton, S. and Nowell-Smith, G. (eds), *Roberto Rossellini: Magician of the Real* (London: British Film Institute, 2000).
Forgacs, D., *Italian Culture in the Industrial Era: 1910–1980* (Manchester: Manchester University Press, 1990).
——— *Rome, Open City* (London: British Film Institute, 2000).
Frears, J. R., *France in the Giscard Presidency* (London: George Allen and Unwin, 1981).
Frei, N., *Adenauer's Germany and the Nazi Past: The Politics of Amnesty and Integration* (New York: Columbia University Press, 2002).
French, P. (ed.), *Malle on Malle* (London: Faber and Faber, 1993).
Friedlander, S., *When Memory Comes* (New York: Noonday Press, 1991).
——— *Memory, History and the Extermination of the Jews of Europe* (Bloomington, IN: Indiana University Press, 1993).
Galli, L., *La Guerra Civile nel Bresciano: Fatti, Documenti, Testimonianze, 1943–1945* (Montichiari: Zanetti, 1988).
Ghirelli, M., *Gillo Pontecorvo* (Firenze: La Nuova Italia, 1971).
Giacovelli, E., *La Commedia all'Italiana: La Storia, i Luoghi, gli Autori, gli Attori, i Film* (Roma: Gremese, 1995).
Gildea, R., *The Past in French History* (London: Yale University Press, 1994).

——— *France since 1945* (Oxford: Oxford University Press, 1996).

Ginsberg, T., *Holocaust Film: the Political Aesthetics of Ideology* (London: Wallflower Press, 2006).

Ginsborg, P., *A History of Contemporary Italy, 1943–1988* (Harmondsworth: Penguin, 1990).

——— *Italy and its Discontents* (London: Allen Lane, 2002).

Ginzburg, N., *Family Sayings* (Manchester: Carcanet, 1984).

Gold, T., *The Lega Nord and Contemporary Politics in Italy* (Basingstoke: Palgrave Macmillan, 2003).

Goldhagen, D., *A Moral Reckoning* (London: Little, Brown, 2002).

Golsan, R., *Memory, the Holocaust and French Justice: The Bousquet and Touvier Affairs* (Hanover, NH: University of New England, 1996).

——— *Memory and Justice on Trial: The Papon Affair* (New York: Routledge, 2000).

——— *The Papon Affair: Memory and Justice on Trial* (London: Routledge, 2000).

——— *Vichy's Afterlife: History and Counter-History in Postwar France* (Lincoln, NE: University of Nebraska Press, 2000).

Gòmez-Reino Cachafeiro, M., *Ethnicity and Nationalism in Italian Politics: Inventing the Padania: the Lega Nord and the Northern Question* (Aldershot: Ashgate, 2001).

Gorrara, C., *Women's Representations of the Occupation in Post-'68 France* (New York: St Martin's Press, 1998).

Greeley, A., *The Catholic Revolution: New Wine, Old Wineskins, and the Second Vatican Council* (Berkeley, CA: University of California Press, 2004).

Grant, K. and Sloniowski, J. (eds), *Documenting the Documentary: Close Readings of Documentary Film and Video* (Detroit, MI: Wayne State University Press, 1998).

Greene, N., *Landscapes of Loss: The National Past in Postwar French Cinema* (Princeton, NJ: Princeton University Press, 1999).

Griffiths, R., *Marshal Pétain* (London: Constable, 1970).

Grosser, A., *Le Crime et la Mémoire* (Paris: Flammarion, 1989).

Gundle, S. and Parker, S. (eds), *The New Italian Republic: From the Fall of the Berlin Wall to Berlusconi* (London: Routledge, 1996).

Haggith, T. and Newman, J., *Holocaust and the Moving Image* (London: Wallflower Press, 2005).

Halls, W.D., *The Youth of Vichy France* (Oxford: Clarendon Press, 1981).

——— *Politics, Society and Christianity in Vichy France* (Oxford: Oxford University Press, 1995).

Hayward, S. and Vincendeau, G. (eds), *French Film: Texts and Contexts* (London: Routledge, 2000).
Hilberg, R., *The Destruction of European Jews* (Chicago, IL: Quadrangle, 1961).
Hirsch, J., *Afterimage: Film, Trauma and the Holocaust* (Philadelphia, PA: Temple University Press, 2004).
Horrowitz, N. (ed.), *Primo Levi: Witnessing, Memory and Writing* (New Haven, CT: University Press of New England, 1999).
Insdorf, A., *Indelible Shadows: Film and the Holocaust* (Cambridge: Cambridge University Press, 1983, 1989 and 2003).
Isnenghi, M. (ed.), *I Luoghi della Memoria: Personaggi e Date dell'Italia Unita*, 3 vols (Bari: Laterza, 1997).
Israel, G. and Nastasi, P., *Scienza e Razza nell'Italia Fascista* (Bologna: Il Mulino, 1998).
Jackson, J., *De Gaulle* (London: Cardinal, 1989).
——— *France: The Dark Years 1940–1944* (Oxford: Oxford University Press, 2001).
——— *The Fall of France: the Nazi Invasion of 1940* (Oxford: Oxford University Press, 2003).
James, G.A., *Mussolini's Intellectuals: Fascist Social and Political Thought* (Princeton, CT: Princeton University Press, 2005).
Kaplan, A., *The Collaborator: The Trial and Execution of Robert Brasillach* (Chicago, IL: University of Chicago Press, 2000).
Kaspi, A., *Les Juifs Pendants l'Occupation* (Paris: Seuil, 1997).
Kedward, H. R., *The Dreyfus Affair: Catalyst for Tension in French Society* (London: Longmans, 1965).
——— *Resistance in Vichy France: A Study of Ideas and Motivation in the Southern Zone, 1940–1942* (Oxford: Oxford University Press, 1978).
Kershaw, I., *The Nazi Dictatorship: Problems of Interpretation*, third edition (London: Edward Arnold, 1993).
Kertzer, D., *The Popes against the Jews* (New York: Vintage Books, 2001).
Klarsfeld, S., *Vichy-Auschwitz: La 'Solution Finale' de la Question Juive en France*, 2 vols (Paris: Fayard, 1983).
Kline, J., *Bertolucci's Dream Loom: A Psychoanalytic Study of Cinema* (Amherst, MA: University of Massachusetts Press, 1987).
Kreidl, J. F., *Alain Resnais* (Boston, MA: Twayne Publishers, 1977).
Laborie, P., *L'Opinion Française sous Vichy* (Paris: Seuil, 1990).
La Capra, D., *Representing the Holocaust: History, Theory and Trauma* (Ithaca, NY: Cornell University Press, 1994).

——— *History and Memory after Auschwitz* (Ithaca, NY: Cornell University Press, 1998).
Lacouture, J., *De Gaulle*, 2 vols (London: Harper Collins, 1990).
______ *Pierre Mendès-France* (New York: Holmes and Meier, 1984).
——— *Mitterrand: Une Histoire de Français*, 2 vols (Paris: Editions du Seuil, 1998).
Lancia E. (ed.), *Dizionario del Cinema Italiano*, vol. 6 (Roma: Gremese, 2002).
Lane, D., *Berlusconi's Shadow: Crime, Justice and the Pursuit of Power* (London: Penguin, 2004).
Langer, L., *Preempting the Holocaust* (New Haven, CT: Yale University Press, 1998).
Lanzmann C. (ed.), *Au Sujet de Shoah: Le film de Claude Lanzmann* (Paris: Belin, 1990).
——— *Shoah: The Complete Text of the Acclaimed Holocaust Film* (New York: Da Capo Press, 1995).
Laubier, C. (ed.), *The Condition of Women in France: 1945 to the Present* (London: Routledge, 1990).
Lehrer, S., *Wannsee House and the Holocaust* (Jefferson, NC: McFarland, 2000).
Lentin, R. (ed.), *Re-presenting the Shoah for the 21st Century* (New York: Berghan, 2004).
Lepre, A., *Storia della Prima Repubblica* (Bologna: Il Mulino, 1993).
Levi, P., *Se Questo é un Uomo* (Torino: Einaudi, 1962).
——— *La Tregua* (Torino: Einaudi, 1962).
——— *I Sommersi e i Salvati* (Torino: Einaudi, 1986).
Lévy, C. and Tillard, A., *La Grande Rafle du Vel d'Hiv* (Paris: Laffront, 1967).
Lévy, B.-H., *Archives d'un Procès: Klaus Barbie* (Paris: Globe, 1986).
Leymarie, M., *Les Intellectuels et la Politique en France* (Paris: Presses Universitaire de France, 2001).
Longo Adorno, M., *Gli Ebrei Fiorentini dall'Emancipazione alla Shoà* (Firenze: Giuntina, 2003).
Loshitzky, Y. (ed.), *Spielberg's Holocaust: Critical Perspectives on Schindler's List* (Bloomington, IN: Indiana University Press, 1997).
Lottman, H.R., *The People's Anger: Justice and Revenge in Post-Liberation France* (Oxford: Clarendon Press, 1989).
Löwy, V., *L'Histoire Infilmable: Les Camps d'Extermination Nazis à l'Écran* (Paris: L'Harmattan, 2001).

Lumley, R. and Foot, J. (eds), *Italian Cityscapes: Culture and Urban Change in Contemporary Italy* (Exeter: University of Exeter Press, 2004).

Luzzatto, A. (ed.), *La Comunità Ebraica di Venezia e il Suo Antico Cimitero* (Milano: Il Polifilo, 2000).

Marcus, M., *Italian Film in the Light of Neo-Realism* (Princeton, NJ: Princeton University Press, 1986).

Marrus, M. and Paxton, R., *Vichy France and the Jews* (New York: Basic Books, 1981).

Medici, A., Morbidelli, M. and Taviani, E. (eds), *Il PCI e il Cinema tra Cultura e Propaganda: 1959–1979* (Milano: Archivio Audiovisivo del Movimento Operaio e Democratico, 2001).

Micciché, L., *Il Cinema Italiano degli Anni '60 e Oltre* (Venezia: Marsilio, 1995).

——— *Luchino Visconti: Un Profilo Critico* (Venezia: Marsilio, 2002).

Michalczyk, J., *The Italian Political Filmmakers* (Cranbury, NJ: Associated University Presses, 1986).

Michel, H. and Wormser, O. (eds), *Tragédie de la Déportation 1940–1945: Témoignages de Survivants des Camps de Concentration Allemands* (Paris: Hachette, 1954).

Michel, H., *Histoire de la Résistance, 1940–1944* (Paris: CHDGM, 1950).

——— *Histoire de la France Libre* (Paris: PUF, 1963).

——— *Vichy: Année '40* (Paris: Robert Laffront, 1967).

Minc, R., *L'Enfer des Innocents* (Paris: Centurion, 1966).

Moeller, F., *The Film Minister: Goebbels and the Cinema in the Third Reich* (Stuttgart: Edition Axel Menges, 2000).

Monaco, J., *Alain Resnais* (Oxford: Oxford University Press, 1978).

Monicelli, F. and Saletti, C. (eds), *Il Racconto della Catastrofe: Il Cinema di Fronte ad Auschwitz* (Verona: Cierre Edizioni, 1998).

Morley, D., *The Nationwide Audience: Structure and Decoding* (London: British Film Institute, 1980).

Morris, A., *Collaboration and Resistance Revisited: Writers and the 'Mode Rétro' in Post-Gaullist France* (New York: Berg, 1992).

Napolitano, L. M. and Tornielli, A., *Il Papa che Salvò gli Ebrei: Dagli Archivi del Vaticano Tutta la Verità su Pio XII* (Casale Monferrato: Piemme, 2004).

Naylor, P., *France and Algeria: A History of Decolonization and Transformation* (Gainesville, FL: University Press of Florida, 2000).

Nierenstein, F., *Gli Antisemiti Progressisti: La Forma Nuova di un Odio Antico* (Milano: Rizzoli, 2004).

Nora, P. (ed.), *Les Lieux de Mémoire*, 6 vols (Paris: Gallimard, 1984–92).

——— and Kritzman, L. (eds), *Realms of Memory: Rethinking the French Past*, vols 1–3 (New York: Columbia University Press, 1996–98).

Northcutt, W., *Mitterrand: A Political Biography* (New York: Holmes & Meyer, 1992).

Nossiter, A., The Algeria Hotel: France, Memory and the Second World War (Boston, MA: Houghton Mifflin, 2001).

Novick, P., *The Resistance Versus Vichy: The Purge of the Collaborators in Liberated France* (London: Chatto & Windus, 1968).

——— *The Holocaust and Collective Memory* (London: Bloomsbury, 2000).

Oliva, G., *La Resa Dei Conti: Aprile-Maggio 1945: Foibe, Piazzale Loreto e Giustizia Partigiana* (Milano: Mondadori, 1999).

Ophuls, M., *Le Chagrin et la Pitié* (Paris: Alain Moreau, 1980).

Ory, P. and Sirinelli, J.-F., *Les Intellectuels en France del'Affaire Dreyfus à Nos Jours* (Paris: Arman Colin, 1982).

Partridge, C., *Senso: Visconti's Film and Boito's Novella: A Case Study in the Relation between Literature and Film* (Lewiston, ME: E. Mellen Press, 1992).

Passerini, L., *Fascism in Popular Memory: The Cultural Experience of the Torino Working Class* (Cambridge: Cambridge University Press, 1987).

Pavone, C., *Alle Origini della Repubblica* (Torino: Bollati Borlinghieri, 1995).

——— *Una Guerra Civile: Saggio Storico Sulla Moralitá della Resistenza* (Torino: Bollati Borlinghieri, 1991).

Paxton, R., *Vichy France: Old Guard and New Order* (New York: Columbia University Press, 1972).

Péan, P., *Une Jeunesse Française: François Mitterrand 1934–1947* (Paris: Fayard, 1994).

Peli, S., *La Resistenza in Italia: Storia e Critica* (Torino: Einaudi, 2004).

Peyrefitte, A., *C'était de Gaulle*, 3 vols (Paris: Éditions de Fallois, 1994–2000).

Picciotto Fargion, L., *Il Libro della Memoria: Gli Ebrei Deportati dall'Italia (1943– 1945)* (Milano: Mursia, 2002).

Pivato, S., *Bella Ciao: Canto e Politica nella Storia d'Italia* (Bari: Laterza, 2005).

Poliakov, L., *Histoire de l'Antisémitisme*, 3 vols (Paris: Calmann-Lévy, 1961–67).

Poppi, M. and Pecorari M. (eds), *Dizionario del Cinema Italiano*, vol. 3 (Roma: Gremese, 1992).

——— *Dizionario del Cinema Italiano*, vol. 4 (Roma: Gremese, 1996).

Presidenza del Consiglio dei Ministri, *Rapporto Generale della Commissione per la Ricostruzione delle Vicende che Hanno Caratterizzato in Italia le Attività di Acquisizione dei Beni dei Cittadini Ebrei da Parte di Organismi Pubblici e Privati* (Roma, 2001).

Pronay, N. and Spring, D.W. (eds), *Propaganda, Politics and Film, 1918–45* (London: Macmillan, 1982).

Pugliese, S., *The Most Ancient of Minorities: The Jews of Italy* (Westpor, CT: Greenwood Press, 2002).

Rashke, R., *Escape from Sobibor* (London: Sphere, 1982).

Raskin, R., *Nuit et Brouillard* (Aarhus: Aarhus University Press, 1987).

Rassinier, P., *Le Véritable Procès Eichmann ou les Vainqueurs Incorrigibles* (Paris: La Vielle Taupe, 1962).

——— *Le Drame des Juifs Européens* (Paris: La Vieille Taupe, 1964).

Reeves, N., *The Power of Film Propaganda: Myth or Reality?* (London: Cassell, 1999).

Ricoeur, P., *Memory, History, Forgetting* (Chicago, IL: Chicago University Press, 2004).

Rioux, J-P., *The Fourth Republic, 1944–1958* (Cambridge: Cambridge University Press, 1987).

——— *La Guerre d'Algérie et les Français* (Paris: Fayard, 1990).

Rizzo, J.-L., *Mendès France ou la Rénovation en Politique* (Paris: Presses de la Fondation Nationale des Sciences Politiques, 1993).

Rodogno, D., *Il Nuovo Ordine Mediterraneo: Le Politiche di Occupazione dell' Italia Fascista in Europa (1940–1943)* (Torino: Bollati Boringhieri, 2003).

Rosenstone, R. (ed.), *Revisioning History: Film and the Construction of a New Past* (Princeton, NJ: Princeton University Press, 1995).

——— *Visions of the Past: The Challenge of Film to our Idea of History* (Cambridge, MA: Harvard University Press, 2001).

Roth, M., *The Ironist's Cage: Memory, Trauma and the Construction of History* (New York: Columbia University Press, 1995).

Roussel, E., *Georges Pompidou* (Paris: P. Lattès, 1994).

Rousso, H., *Un Château en Allemagne: La France de Pétain en Exil, Sigmaringen 1944–1945* (Paris: Éditions Ramsay, 1980).

——— *The Vichy Syndrome: History and Memory in France since 1944* (Cambridge, MA: Harvard University Press, 1991).
——— *La Hantise du Passé: Entretien avec Philippe Petit* (Paris: Textuel, 1998).
——— *Vichy: l'Événement, la Mémoire, l'Histoire* (Paris: Gallimard, 2001).
Sarfatti, M., *Mussolini Contro gli Ebrei: Cronaca dell'Elaborazione delle Leggi del 1938* (Torino: S. Zamorani Editore, 1994).
——— *Gli ebrei nell'Italia fascista: vicende, identità, persecuzione* (Torino: G. Einaudi, 2000).
Schwarz, D., *Imagining the Holocaust* (New York: St Martin's Press, 1999).
Segre, B., *Gli Ebrei in Italia* (Milano: Fenice 2000, 1993).
Servant, P., *Le Mythe Pétain: Verdun ou les Tranchées de la Mémoire* (Paris: Payot, 1992).
Shennan, A., *De Gaulle* (London: Longman, 1994).
Sherman, D.J., *The Construction of Memory in Interwar France* (Chicago, IL: University of Chicago Press, 1999).
Short, K.R.M. (ed.), *Film and Radio Propaganda in World War Two* (Knoxville, TN: University of Tennessee Press, 1983).
Simmons, H.G., *The French National Front: The Extremist Challenge to Democracy* (Oxford: Westview, 1996).
Simsi, S., *Ciné Référence: Les Films et les Chiffres* (Paris: Dixit, 2000).
Singer, C., *Vichy, l'Université et les Juifs: Les Silences et la Mémoire* (Paris: Les Belles Lettres, 1992).
Sluga, G., *The Problem of Trieste and the Italo-Yugoslav Border: Difference, Identity, and Sovereignty in Twentieth-Century Europe* (Albany, NY: State University of New York Press, 2001).
Solinas, P.-N. (ed.), *Gillo Pontecorvo's The Battle of Algiers* (New York: Scribner, 1973).
Sorlin, P., *European Cinemas, European Societies, 1939–1990* (London: Routledge, 1991).
——— *Italian National Cinema 1896–1996* (London: Routledge, 1996).
Spiegelman, A., *The Complete Maus: A Survivor's Tale* (London: Penguin, 2003).
Staiger, J., *Interpreting Films: Studies in the Historical Reception of American Cinema* (Princeton, NJ: Princeton University Press, 1992).
——— *Perverse Spectators: The Practices of Film Reception* (New York: New York University Press, 2000).

Steinberg, J., *All or Nothing: The Axis and the Holocaust, 1941–1943* (London: Routledge, 2002).
Stille, A., *Benevolence and Betrayal: Five Italian Jewish Families under Fascism* (London: Vintage, 1993).
Stora, B., *La Gangrène et l'Oubli: La Mémoire de la Guerre d'Algérie* (Paris: La Découverte, 1992).
——— *Imaginaires de Guerre: Algérie–Viètnam, en France et aux Etats-Unis* (Paris: La Découverte, 1997).
——— *Algeria 1830–2000* (Ithaca, NY: Cornell University Press, 2001).
Stow, K., *The Jews in Rome* (Leiden: Brill, 1995).
Sweets, J., *The Politics of Resistance in France, 1940–1944* (DeKalb, IL: Northern Illinois University Press, 1976).
——— *Choices in Vichy France* (Oxford: Oxford University Press, 1986).
Taguieff, P.-A., *Rising from the Muck: The New Anti-Semitism in Europe* (Chicago, IL: Ivan R. Dee, 2004).
Truffaut, F., *The Films of my Life* (New York: Simon & Schuster, 1978).
Van der Knaap, E., *Uncovering the Holocaust: the International Reception of Night and Fog* (London: Wallflower Press, 2006).
Vanderwolk, W., *Rewriting the Past: Memory, History and Narration in the Novels of Patrick Modiano* (Amsterdam: Rodopi, 1997).
Vice, S. (ed.), *Representing the Holocaust* (Portland, OR: Vallentine Mitchell, 2003).
Vidal-Nacquet, P., *Les Assassins de la Mémoire* (Paris: La Découverte, 1982).
——— *The Jews: History, Memory and the Present* (New York: Columbia University Press, 1996).
Virgili, F., *Shorn Women: Gender and Punishment in Liberation France* (Oxford: Berg, 2002).
Warner, G., *Pierre Laval and the Eclipse of France* (London: Eyre & Spottiswoode, 1968).
Wiedmer, C.A., *The Claims of Memory: Representations of the Holocaust in Contemporary Germany and France* (Ithaca, NY: Cornell University Press, 1999).
Wieviorka, A., *Déportation et Génocide: Entre la Mémoire et l'Oubli* (Paris: Hachette Littératures, 1992).
——— *Auschwitz: 60 Ans Après* (Paris: Robert Laffront, 2005).
Williams, A., *Republic of Images: A History of French Filmmaking* (Cambridge, MA: Harvard University Press, 1992).

Wilson D. (ed.), *Cahiers du Cinéma – Vol. 4: 1973–1978: History, Ideology, Cultural Struggle* (London: Routledge, 2000).

Winock, M., *La France et les Juifs: De 1789 à Nos Jours* (Paris: Seuil, 2004).

Wolf, J., *Harnessing the Holocaust: The Politics of Memory in France* (Stanford, CA: Stanford University Press, 2004).

Young, J.E., *Writing and Rewriting the Holocaust* (Bloomington, IN: Indiana University Press, 1988).

——— *Holocaust Memorials and Meaning* (New Haven, CT: Yale University Press, 1993).

Ziv, A. and Zajdman, A. (eds), *Semites and Stereotypes: Characteristics of Jewish Humour* (Westport, CT: Greenwood, 1993).

Zuccotti, S., *The Italians and the Holocaust* (New York: Basic Books, 1987).

——— *The Holocaust, the French and the Jews* (New York: Basic Books, 1993).

——— *Under his Very Windows: The Vatican and the Holocaust in Italy* (New Haven, CT: Yale University Press, 2000).

JOURNAL ARTICLES

Altman, C.F., 'Lacombe, Lucien: Laughter as Collaboration', *French Review*, 49, 4 (1976), pp.549–58.

Ben-Ghiat, R., 'The Secret Histories of Roberto Benigni's *Life is Beautiful*', *Yale Journal of Criticism*, 14, 1 (2001), pp.253–66.

Binetti, V., 'Marginalità e Appartenenza: La Funzione dell'Intellettuale tra Sfera Pubblica e Privato nell' Italia del Dopoguerra', *Italica*, 74, 3 (Autumn 1997), pp.360–74.

Bowles, B., 'German Newsreel Propaganda in France', *Historical Journal of Film, Radio and Television*, 24, 1 (March 2004), pp.45–68.

Bruhn Jensen, K., 'The Past in the Future: Problems and Potentials of Historical Reception Studies', *Journal of Communications*, 43, 4 (Autumn 1993), pp.20–8.

Brunette, P., 'Just how Brechtian is Rossellini?', *Film Criticism* 3, 2 (1979), pp.30–42.

——— 'Rossellini and Cinematic Realism', *Cinema Journal* 25, 1 (1985), pp.34–49.

Dumling, A., 'Eisler's Music for Resnais's *Night and Fog*: A Musical Counterpoint to the Cinematic Portrayal of Terror',

Historical Journal of Film, Radio and Television (October 1998), pp.575–84.

Ellsworth, E., 'Illicit Pleasures: Feminist Spectators and *Personal Best*', *Wide Angle*, 8, 2 (1986), pp.45–56.

Flanzbaum, H., '"But wasn't it terrific?": A Defense of Liking *Life is Beautiful*', *Yale Journal of Criticism*, 14, 1 (2001), pp.273–86.

Foot, J., 'Cinema and the City: Milano and Luchino Visconti's *Rocco and his Brothers* (1960)', *Journal of Modern Italian Studies*, 4, 2 (Summer 1999), pp.209–35.

Fresco, N., "Les Redresseurs de Morts", *Les Temps Modernes*, 407 (June 1980), pp.2150–211.

——— 'Parcours Du Ressentiment: Pseudo-Histoire et Théorie sur Mesure dans le "Révissionisme" Français', in *History and Theory*, 28, 2 (May, 1989), pp.173–97.

Gilman, S., 'Is Life Beautiful? Can the Shoah be Funny? Some Thoughts on Recent and Older Films', *Critical Inquiry* (Winter 2000), pp.279–308.

Gundle, S., 'The "Civic Religion" of the Resistance in Post-War Italy', *Modern Italy*, 5, 2 (November 2000), pp.113–32.

Hutton, P., 'Recent Scholarship on Memory and History', *History Teacher*, 33, 4 (August 2000), pp.533–48.

——— 'Sigmund Freud and Maurice Halbwachs: The Problem of Memory in Historical Psychology', *History Teacher*, 27 (1994), pp.145–58.

Jankowski, P., 'In Defence of Fiction', *Journal of Modern History*, 63, 3 (September 1991), pp.457–82.

Kedward, H.R., 'Patriots and Patriotism in Vichy France', *Transactions of the Royal Historical Society*, 32 (1982), pp.175–92.

Kertzer, A., 'Like a Fable, not a Pretty Picture: Holocaust Representation in Roberto Benigni and Anita Lobel', *Michigan Quarterly Review*, 39, 2 (Spring 2000), pp.279–300.

Klein, K.L., 'On the Emergence of "Memory" in the Historical Discourse', *Representations*, 69, Special Issue: 'Grounds for Remembering' (Winter 2000), pp.127–50.

Krantz, C., 'Teaching *Night and Fog*: History and Historiography', *Film History*, 15, 1 (February 1985), pp.2–15.

Lewin, R., 'Paul Rassinier ou la Conjonction des Extrêmes', *Silex*, 36 (1984), pp.85–93.

Lindlof, T., 'The Qualitative Study of Media Audiences', *Journal of Broadcasting and Electronic Media*, 35, 1 (Winter 1991), pp.23–42.

Monticelli, S., 'National Identity and the Representation of Italy at War: The Case of Combat Film', *Modern Italy*, 5, 2 (November 2000), pp.133–46.

Nora, P., 'Between Memory and History: Les Lieux de Mémoire', *Representations*, 26, Special Issue: 'Memory and Counter-Memory' (Spring 1989), pp.7–24.

Revue d'Histoire de la Shoah: Le Monde Juif, 176 (July–December 2002).

Revue d'Histoire de la Shoah: Le Monde Juif, 181 (July–December 2004).

Rodogno, D., 'Italiani Brava Gente? Fascist Italy's Policy Toward the Jews in the Balkans, April 1941–July 1943', *European History Quarterly*, 35, 2 (April 2005), pp.213–40.

Rothberg, M., '"We were talking Jewish": Art Spiegelman's *Maus* as Holocaust Production', *Contemporary Literature*, 35 (Winter 1994), pp.661–87.

Schwabsky, B., 'Art Spiegelman: Un Subtil Sens de l'Equilibre', *Art Press*, 194 (September 1994), pp.27–32.

Sluga, G., 'Trieste: Ethnicity and the Cold War, 1945–1954', *Journal of Contemporary History*, 29 (1994), pp.285–304.

Viano, M., '*Life is Beautiful*: Reception, Allegory and Holocaust Laughter', *Annali d'Italianistica*, 17 (1999), pp.155–72.

Vinen, R., 'Pétain's Hollow Crown', *History Today* (June 1994), pp.13–19.

Wagstaff, C., 'Forty-Seven Shots of Bertolucci's *Il Conformista*', *The Italianist*, 2 (1982), pp.76–101.

——— 'The Construction of Point of View of Bertolucci's *Il Conformista*', *The Italianist*, 3 (1983), pp.64–71.

——— 'Bernardo Bertolucci, Intravenous Cinema', *Sight and Sound*, 4 (1994), pp.18–21.

Wellers, G. 'La "Solution Finale de la Question Juive" et la Mythomanie Néo-Nazie', in *Revue d'Histoire de la Shoah: Le Monde Juif*, 86 (1977), pp.41–84.

Index